ROCK 'N' POP'S GREATEST COURT BATTLES

POP GOES *to* COURT

For Alyssa, a wonderful new life

ROCK 'N' POP'S GREATEST COURT BATTLES

POP GOES *to* COURT

BRIAN SOUTHALL

OMNIBUS PRESS

LONDON / NEW YORK / PARIS / SYDNEY / COPENHAGEN / BERLIN / MADRID / TOKYO

Copyright © 2008 Omnibus Press
(A Division of Music Sales Limited)

Cover designed by Fresh Lemon
Picture research by Sarah Bacon

ISBN: 978.1.84772.113.6
Order No: OP52206

Exclusive Distributors
Music Sales Limited,
14/15 Berners Street,
London, W1T 3LJ.

Music Sales Corporation,
257 Park Avenue South,
New York, NY 10010, USA.

Macmillan Distribution Services,
56 Parkwest Drive,
Derrimut, Vic 3030,
Australia.

Every effort has been made to trace the copyright holders of the photographs in this book but one or two were unreachable. We would be grateful if the photographers concerned would contact us.

Typeset by: Phoenix Photosetting, Chatham, Kent
Printed by Gutenberg Press Ltd, Malta

A catalogue record for this book is available from the British Library.

Visit Omnibus Press on the web at www.omnibuspress.com

Contents

Preface

Dark and dingy clubs, swanky theatres, big city stadiums and festivals promoting love and peace; these are the sorts of places where you expect to catch sight of the biggest names in rock and pop music. But over the years – and the past half-century in particular – a different and perhaps more mundane and austere location has been the venue for a series of headline- and attention-grabbing performances.

In hallowed halls of justice around the world, legal tussles involving star names, plus their families, friends, partners, critics, mentors and fans, have allowed the media and the public a rare insight into matters that, but for a lawsuit, would have remained locked in the file marked "private and confidential".

Arguments over contracts, wills, newspaper articles, agreements (written and unwritten), trademarks and technology, plus tragic suicides, have all had to go to court to be resolved, and watching the rich and the famous settle their differences in open court is what, for many fans and pundits, makes the business of rock and pop truly entertaining.

The public airing of details about finances, friendships, partnerships and sexual preferences can be a very necessary part of winning legal satisfaction.

After all, we should never forget that it was in an English high court where the career of the world's most popular and successful group finally came to a shuddering halt.

The legal break-up of The Beatles is just one in a series of high profile court cases in which the lives and times of a host of the world's most successful and most popular musicians have been exposed and examined under scrutiny from both the media and the public.

Even before pop music began to take hold in the Fifties, the big-time actors and singers who had their names up in lights were all contracted to major film studios and record labels. And almost without exception, each one of them had an agent and/or a manager and, somewhere in the background, there would also have been a lawyer. At the first sign of a dispute over money, billing, co-stars or contracts, the legal eagles would have been called into action.

Sometimes these differences were settled out of court, with most of the juicy details being kept secret and with nobody ever taking the blame. But when it was impossible to settle privately – either in or out of court – then the full weight of the law was brought to bear in what was usually a high-profile, well-publicised and, more often than not, hurtful legal encounter.

And in the modern era of pop and rock music it has been no different. For years, judges have sat in judgement as the stars – and often those nearest and dearest to them – have fought over things said and done or, in some cases, not done.

While a good many of these legal differences of opinion are centred around contract disputes and issues involving royalty payments and composing credits, the subject of wills, suicides, trademarks, libels and memorabilia also figure in cases involving popular publications, a disgruntled politician, world-renowned companies and an impressive collection of some of the biggest names in the entertainment business.

The Beatles, The Smiths, Ozzy Osbourne, Elton John, George Michael, The Spice Girls and U2 are among those who have been forced into the courts of law to either state their cases or clear their names. At the same time, businesses operating on behalf of legends such as Elvis Presley and Jimi Hendrix have been publicly scrutinised in the name of justice.

The pages of *Pop Goes To Court* trace and chronicle some of the most famous, notorious, important and amusing court cases involving the great and the good of rock and pop ever to be set before judges and juries.

It was Charles Dickens who wrote "the law is an ass". Whether those words, as uttered by Mr Bumble in *Oliver Twist*, are true or not, it seems that turning to the legal system is still a popular or, maybe in some cases, last port of call for artists, managers, companies, fans and families when all other more reasonable (and cheaper) options have been exhausted.

Even as the finishing touches were being put to this collection of music-related legal spats, there came news of two more fascinating and entertaining disputes that were only at the embryonic stage but could yet turn into full-scale court cases.

Morrissey – star of a high-profile 1996 high court appearance involving The Smiths – issued two writs against *New Musical Express* and its editor, Conor McNicholas, alleging defamation over quotes attributed to the singer in a November 2007 issue of the music magazine.

Reporting news of the legal proceedings in its November 30 issue, *The Times* began its story with the less than complimentary sentence, "Bigmouth has struck again and, heaven knows he's miserable now."

After suggesting that the ex-Smiths front man took a "naïve and inflammatory" stance on immigration and employed language that "dangerously echoes" the British National Party's manifesto, *NME* stood accused of misquoting Morrissey and taking his words out of context.

A week or two earlier there was news of a dispute in America over a made-up word that appeared as the title of both a best-selling album and a top-rated US television show.

The Red Hot Chili Peppers issued *Californication* in 1999 and hit the charts with both the album and the title-track single. In 2007, a TV series of the same name, starring *X-Files* actor David Duchovny, was aired in both the US and the UK and the four-piece rock band began proceedings against the show's makers, Showtime, for damages. They also took out an injunction to stop the TV network from using the word.

While the band's singer, Anthony Kiedis, went on record to claim that "*Californication* is the signature CD, video and song of the band's career", there were stories of the word – a combination of California and fornication – appearing as far back as 1972, when it was defined as "haphazard, mindless development that has already gobbled up most of Southern California".

Who will win? We'll have to wait and see, but it may not necessarily be "he who dares" to go to court. The fact that there are always prosecuting and defending counsels arguing over their interpretation of the same facts means that taking legal action is, and always will be, a lottery.

Having right on your side is not always enough. A highly publicised, possibly even sensational, court case can test the patience of even the most devoted fans when they hear and read about the antics and attitudes of their heroes.

Sometimes winning isn't everything … but it's usually a lot cheaper than losing!

Chapter 1

LIBERACE

Took offence at what the papers said about him

There are a whole load of things we know about Wladziu Valentino Liberace: he had a piano-shaped swimming pool, a taste for rhinestone and fur outfits, and he stuck a candelabra on his piano as part of his stage act. And, as was mentioned in every obituary, he died from Aids and never married. Funny that!

By themselves, these last two facts did not necessarily make the enormously successful and popular entertainer, whose career spanned five decades, homosexual, but, in the Fifties – when homosexuality was still illegal – the world of nudge-nudge-wink-wink had him down as gay whether he liked it or not.

And, as the world was to find out in 1959, the man with the dimpled grin, camp innuendos and over-the-top showbiz lifestyle was not best pleased by accusations about his sexuality.

At his peak, Liberace rivalled Elvis Presley as a major draw on America's live concert circuit. As far back as 1952, he attracted a record-breaking 22,000 fans to the famous Hollywood Bowl where, for the first time, he appeared in a white evening suit.

It was the start of something very big indeed.

He added a $10,000 black mohair suit with diamond-studded buttons to his wardrobe and, by the end of the decade, he'd assembled a collection of 60 suits, 80 pairs of shoes and a gold lamé dinner jacket, which, bizarrely, he strenuously maintained had not been designed by Christian Dior.

All this excess – including having a replica of the ceiling of the Sistine Chapel painted in his bedroom – brought him regular earnings of over a million dollars a year from television and concert appearances, plus millions more from record sales, endorsements and investments.

With his brother George at his side as both orchestra leader and the butt of his jokes, Liberace used his enormous wealth to occasionally mock his audience. "I've had so much fun tonight that honestly I'm ashamed to take the money – but I will", and, "Do you like my outfit? You should – you paid for it" were just two of the gags that endeared him to his fans.

Liberace, whose father was a French horn player who had performed with John Philip Sousa, added to his appeal to the middle-aged mothers of America by doting on his own mother. His fans responded by sending him 27,000 valentine cards each year and around 12 offers of marriage every month.

In the midst of all this excess and activity, Liberace consistently denied he was homosexual, which brought a backlash from the early gay liberation movement, whose members disapproved of his apparent closet homosexuality.

However, the man who was ultimately destined to suffer the wrath of the offended and outraged piano-player from Wisconsin was a state-educated boy with ambitions to join the Navy. Poor eyesight put paid to William Connor's naval aspirations, however, and he was forced to work as a messenger in a London store.

Displaying a growing love and skill for writing, Connor eventually joined an advertising agency and, at the age of 26, finally earned a position with the *Daily Mirror*, one of Britain's most popular daily newspapers, where he was soon given a daily column written under the name Cassandra.

After service in Italy and North Africa during World War II, Connor returned to the *Mirror* in 1946 and immediately took up the pen. With the phrase, "As I was saying when I was interrupted ...", he resumed his regular Cassandra column. In the autumn of 1956, he turned his attention to Liberace, the classically trained pianist who once jumped out of a giant Fabergé egg dressed in a costume of feathers.

Liberace sailed into England on September 25 – complete with 30 crates of outfits, a Perspex piano and his mum – to be met by over 3,000 excited women. Thousands more – described at the time as "screaming bobby-soxers" – mobbed his train when it arrived at London's Waterloo station.

The very next day Connor wrote a blistering attack on Liberace under the heading "Yearn – Strength Five", a reference to a drink the writer had tasted in Berlin in 1939 called Windstärke Fünf, which was the most powerful alcoholic concoction made in Germany.

The article continued: *"I have to report that Mr Liberace, like Windstarke Funf, is about the most that man can take. But he is not a drink, he is yearning – wind strength five. He is the summit of sex – the pinnacle of masculine, feminine and neuter. Everything that he, she and it can ever want.*

"I spoke to sad but kindly men on this newspaper who have met every celebrity arriving from the US for the past thirty years.

"They all say that this deadly, winking, sniggering, snuggling, chromium-plated, scent-impregnated, luminous, quivering, giggling, fruit-flavoured, mincing, ice-covered, heap of mother love has had the biggest reception and impact on London since Charlie Chaplin arrived at the same station, Waterloo, on September 12th, 1921.

"This appalling man – and I use the word appalling in no other than its true sense of terrifying – has hit this country in a way that is as violent as Churchill receiving the cheers on VE day.

"He reeks with emetic language that can only make grown men long for a quiet corner, an aspidistra, a handkerchief and the old heave-ho.

"Without doubt this is the biggest sentimental vomit of all time. Slobbering over his mother, winking at his brother and counting the cash at every second, this superb piece of calculating candy-floss has an answer for every situation.

"Nobody since Aimee Semple-McPherson* has purveyed a bigger, richer, more varied slagheap of lilac-covered hokum. Nobody anywhere ever made so much money out of high speed piano playing with the ghost of Chopin gibbering at every note.

---

* An American evangelist who built up a million-dollar business, including a private radio station, and had supporters dressed as angels.

3

"There must be something wrong with us that our teenagers longing for sex and middle-aged matrons fed up with sex alike should fall for such a sugary mountain of jingling claptrap wrapped up in such a preposterous clown."

On October 18, Liberace again featured in Connor's Cassandra column when, under the heading "Calling All Cussers", he wrote: *"In their daily programme of events called 'Today's Arrangements', The Times was yesterday at its impassive unsmiling best.*

"It said: 'St Vedast's, Foster Lane: Cannon C.B. Mortlock, 12.30; St Paul's Covent Garden: the Rev Vincent Howson, 1.15; St Botolph's, Bishopsgate: Preb H.H. Treacher, 1.15; All Souls Langham Place: Mr H.M. Collins 12.30; Albert Hall: Liberace, 7.30."

"Rarely has the sacred been so well marshalled alongside the profane."

These two collections totalling just a few hundred words, printed in a newspaper with a daily circulation of over four and a half million, were destined to bring Liberace and Connor face to face in London's Royal Courts of Justice nearly three years later.

Within days of the article being published, the American entertainer had sought legal advice from his American lawyer, John Jacobs, and they decided to sue for libel, which Jacobs defined legally as, "to defame or expose to public hatred, contempt or ridicule by a writing, picture or sign". However, despite their enthusiasm for action, the musician's heavily booked touring schedule meant the earliest date for a court hearing would be June 1959.

Reflecting on his emotions on the day the high court proceedings began, Liberace wrote in his autobiography, "I find it difficult to put into words how I felt that Monday, June 8, 1959, as I sat in an English courtroom, Queens Bench Number Four, surrounded by black-robed, white-wigged gentlemen, and prepared to hear myself vilified, as well as defended, and waited to find out whether I'd done the right thing or the wrong one in following the insistence of my conscience and the confirmation of my attorney."

The court was gathered before Mr Justice Sir Cyril Salmon, whose wife was apparently gathered in the gallery alongside loyal fans and curious onlookers to hear the evidence given to the jury of 10 men and two women.

Liberace was represented by Gilbert Beyfus QC, recognised at the time as the oldest practising barrister on the south-eastern circuit and known within the corridors of the law as "The Fox". This nickname failed to impress Liberace, who described the 76-year-old barrister as looking like "a toothless old lion".

In fact, the American plaintiff was so dismayed and perhaps even disappointed with his counsel that he added, "My heart sank, I knew then and there that I didn't have a prayer."

Opposing him was Gerald Gardiner QC, who had recently been elected chairman of the General Council of the Bar, and, on behalf of both Cassandra and the *Daily Mirror*, he claimed that the statements of fact in the articles were true and the expressions of opinion were fair comment.

London was about to endure and/or enjoy the most sensational libel trial since 1895, when Oscar Wilde had sued his male lover's father for libel over allegations that he was a homosexual. Unsuccessful in that case, the playwright and society wit was subsequently convicted of committing sodomy and sentenced to two years in prison, famously served at Reading Gaol.

Now Liberace's fans around the world waited with bated breath as their hero stood to be paraded, questioned and accused before a judge and jury in a London courtroom.

Beyfus opened his case by telling the court that the alleged libel was "as vicious and violent attack on a plaintiff as can well be imagined, written by as vicious and violent writer as has ever been in the profession of journalism in the City of London".

With his opening gambit made, Beyfus went on to explain that the origin of Connor's nom de plume (which Liberace some time later dubbed a "nom de slur") was a Trojan princess who constantly prophesised evil. Connor later expanded upon this description, telling the court that Cassandra was in fact, "a sometime gloomy prophetess who was always right but, because of a curse from the Gods, nobody ever believed her".

Liberace's counsel then addressed the subject of his client's "elaborate wardrobe of what might be called fancy dress" and, turning his attention to the styles and fashions of the day, he dragged into the debate soldiers, knights of the realm and even members of the legal profession.

"In these days of somewhat drab and dreary male clothing, remember the Guards at Buckingham Palace, the Horse Guards in Whitehall, the Beefeaters at the Tower, the uniforms of the Privy Counsellors, Knights of the Garter and Peers of the Realm.

"Look at the Hunt Ball, when tough hunting men prance around in pink coats with silk lapels of different colours. Some add dignity, all add colour," Beyfus said, before turning to look around the courtroom for further inspiration. "Look at me, my lord and my learned friends, dressed in accordance with old traditions. We do not dress like this in ordinary life, nor does Liberace."

He summed up his client's undoubted showmanship and the candelabra he used in his act as "a trademark, something like Maurice Chevalier's straw hat".

Finally, having read out loud the offending article written by Connor, Beyfus gave the court his interpretation of the piece. "It was as savage a diatribe as can be imagined. It meant, and was intended to mean, that Liberace was a homosexual. That is as clear as clear can be, otherwise I venture to suggest the words have no meaning at all."

Beyfus finished his opening speech by describing Connor as "a literary assassin who dips his pen in vitriol, hired by this sensational newspaper to murder reputation and hand out the sensational articles on which its circulation is built".

When Liberace took the stand on the first day, he spent time outlining how his career had developed and how his success inspired him towards a glamorous lifestyle. He also confirmed that he had made a deliberate attempt to keep the offending *Daily Mirror* article away from his mother who, when she did finally see it, fell ill.

At this point, Beyfus asked Liberace the question the whole court and the entire country had been waiting for. "Are you homosexual?" to which Liberace replied, "No, sir."

Gardiner, for Cassandra and the *Daily Mirror*, immediately objected to the introduction of the question of homosexuality. "There is no suggestion and never has been anything of the kind."

Beyfus then took it a stage further. "Have you ever indulged in homosexual practices?" and Liberace's reply was, "No, sir, never in my life."

Asked by his counsel what his feelings were towards homosexual acts, Liberace continued with his denial. "My feelings are the same as anyone else's. I am against the practice because it offends convention and offends society."

So there it was in open court. Liberace was not homosexual and had never committed a homosexual act. The preening, primping, winking and over-the-top camp excesses were all part of an act that, he told the court, he had tried his best to fill with "sincerity and wholesomeness".

In cross-examination, Gardiner asked the American star if he thought an earlier *Daily Sketch* article that said, "even bankers behave like bobby-soxers at Liberace's playing", suggested that he was homosexual. Again, Liberace said no.

As arguably the most sensational libel trial in 50 years, the reports in the next day's newspapers of the opening day in court wallowed in the welter of innuendo and homosexual references.

They offered up such headlines as – "Liberace Called 'The Summit Of Sex'" and "Newspaper Sued Over Summit Of Sex", plus "I'm Not A Sex Appeal Artist", while the rather staid *New York Times* preferred the more factual "Liberace Denies He Is Homosexual".

Yet even the cruellest of these headlines was nothing compared to an American magazine called *Hush-Hush*, which, two years before the trial started but after the publication of Cassandra's column, had carried the banner headline posing the question: "Is Liberace A Man?"

Two other American scandal sheets – *Hollywood Confidential* and *Rave* – had added fuel to the fire and tested Liberace's resolve with salacious articles carrying sensational headlines questioning his sexuality.

Hollywood Confidential stated in its headline: "Why Liberace's Theme Song Should Be 'Mad About The Boy'", while *Rave* offered the banner: "Liberace: Don't Call Him Mister!" Other American publications, both scandal sheets and more reputable papers, had on more than one occasion referred to the pianist and entertainer as "a sissy", "a mama's boy" and even "a homosexual".

Opening day two of the case, Gardiner asked Liberace about sex appeal – "I deny that I trade on it," said the pianist; his fans – "I love my fans and

I believe they love me"; and scent – "I do not use scent but I do use after-shave lotions, deodorants and eau de cologne, all well-groomed men do."

Shown an article written by *Daily Mirror* showbiz writer Donald Zec, Liberace denied suggestions that he did a "springy little walk round the piano" or that he imitated a showgirl lifting her skirt coyly, and that he owned a parakeet that screeched the name Liberace. "I have a parakeet but it doesn't speak a word," he said.

The performer told the court that he was in fact grateful to Zec for the fact that he did not use in his article the expression, "he, she, it, masculine, feminine or neuter" or "fruit-flavoured". The phrases were all part of Cassandra's allegedly libellous column and, according to Liberace, were all "expressions which in America are termed homosexual".

He further confirmed to Gardiner that none of the press reviews he had received in America had ever used "expressions denoting homosexuality".

Turning to Liberace's personal hygiene, Gardiner was keen to find out whether the American entertainer used "scent or scented lotion", and was informed that Liberace did indeed use scented aftershave lotions and underarm deodorants.

Defence counsel suggested that when Liberace came into a room "a noticeable odour comes with you", to which the plaintiff replied: "I would not say it is an odour. I would say it is a scent of good grooming, that I smell clean and fresh." He added that the reference to scents in the *Daily Mirror* article implied an accusation that he was a homosexual.

Getting to the crux of the matter, Gardiner then asked Liberace whether the words, "He is the summit of sex – the pinnacle of masculine, feminine and neuter. Everything that he, she and it can ever want" seriously suggested that he was homosexual?

In reply, Liberace told the court: "That is the interpretation that was given and understood without exception by everyone I have company with."

Quoting again from the offending Cassandra article, Gardiner suggested that the statement saying that Liberace exuded love meant that he had great sex appeal and that he attracted all sections of the community, but not in any improper sense.

Liberace's response was to claim that the feature was, "The most improper article that has ever been written about me. It has been widely quoted in all parts of the world and has been reproduced exactly as it appeared in the *Daily Mirror*.

"It has been given the interpretation of homosexuality. One paper had the headline, 'Is Liberace A Man?'"

Gardiner's reply was to suggest that readers must have filthy minds if they thought the words implied that Liberace was homosexual. Liberace retaliated by saying that the phrase "fruit-flavoured" was one commonly directed at homosexuals and added, "The reason I am in court is that this article attacked me below the belt on a moral issue."

Moving on to the phrase "summit of sex", Gardiner argued that it was simply Cassandra's description of the "universality of your appeal" and nothing to do with being homosexual, which prompted Liberace to argue: "People have given it that interpretation. It has caused me untold agonies and embarrassment and has made me the subject of ridicule.

"On my word of God, on my mother's health, which is so dear to me, this article only means one thing, that I am a homosexual and that is why I am in this court."

Liberace's evidence lasted six hours, and he was followed into the witness box by a variety of witnesses called by Beyfus on his client's behalf.

First up was writer Dail Ambler, who said that she had been to interview Connor (Cassandra) about his pet cat just after the writ for libel had been issued. She alleged that Connor laughed about it and said that it was a libel for which Liberace would get a lot of money from the *Daily Mirror* and that the libel was in the phrase "he, she or it".

When she asked Connor why he had written it and why it had been printed, she told the court that Connor had told her: "They think it will be worth it for a week's publicity", and then added, "I don't know who will look the bigger buffoon in the witness box, he or me."

Actress Cicely Courtneidge and cabaret star Hélène Cordet both gave evidence that they had seen performances by Liberace and neither of them considered the shows to be sexy or suggestive, while comedian Bob Monkhouse gave the court a sample of his impersonation of the American performer which he used in his stage act, adding that Liberace had seen the performance and had been "enormously helpful".

Midway through the third day of the libel case, Gardiner opened the defence on behalf of the *Mirror* and Cassandra with an argument for free speech and democracy. "It [free speech] was not a special right of newspapers but it was everyone's right to say what they thought on any matter of public interest.

"A democracy cannot really work in any other way because public opinion has to be formed and public opinion grows out of expressions of differences of opinion."

He added that the question before the jury was not whether they agreed with what Cassandra had said but whether he held that opinion honestly.

Acknowledging that Connor was a serious man who took a slightly gloomy view of life and was very conscious of cruelties and suffering, Gardiner added: "He is usually standing up for the poor and downtrodden, sometimes blaming, sometimes praising."

Adding that Connor had never had a court verdict given against him, Gardiner told the court that there had, however, been four actions against the writer over articles he had written in the *Daily Mirror*. In one case, £50 was paid to Oswald Mosley, founder of the British Union of Fascists, while an action by "a Soho gentleman" was subsequently dropped as was a case brought by a property dealer, but a fourth case was settled with an out of court payment of £250.

Gardiner confirmed to the jury that Connor had seen one and a half of Liberace's films, which were shown on British television in 1956. "I say one and a half, in fact he saw one whole show and as much of the second as he could stomach."

Gardiner argued that Connor's *Mirror* article, apart from the opening paragraph, had not said anything that had not been said before in all the newspapers. Claiming that the substance of this criticism of Liberace was that nobody thought much of his piano playing, Gardiner added, "There are also many people who did not like his professional charm, which makes some people rather sick."

After stating that Connor did not ask the jury to necessarily agree with what he had written, Gardiner called the veteran *Mirror* columnist to the witness box to give evidence.

Confirming that he wrote the first of the articles complained of in the libel action after seeing photographers and reporters who had been to Waterloo to cover Liberace's arrival, reading their copy and all the cuttings and comments available, Connor said it was an "honest opinion".

Asked what he intended when he wrote the phrase: "He is the summit of sex, the pinnacle of masculine, feminine and neuter", Connor told the court: "What I had in mind was that by using his sex appeal he was the greatest exponent in show business and had received audiences which were world records."

He went on to explain that the phrase, "everything that he, she and it can ever want", was a reference to the comprehensive nature of Liberace's techniques designed to apply to the whole community – "the full circle".

After explaining that he viewed Liberace's performances with "a feeling of astonishment to begin with and then nausea", Connor was asked by his counsel whether he had any intention at any time of imputing homosexuality to Liberace. His reply came in three words – "None at all."

Gardiner then focused his attention on phrases used in Connor's first *Mirror* article. He put them to the journalist one by one, asking what he meant by each description.

Deadly – "He overwhelms one, he attacks the senses."

Winking, sniggering, giggling, snuggling – "I had read a number of reports which contained these adjectives and I had observed him doing these very things on television."

Chromium-plated – "To my mind chromium-plated means a bright, light-reflecting surface. In his performance he seemed to have these light-reflecting surfaces such as a completely white suit of tails, a candelabra, an enormous ring on his finger."

Scent-impregnated – "The question of scent had been mentioned in the *Daily Mirror*, *Daily Express* and *Evening Standard*."

Fruit-flavoured – "That was part of the impression of confectionery which Mr Liberace conveyed to me. Over-sweetened, over-flavoured, over-luscious and just sickening."

Heap of mother love – "I think Mr Liberace was dealing with what I think is the closest bond between human beings. The positive relationship between humans begins in friendship, develops to affection and then comes love. There are various degrees of love. There is sexual love

11

which provides its own immediate pleasures, but there is something much more tender and important, the love of a mother and her child. It survives the disagreements of the parents who made it, it survives poverty, it survives war. When I see this on the stage at the London Palladium by a 40-year-old man in company with his mother, whom he may love, I regard that as profane and wrong."

Appalling and terrifying – "I am always suspicious of people gathered together in large numbers. I saw the Nuremberg rallies, people persuaded by propaganda, searchlights, speeches by Goering, driven by the herd instinct. That is a bad thing. When I saw these young and impressionable people gathering outside Waterloo Station I did not like it."

Counting the cash at every second – "I think that is an exaggeration. I think he probably counts it once a month just to see how many millions there are."

Candy floss – "Again his sugary performance."

Connor admitted to the court that he said jokingly to Dail Ambler that it would be interesting "to see who was the bigger buffoon in the box", but he denied making any of the other statements about Liberace and the libel case as she claimed in her evidence.

Now it was the turn of Beyfus to cross-examine Connor, and he began by suggesting that the journalist had a reputation for being a violent and vitriolic writer and that the *Mirror* was a sensational newspaper. Connor denied both suggestions, but confirmed that he was in a position to be able to write independently what be believed to be right.

Before the hearing adjourned at the end of the third day, the foreman of the jury replied to the invitation that jurors could watch recordings of Liberace's television shows if they hadn't seen them before. He told the judge that only two members of the jury had not seen the shows and they didn't think it was necessary to watch them now.

The next day, turning to a sequence in a television show in which a woman dressed as a nun knelt in front of the Madonna while Liberace played 'Ave Maria', Connor confirmed his objection to the scene, saying that when the woman dressed as a nun began to writhe in front of the Madonna, he felt a sacred occasion was being misused by Liberace.

Beyfus then moved on to suggest to Connor that the articles in question were written to "express your detestation of Liberace". Replying,

Connor stressed that he did not detest Liberace and added, "In his personal capacity he is entirely unknown to me but I strongly dislike what he does on stage, in the concert hall and on television." He then said that he thought the article would reduce Liberace to his correct proportion – "as a preposterous clown".

Moving on to the issue of the suggestions of homosexuality in the article, Beyfus confronted Connor by asking if the words "summit of sex, pinnacle of masculine, feminine and neuter" were not meant to suggest Liberace was a homosexual. The journalist stood by his claim that they were intended to describe the universality of the pianist's appeal.

Liberace's counsel took things a stage further and suggested to Connor that he knew that the word "fruit" was American slang for a homosexual. "I did not," said Connor, adding, "I am well acquainted with many hostile words including those imputing homosexuality, but I did not know that 'fruit' was one of them. It came as a bit of a surprise to me."

His use of the phrase "fruit-flavoured" was, according to the newspaper man, in association with other confectionery adjectives.

After five hours in the witness box, Connor's day in court finally came to an. Next, the revue artist Jimmy Thompson took the stand to talk about his "skit" on Liberace in which he described the latter as "a sort of Winifred Atwell combining aspects of Vera Lynn".

Referring to lines from Thompson's script for his Liberace act, Beyfus quoted from a section referring to marriage proposals to Liberace. "I get more and more. They propose by the score. And at least one or two are from girls."

Thompson explained that the words were intended to reflect on the persons making the proposals rather then the person who received them. Covering a section that read: "My fans all agree that I'm really most me. When I play the sugar-plum fairy", Thompson said he knew the word "fairy" was slang in America for homosexual but was unaware that it was in Britain.

Ending the fourth day's proceedings on Friday, June 12, Mr Justice Salmon suggested that the members of the jury should not watch Liberace's performance on television's *Sunday Night At The London Palladium* set for broadcast two days later on June 14.

"It is long after these matters which are now in issue and it might convey a right or wrong impression in your mind, so I think it probably better if you do not see it."

Called to the witness stand by defence counsel Gardiner, *Daily Mirror* columnist Donald Zec said that after a press conference in Cherbourg, France, he had made a reference to Liberace as "fragrantly perfumed with toilet water", but had not meant to suggest that the entertainer was necessarily wearing perfume.

He also admitted that a previous article he had written, after visiting Liberace's home in Hollywood, had been "very satirical", and that when Liberace embraced him in France and thanked him for the article, he was surprised. "To thank me so warmly if he had read the article, suggested that he put much greater value on publicity than he did on his personal feelings.

"If he hadn't read the article, it seemed to me to be palpably insincere," said Zec, the paper's major show-business writer.

Also called for the defence was fellow *Daily Mirror* writer Patrick Doncaster, who gave evidence about a meeting in pianist Winifred Atwell's dressing room at the London Palladium in October 1956. Doncaster and other journalists were joined backstage by Liberace and writer Dail Ambler, who had given evidence on the second day of the libel trial.

According to Doncaster, one of the *Mirror*'s senior feature writers, Ambler said in a loud voice: "If Randolph Churchill can get £5,000 from the *People*, Liberace should get something from the *Mirror*. I hear the *Mirror* has a million."

Doncaster told the court that he then asked Liberace if he was going to sue the *Daily Mirror* over the Cassandra remarks and the performer said he was not.

The final defence witness was Cassandra's boss, Hugh Cudlipp, editorial director of the *Daily Mirror* and *Sunday Pictorial*, who confirmed at the outset that Connor had complete freedom to express his views unless the editor objected.

Stating that a poll conducted six years earlier had shown that about half of the *Mirror*'s readers regularly read Cassandra, Cudlipp added, "Cassandra's views are frequently opposed to those of the paper. That is usual on the progressive and better papers."

Near to the close of day five, Cudlipp admitted to Liberace's counsel that he did not entirely agree with Cassandra's views of Liberace, but he agreed that he had the right to express them.

Before the opposing counsels could begin their closing addresses on the sixth day of the action, Mr Justice Salmon told the court that there were five questions that the jury in the case had to consider.

Firstly, did the words complained of in the September 26th *Daily Mirror* article by the defendant mean that the plaintiff was a homosexual? Secondly, without this meaning, were the words true in so far as they were fair comment, in so far as they were expressions of an opinion?

Next, if the answers to the first two questions were both in favour of Liberace, how much of the damages were attributable to the imputation of homosexuality?

Moving on to the Cassandra Column printed on October 18, the judge asked whether these words were fair comment and reminded the jury that they would also need to consider the question of damages in this incident.

In his closing speech on behalf of the defendant, Gardiner suggested that the plaintiff "appears to have a bee in his bonnet about people charging him with homosexuality".

Referring to the sentence, "Everything he, she or it can ever want," counsel added: "It was fantastic to suppose that any reasonable person reading the sentence would have said, 'Oh, I never knew that Mr Liberace went to bed with men'."

He ended by saying that Connor was simply saying what he honestly thought on a subject on which he felt strongly.

Concluding the case for Liberace, Beyfus, after questioning the honesty of Connor as a witness, stated: "I suggest that this man studiously and carefully sorted out phrases which would convey the idea that Liberace was a homosexual but at the same time enabling him to go into the witness box and be spared the consequences."

He finished his speech by claiming that the *Daily Mirror* was vicious and violent, venomous and vindictive, salacious and sensational, ruthless and remorseless, before telling the jury: "Let your award of damages be such a sum to make the directors think when they deal with their balance sheets."

The essence of Mr Justice Salmon's summing up centred on the issue of freedom of speech, which he described as, "The freedom of everyone to state their honest opinion about any matter of general importance – a right which is common to us all."

He stressed the only real question facing the jury was what the words in the first article written by Cassandra meant to the ordinary man. "Liberace had to satisfy the jury – if they were to answer in his favour – that the words complained of meant that he was a homosexual, a sexual pervert who indulged in sexual practices with other men."

He went on: "If the jury thought all that the words meant was that Liberace seemed to have a tremendous attraction not only to women but also for men and possibly for some homosexuals, that did not mean Liberace was a homosexual."

Acknowledging that the words used by Cassandra were ironic and derisive, he asked the jury to decide whether their meaning was that Liberace was a homosexual or that he had astonishing universal appeal.

Adding that the question of whether a man was a sexual pervert was a matter of fact, the judge concluded: "If one stated untruthfully that a man was a homosexual it was no defence to say one honestly believed what was stated. On the other hand, to say that a man's behaviour was nauseating was a matter of opinion."

Advising the jury on the subject of damages, Mr Justice Salmon said much would depend on whether the jury thought the words meant Mr Liberace was a homosexual. Confirming that this was an allegation that the defendants said was "rubbish", he warned the jury: "In considering damages you must not be niggardly – on the other hand, you must not be extravagant."

After deliberating for nearly three-and-a-half hours, the jury finally returned to give answers to the five questions the judge had put to them earlier.

Firstly, did the words complained of in the defendant's publication of September 26, 1956 in the ordinary and natural meaning mean that the plaintiff is a homosexual? The jury answered – *YES*

Secondly, without this meaning, were the words complained of a) true in so far as they are statement of fact, and b) fair comment in so far as they are expressions of opinion? The answer from the jury to both these questions was – *NO*.

On the question of damages for the September 26th article, the jury agreed on £8,000, with £2,000 of these damages attributable to the imputation of homosexuality.

Regarding the fourth question as to whether the article published on October 18, 1956 was fair comment, the jury decided – *CASE NOT PROVED*, and, on the final question of damages in respect of that article, their response was – *NO ANSWER*.

So the jury agreed that Cassandra's words meant that the 40-year-old American pianist was a homosexual and that the words in the article were neither true nor fair comment.

They awarded £2,000 of the total £8,000 damages – the highest ever awarded in a British high court – for the suggestion that he was homosexual, but agreed that the October article was fair comment and costs in this article were awarded to the *Daily Mirror* and Cassandra.

The costs, awarded against the *Mirror* and Cassandra in the main case, were reckoned to be in excess of £27,000.

Having heard the jury's decisions, Mr Justice Salmon, in his judgement, quoted the words applied to Liberace in the article – "sniggering, snuggling, scent-impregnated, giggling and mincing" – and commented: "I am quite unable in these circumstances to say that the words were not capable of the meaning that the jury has attributed to them."

After giving his final judgement, the judge shocked the court by admitting that during the trial he had received a number of anonymous letters. "All except one appear to have been written by lunatics and they have gone straight into the wastepaper basket," he told the court. "The one letter was a sinister and squalid attempt to pervert the course of justice and I intend to send this to the Director of Public Prosecutions for his consideration."

Leaving the court through huge crowds, which brought traffic around the high courts to a standstill, the smiling and victorious Liberace issued a statement that said: "Mr. Liberace is delighted that his reputation has been vindicated by the verdict of a British jury." Later, on the subject of his record award, he famously quipped, "I cried all the way to the bank."

The defeated but unbowed Connor was granted a knighthood by Prime Minister Harold Wilson in 1965. He died in April 1967, while Liberace lived on for a further 20 years until February 1987.

However, in 1982 the 63-year-old American entertainer was sued for $113 million after a bitter split with his live-in boyfriend Scott Thorson and, while much of the palimony claim was dismissed, Thorson was awarded an out-of-court settlement.

Liberace continued to deny all accusations and suggestions that he was homosexual up to the time of his death of complications attributed to AIDS.

Upon hearing this news the *Daily Mirror,* nearly three decades after it was defeated in court, ran an article suggesting that his estate might like to return the money he was awarded in 1959 for being called a homosexual. They never did.

Chapter 2

THE MOVE

*Their promotional postcard upset the
country's top politician*

Pop manager Tony Secunda had an irrepressible love of scams and
publicity stunts as a means of furthering the careers of those artists
who put their faith and trust in this ex-public schoolboy turned would-
be entrepreneur.

After helping the Birmingham-based group The Moody Blues to the
top of the charts in early 1965 with 'Go Now', Secunda quickly turned
his attention to another rapidly emerging Midlands outfit.

His initial idea after taking The Move under his belt was to convince
them that a wild stage act, complete with Chicago gangster-style outfits,
was the first step towards making them million sellers and household
names. His style was all about controlling his charges and, in The Move,
he found a group whose members were considered by many to be mal-
leable. He duly turned them into "psychedelic anarchists" who went
along with his numerous and various publicity stunts.

He was right in one respect – The Move would eventually become
the stuff of headlines. But it would have nothing to do with their music,
appearance or stage antics and all to do with Secunda's obsession with

madcap ideas, all intended to make them stand out from the hundreds of other successful but not quite superstar groups that littered the theatres, clubs and pubs of Britain in the Sixties.

After Roy Wood, Carl Wayne, Bev Bevan, Chris "Ace" Kefford and Trevor Burton had steered The Move to huge local success, the band turned to Secunda in early 1966 to take them to the next level – exposure on the all-important London scene and a possible major record deal.

Secunda booked them at the famous and fashionable Marquee club in Soho, but their residency was brought to an abrupt end when the management objected to The Move's habit of smashing up television sets on stage and setting off fireworks; three fire engines were called to the club during one particularly lively night.

The group even took to including in their act a life-sized effigy of Prime Minister Harold Wilson, which was torn to pieces during the show. Looking back on these antics, lead singer Wayne once commented: "Secunda was a creative genius. In many ways he was able to bring out the best in everybody by bringing out the worst."

As an indication of what was to come, Secunda initially got the group to tow a fake H-bomb around Manchester in a supposed anti-Vietnam War protest, to promote their first single 'Night Of Fear', released late in 1966.

Even then, not all of the group were happy with the stunts and the image Secunda was busy creating for his charges. "In Trevor, Ace and me," acknowledged Wayne, "he had the animals who would do what he wanted. But I think Roy was slightly embarrassed by the stunts."

By the time The Move's third single was set for release in August 1967, Secunda had dreamed up a promotional plan that would exceed even his wildest dreams in terms of headlines and column inches.

'Flowers In The Rain' earned itself a place in pop history by becoming the first single played on the BBC's brand new, flagship pop station Radio 1, when Tony Blackburn hosted the early morning show on September 30, 1967.

By that time the record, written by Wood, the group's main songwriter, had entered the British charts and earned The Move their third successive hit after 'Night Of Fear' and 'I Can Hear The Grass Grow', peaking at number two in early October.

However, along with the adulation and the royalty cheques, The Move also received notice of a libel suit from an unlikely yet powerful individual who, in fact, held the highest elected office in the land. Prime Minister Harold Wilson had seemingly taken great offence at Secunda's best efforts to promote the single's two minutes and 17 seconds of psychedelic pop, which came complete with thunderclaps and the sound of pouring rain.

For reasons that nobody really understood, Secunda had decided to issue to the media and the music industry a promotional postcard for 'Flowers In The Rain' that featured a cartoon (and this is the legal phrase that remains in place today) of "the Labour PM in a state of undress with a woman who was not his wife".

There had long been rumours of a supposed relationship between Wilson and his personal secretary, Marcia Williams – which both consistently denied – and even though the postcard did not identify the woman it reportedly featured the words, "Harold's very personal secretary".

The postcard, of which the initial order was for just 500 copies, also carried the message: "Disgusting, despised and despicable though Harold may be, beautiful is the only word to describe 'Flowers In The Rain' by The Move."

There were also suggestions that Secunda and his associates persuaded Labour MP and future Party leader Michael Foot to take a quantity of the postcards and distribute them in the House of Commons.

The record was the band's first release after their move from Deram to the EMI-owned Regal Zonophone label, which had previously found fame as a home to recordings by Salvation Army bands and popular music-hall acts such as Gracie Fields and George Formby. It was now facing a potential sales and promotional backlash in the face of a damaging lawsuit.

The result was that Prime Minister Wilson instructed his lawyers to seek an injunction banning the use of the postcard and, in the first week of September, he was granted an interim injunction against The Move and Secunda, halting distribution of what was called "a cartoon postcard promoting 'Flowers In The Rain'."

The fact they were named in the action was something of a surprise to the group, as they had not been told about the postcard campaign by Secunda and were completely unaware of its existence until the nation's top politician brought down the full weight of the law on their young shoulders.

Harold Wilson had been elected Prime Minister in 1964 and became Britain's first Labour Premier for over 13 years, during which time four Conservatives had served in the highest office. Although a Yorkshireman by birth, Wilson's constituency was Huyton in Liverpool, the birthplace of the nation's Sixties beat music boom, which was by now exploding into an international phenomenon.

A dour man but a shrewd politician, Wilson quickly grasped the value of appealing to teenagers who might turn out to be Labour supporters when they reached the then official voting age of 21. Years before Tony Blair ever opened the doors of 10 Downing Street to the great and good of the Nineties celebrity scene, Wilson understood all about mixing and mingling with pop stars, footballers and film stars.

England won the 1966 World Cup during his time in office and politicians throughout the land feted the winning soccer team. A year before that, Wilson had made the landmark decision to recommend that the biggest-selling pop group in the world be honoured for their services to music and the country.

There were those who believed that Marcia Williams – considered by many commentators to be as influential in the Sixties as Alastair Campbell would be three decades later – in some way influenced Wilson in his decision to put forward John Lennon, Paul McCartney, George Harrison and Ringo Starr for the 1965 Queen's Birthday Honours list.

The fact that they were awarded MBEs (Member of the British Empire) brought a salvo of protests from medal holders including former Canadian MP Hector Dupuis, who wrote: "The British house of royalty has put me on the same level as a bunch of vulgar numbskulls."

Even before that Wilson had made himself available to present The Beatles with their Variety Club of Great Britain Show Business Personalities of the Year Awards in March 1964. Attempting to play down the event as a potential vote winner, Wilson told the assembled showbiz audience, "I will refrain from making any political capital out of The Beatles," but he still went to great lengths to make the point that they were a valuable export commodity for the country and had succeeded during a time when Labour was in power.

But even the patience of the first pop-loving Prime Minister was tested by Secunda's cheap and, some would say, tacky publicity stunt. In the light of the injunction granted in the first week of September 1967, Secunda saw sense and moved to lessen the damage by winning his own injunction – in the name of The Move – against a German magazine that was intent on reproducing the postcard in a forthcoming issue.

Talking to *Melody Maker* in the same month, Secunda also confirmed that there was a growing black market for the postcards. "I have already been offered £2 for one of the cards but the injunction stops me from selling or giving any away."

While he may not have been running scared, even Secunda understood the gravity of the situation. Prime Ministers did not issue writs for libel and risk airing their personal business in open court unless they were seriously upset.

The first injunction granted to Wilson ran until September 6, and followed the action brought by solicitors Goodman Derrick & Co., led by the Prime Minister's solicitor and good friend Lord Goodman, who also acted as an adviser to The Beatles and their manager, Brian Epstein.

The court heard that The Move were using a postcard that was alleged to libel Wilson as promotional material, and, bizarrely, Secunda even sent one of the cards to the PM's official residence at 10 Downing Street, while it was claimed that others went to newspapers and people in the "pop" business.

A week later, Wilson was granted a second injunction that further prevented the members of The Move from issuing the postcard until a high court had decided whether it was libellous or not.

Not surprisingly, the best-selling satirical magazine *Private Eye* went to town when Wilson took action against The Move and produced a front cover with the banner heading, "Exclusive – The Card Wilson Wants To BAN!" alongside a spoof cartoon showing the Prime Minister in bed with George Wigg, the then Postmaster General, with Mrs Wilson peering through a curtain.

In the cartoon, credited to lauded artist Gerald Scarfe, Wilson was captioned a "humourless twit", while the magazine's Colour Section editorial wrote: "We must, with due regret, apologise to those readers who are under the impression that the card on our cover showing the Prime Minister and the Paymaster General consenting together in an unusual manner, is in fact the genuine article, i.e. the postcard put out by The Move to promote their latest waxing."

The magazine, edited by Richard Ingrams, continued: "After examination of this, we decided that it was altogether so innocuous and so badly produced that it would be inadvisable from every point of view to give it further currency."

Private Eye further posed the question: "Why then has Wilsundra (the magazine's pet name for the Prime Minister) used the mighty sledgehammer of the law to crack such a tiny nut? The fact is that since Profumo he has been hysterically frightened of the slightest possible hint of trouble on the sex front."

When the court hearing opened, Wilson sought damages from the five band members and their manager, while the *Daily Express* of September 7 was seemingly more interested in letting the public know just how pop stars dressed for a court appearance.

It wrote that, "Between them The Move mustered a collection involving lime green trousers, white boots, a couple of lace shirts, black velvet jacket, two floral tunics and five pairs of tinted glasses," and also reported that the group described themselves as "psychedelic anarchists".

In the final days of the month, press reports were confidentially forecasting an early out-of-court settlement of the case involving the postcard, which was reported to "show Wilson kneeling on a bed in the nude".

Finally, on October 12, Secunda, Wood, Wayne, Ireson (Trevor Burton's real name), Kefford and Bevan found themselves called to London's High Court in the action brought by a man named simply as James Harold Wilson, who was not in court. Also named in the libel action were postcard designer Neil Smith, C.C.S Advertising Associates and printers Richard Moore & Leslie.

In the proceedings before Mr Justice Melford Stevenson, the Prime Minister was perhaps surprisingly represented by Quintin Hogg QC, a

Conservative MP and former Tory Minister who had once tried to defend the antics of adulterous Conservative MP John Profumo with model-cum-call girl Christine Keeler.

The three members of The Move – Ireson, Kefford and Wood – who were under the age of 21 were sued through their parents and, together with the underage Smith, were referred to in court as "infants". They were all represented by Mr Richard Hartley, who also acted for Wayne, Bevan and manager Secunda.

Hogg told the court that the postcard published to promote the record 'Flowers In The Rain' – "a song and dance number which had nothing to with public affairs" – contained a libel on the Prime Minister that would have warranted criminal proceedings.

He also confirmed that Wilson had been aware of false and malicious rumours about his personal character and integrity, which had been circulating for some years, and he had, up to now, contemptuously ignored them. However, according to Hogg, Secunda commissioned the designer, advertising agency and printers to produce what amounted to a "violent and malicious personal attack on the Prime Minister".

While Hogg gave no details of the rumours, nor did he clarify what was actually on the offending postcard, newspaper reports of the court action said the card included a sketch of Mr Wilson in the nude. There were subsequent and conflicting reports as to whether the nude caricature of Wilson was actually on a bed or in a bath, but either way the woman in the picture was consistently referred to as "a woman who was not his wife".

Secunda, according to Hogg's statement in court, had purported to justify his action in producing and distributing the postcard through the open post in various press interviews, "on the inconsistent pleas that it was meant as a joke and that it was inspired by his [Secunda's] dislike of the Prime Minister".

Speaking on Wilson's behalf, Hogg told the High Court and the judge that the postcard and its contents were one step too far for the Prime Minister. "Unfortunately, in order to found their attack on the plaintiff – a deliberate and gratuitous attack which had nothing to do with the subject matter of the recording – use was made of these rumours which the plaintiff has always considered it right to treat with the contempt they deserve."

Emphasising the Prime Minister's concern about the postcard and its public distribution, Hogg added: "In the present instance the scurrility of the card coupled with the extent of the circulation left him (Wilson) with no alternative but to assert his legal rights and thereby to make plain his determination to establish the complete falsity of these rumours."

It was obvious to everybody in the court and in the music business that Secunda's "joke" postcard had backfired, and it represented the final straw for Prime Minister Wilson in the light of the continuing rumours about his private life. Since the issue of the first writ on September 1 and the subsequent injunctions halting the distribution of the postcard, negotiations had obviously gone on between counsels representing Wilson, The Move, Secunda and the other defendants, which resulted in a swift ending to the High Court action.

Hogg was able to confirm to Judge Stevenson that: "The defendants have now realised the unacceptable nature of their conduct and, it is fair to say, have never at any time suggested that there was any word of truth in any of the suggestions contained in the libel."

Accepting a settlement that would have a long-lasting impact on the group's finances − and those of composer Wood in particular − Hogg explained that Wilson never intended to be harsh or vindictive and had accepted extremely generous terms of settlement from the defendants. But he finished by adding: "In view however of the wide dissemination of the postcard he wishes me to make it clear that he would not necessarily take the same lenient view on any subsequent occasions."

In addition to offering their apologies to Wilson, the defendants agreed to pay the Prime Minister's costs, which were variously calculated to be between £2,000 and £3,000, while C.C.S., which confirmed that they had handed over all remaining copies of the postcard along with the glass negative plates, and Richard Moore & Leslie paid agreed damages.

The judge, an outspoken public critic of the permissive society of the Sixties, also placed a ban on any representation or any disclosure of the postcard's contents, a restriction that remains in place to this day.

However, for the members of the band − who spent the night before the proceedings playing a concert in Sheffield and arrived at court in a hired Rolls Royce five minutes after the proceedings had ended – there was an added financial penalty in the settlement.

While expressing their appreciation of the generous attitude displayed by Wilson in the case, The Move agreed that all their royalties from 'Flowers In The Rain' would go to charities nominated by the Prime Minister in perpetuity.

At the time, it was reckoned that the Spastics Society and the Amenity Funds of Stoke Mandeville Hospital would receive around £10,000 based on sales of approximately 200,000 records up to October 1967.

Over the past 40 years the two charities have continued to receive payments, including Wood's personal publishing royalties as the composer of 'Flowers In the Rain', and these have by now undoubtedly run into hundreds of thousands – perhaps even millions – of pounds.

Fresh from court, the members of The Move were quick to confirm their political standpoint to waiting reporters: "We've no faith in any political sides at all. We'd vote for people like Frank Zappa, Jimi Hendrix, you know."

Secunda, whose role as manager and mentor to the group was in jeopardy after the case, denied that the postcard had been a publicity stunt: "Wilson started legal proceedings, we did it as a cartoon, remember that. It wasn't intended to be anything but that."

But it was not all bad news for The Move. In the same week as they were hauled before the High Court to face the wrath of the Prime Minister, it was announced that they had signed to A&M Records in America and, under a deal that was reported to be worth $2 million, 'Flowers In The Rain' was planned as the first single release.

For the band members, the period after the court case was a time for reflection on their relationship with Secunda. Wayne saw the case as the beginning of the end for The Move. "We were suddenly thrown into the High Court of Justice and we were defenceless. Had we been sensible we'd have taken council (sic) and listened to what we should have said. Instead we admitted to something that we didn't actually do – all because we thought it was good fun to do.

"It was Secunda's bag and we should have quickly stepped away from it. It was a stunt too far but by then of course, we couldn't."

Even with the royalties going to charity, the band continued to play the song in their live shows and it was still featured on radio. Talking to *Rolling Stone* magazine, Wood later made clear how he felt about it all. "The sick thing is that we had to promote the single all the same."

Drummer Bevan was similarly unimpressed with their manager's initiative in producing the libellous postcard. "We didn't even know he was going to do it and, while the other stunts were fun, this was beyond a joke and we were terrified. We were frightened of what Secunda might do next and we split with him."

In fact, the band's parting of the ways with their occasionally inspirational manager was finally brought about in part by the planned follow-up single to the notorious 'Flowers In The Rain'.

While releasing 'Cherry Blossom Clinic', a song written by Wood about the delights of a mental institution, was considered potentially controversial, it was the idea of featuring as the B-side 'Vote For Me' – a song that could have constituted a dig at PM Wilson and the political establishment – that brought things to a head.

The record was cancelled and soon after so was The Move's contract with Secunda. According to Wayne, who died aged 61 in 2004, it signalled the end of a bright future for one of the most successful groups to come out of Britain's second city. "I do believe that when Tony Secunda went – and we got rid of Secunda because we got scared – that was the end of it. We dug our own graves because I think ultimately Secunda could have got us through."

But it was not to be. Secunda went on to manage Marc Bolan, Steeleye Span and Marianne Faithfull before moving to California, where he died in 1995, aged 54. Writing Secunda's obituary in *The Independent* newspaper, respected rock writer Chris Welch described the man who was brought to court and to his knees by a British Prime Minister as: "One of an elite corps of pop managers who galvanised the Swinging Sixties and helped shape the course of popular music."

Meanwhile, The Move – who were voted 18th Best British Vocal Group and eighth Best New Group in the 1967 *New Musical Express* Awards – lasted without further major incident until 1971, by which time Kefford, Burton and Wayne had all left. Wood and Bevan soldiered on, producing seven more hit singles and three albums.

28

Despite their $2 million American recording deal, the band consistently failed to even dent the lower reaches of the US charts. Ultimately, Wood launched his much-vaunted Electric Light Orchestra with fellow Brummie Jeff Lynne. However, after less than 12 months, Wood moved on to form Wizzard.

In April 2007, Marcia Williams – who had been elevated to a peerage in 1974 and took the title Lady Falkender – brought the rumours of her alleged affair with Harold Wilson back into the public eye when she sued the BBC over the drama documentary *The Lavender List*, which repeated the suggestions of a relationship in association with Wilson's 1976 resignation honours list.

The programme, which was broadcast on BBC4, cost the corporation £75,000 in damages to Lady Falkender, plus total costs estimated at £200,000 and an undertaking that it would never be screened again.

So, at the end of the day, both The Move and the BBC paid through the nose for their ill-advised and damaging productions featuring references to Prime Minister Harold Wilson and his loyal personal secretary.

Chapter 3

THE BEATLES

How it all came to an end for the world's biggest group

For eight years from 1962, The Beatles ruled the world as the biggest pop music act of the decade. They overshadowed every other collection of musicians who got together after them in the hope of achieving just the smallest taste of the Fab Four's extraordinary global success.

From 'Love Me Do' and 'Please Please Me' to the final 'Let It Be' single and album release in 1970, John Lennon, Paul McCartney, George Harrison and Ringo Starr stood heads and shoulders above everybody else. They sold records by the millions, attracted crowds in their ten of thousands and won literally hundreds of awards.

But somewhere along the line the glitter faded and the fame, fortune and adulation turned into a millstone around the necks of the four most famous musicians Britain has ever produced.

For years pundits, critics and fans have theorised how and why and when it all started to go wrong. Was it the death of manager and mentor Brian Epstein? Maybe it was John bringing Yoko Ono into the fold while Paul linked with Linda Eastman? Perhaps it was the pressure of running their bizarre Apple company and dealing with the new men in suits who came into their lives? Or did they finally just fall out of love?

After Epstein's death in 1967, Starr admitted, "We wondered what we were going to do. We were suddenly like chickens without heads." Lennon observed that Yoko and Linda never had an argument and then posed the question, "How can two women split up four strong men? It's impossible." Looking back at Apple, Harrison told the world, "I've no idea who thought of Apple first. It was a bad idea, whoever thought of it. The idea of it was much better than the reality." While McCartney admitted, "I'd fallen out with the other three over the [Allen] Klein thing," and then added for good measure, "I didn't leave The Beatles. The Beatles have left The Beatles, but no one wants to be the one to say the party's over."

Certainly, during recording sessions in 1968 and 1969, both Starr and Harrison walked out of the group, albeit briefly, in the lead-up to American music lawyer Allen Klein – known to many in the music business as "notorious" – being appointed as the group's business manager in February 1969.

At around the same time, McCartney's future father-in-law, Lee Eastman, and his company were named as counsel for Apple. By April it was clear there were two very different sides involved in the business of The Beatles, and a letter dated April 18 sent to Eastman confirmed the rapidly disintegrating situation.

Dear Mr Eastman,

This is to inform you of the fact that you are not authorised to act or hold yourself out as the attorney or legal representative of "The Beatles" or any of the companies which The Beatles own or control.

We recognise that you are authorized to act for Paul McCartney, personally, and in this regard we will instruct our representatives to give you the fullest co-operation.

We would appreciate you forwarding to
ABKCO Industries Inc
1700 Broadway
New York
N.Y.

all documents, correspondence and files which you hold in your possession relating to the affairs of The Beatles, or any of the companies which The Beatles own or control.

The letter was signed "very truly yours" by John Lennon, Richard Starkey and George Harrison.*

In September, The Beatles had got together at their Savile Row offices for a serious meeting to discuss Apple business. Paul recalled afterwards, "The group was getting very tense. It was looking like we were breaking up."

And as if to prove McCartney right, Lennon chose the meeting to tell his colleagues what he thought of the suggestions that they should go back on the road playing small clubs. "I think you're daft. I want a divorce just like I had from Cyn [Cynthia Powell, Lennon's first wife]."

Even though McCartney claimed he didn't leave The Beatles, by releasing his first solo album in April 1970 alongside the group's *Let It Be*, he became the first Beatle to publicly nail his colours to his own mast. On April 10, this was made official with the glaring headline: "Paul Quits The Beatles".

In fact, the release of the *McCartney* album was one of the things that set the alarm bells ringing for the singing songwriting bass player. The inclusion of the words, "An ABKCO-managed company" in relation to Apple on the sleeve added to his growing sense of anger and frustration.

In August 1970, he sent a letter to *Melody Maker* that made abundantly clear his position regarding the future of The Beatles. "In order to put out of its misery the limping dog of a news story which has been dragging itself across your pages for the past year, my answer to the question: 'Will the Beatles get together again?' is No."†

So, with Lennon off working with the Plastic Ono Band, Starr completing his *Sentimental Journey* solo album and Harrison producing

---

* This letter was sold for £48,000 at a London auction in May 2005.
† In 1985, this letter came up at auction at Sotheby's and was bought by McCartney himself for £10,000.

THE SINGLE MEN ARE HOHOS

Hare Krishna projects and touring with Delaney & Bonnie & Friends, The Beatles had definitely come to an end in a creative and musical sense... but there were still a whole bunch of legal issues to be resolved.

Again it was McCartney who took the initiative and, on the last day of December 1970 – almost eight years to the day after their debut single peaked at number 17 in the charts – he filed a suit in the Chancery Division of the High Court against the rest of the group, seeking to dissolve the partnership known as The Beatles & Co.

While McCartney had opted for the Eastmans to look after his affairs, Lennon, Harrison and Starr decided to stay with Klein, and for McCartney this left him with no real alternative. "I wanted to sue Klein but the only recourse was to sue my former mates," was how he described the situation.

High Court case 1970 No. 6315 was all set to be a major and very messy public divorce that, in McCartney's eyes, pitted him against the world. "So it was three against one. Never mind three against one. It was me against three million as far as I was concerned."

In his writ, McCartney also asked that the affairs of the partnership – which was launched in 1967 on the eve of the release of *Sgt. Pepper's Lonely Hearts Club Band* – be wound up, that accounts and inquiries be taken (in particular of dealings between the partners) and that a receiver should be appointed to collect debts accruing to the partnership of The Beatles & Co. McCartney also requested costs in his action.

Named as defendants in the action were Lennon, Harrison, Starr (Richard Starkey) and the company Apple Corps., formed in 1968, which was overseen by Klein in his capacity as the group's manager.

An independent music industry lawyer assessed the action at the time and concluded that the appointment of a receiver would be the first step and, assuming there were no objections, one would be appointed to report back to the court. "The court will decide who should take what when the receiver has looked in the accounts. In The Beatles' case it would be a fairly long and involved business because their affairs are pretty far-flung."

He also suggested that, "It seems like a simple dissolution of partnership case, rather like winding up a company."

Proceedings got under way on January 19, 1971 when McCartney's counsel, David Hirst QC, told the judge, Mr Justice Stamp, that Klein was a man "of bad commercial reputation" who was to blame for the serious state of The Beatles' finances. Hirst confirmed to the court that his client had never accepted Klein as manager or trusted him, and had strongly opposed his appointment. In making McCartney's case for the appointment of a receiver to act as "caretaker" of the assets of The Beatles & Co., Hirst said that Klein had "drawn down the shutters on any information about the financial position, despite repeated requests from Paul, his legal advisers and his accountants".

Describing The Beatles' financial position as "very, very serious", counsel, while acknowledging that the group's income had to be measured in millions of pounds, stated: "The latest accounts suggest there probably is not enough in the kitty to meet even the individual Beatles' income tax and surtax liability, let alone the Apple company's corporation tax."

With none of the Beatles in court, Hirst continued to outline McCartney's concerns. "So grave was the deficiency of accounts and so substantial the potential tax liability that it is submitted that a receiver ought, at all events, to be appointed." He added that the previous evening draft accounts had been delivered to McCartney's solicitor revealing a "grave state of affairs".

While McCartney was, according to Hirst, concerned that his artistic freedom would be interfered with, the court heard that McCartney's debut solo album had earned the bass player £487,000 in royalties.

Counsel for McCartney told the judge that his client's partners (Lennon, Harrison and Starr) had, against his wishes and in breach of their partnership agreement, appointed Klein's company, ABKCO, as their exclusive business managers "at a fee of no less than 20% of the gross income".

Figures showed that the net combined profits of The Beatles' partnership for the year ended March 31, 1968 were £1.5 million. The accounts received on the eve of the hearing showed the total amount credited to the four members of The Beatles was £738,000, of which £678,000 was owing in income tax, explained Hirst, who added that The Beatles were also liable to pay a surtax of £500,000.

The final shot in the one-day hearing came from A.J. Balcombe QC, counsel for Klein, who protested at the "extremely adverse comments" that had been made in court about his client.

The judge was seemingly unmoved and adjourned the full hearing for a month, during which time the royalty income of The Beatles would remain frozen.

When the hearing reconvened on February 19, it was in court number 16, a room with a public gallery that was not open to visitors. McCartney was in court, having listened to the urgings of his father-in-law, Lee Eastman, who apparently told him in no uncertain terms what was at stake. "It's all or nothing. You could end up a free man, or working the rest of your life for Allen Klein."

His appearance, according to close associates from Apple, also earned McCartney two shillings (10 pence) from a bet with a courtroom usher who had his money on Lennon and Yoko Ono turning up to make their points in public.

Hirst went over issues he had raised during the January hearing and confirmed to Mr Justice Stamp that the essence of The Beatles & Co. partnership was an agreement to perform together as a group. He added that they had not done so for nearly two years and "never would again".

He informed the court that each of The Beatles had a 5% share in The Beatles & Co. while Apple Corps held the remaining 80%. Stressing that McCartney considered Klein to be a man of very bad commercial reputation, Hirst said, "Mr Klein has paid himself commission out of the funds to which he is not entitled and has asserted an entitlement to even more."

Moving on to the fact that Klein had been convicted a month earlier by a New York court on 10 tax offences, Hirst added, "This has not enhanced our confidence in him."

There were, according to Hirst, three events in early 1970 that made McCartney decide to leave The Beatles. Firstly, that Klein had tried to delay the release of McCartney's solo album on the grounds that it was in breach of the partnership agreement. (It transpired that the agreement, which Klein had uncovered, only prevented The Beatles from appearing alone or with other artists and had nothing to do with solo recordings.)

McCartney's second reason, according to Hirst, was the fact that ABKCO altered his song 'The Long And Winding Road' on the *Let It*

Be album without consulting him. Finally, he complained that ABKCO, without McCartney's authority, transferred the rights of the film *Let It Be* from Apple to United Artists.

In a letter read out to the court, *Let It Be* producer Phil Spector – the man behind the legendary "Wall of Sound" and classic hits such as 'Be My Baby', 'You've Lost That Lovin' Feelin'' and 'River Deep Mountain High' – wrote to The Beatles about the track 'The Long And Winding Road'. "This has strings, voices, horns and Ringo's drums overdubbed. I like it as a title for the album instead of *Let It Be* but that's just a personal preference." The letter ended, "If there's anything you'd like done to the LP let me know and I'll be glad to help. Naturally little things are easy to change, big things would be a problem."

McCartney's reply to Klein, dated April 14, 1970 and addressed to Apple Corps at 3 Savile Row, was also read out. It began, "In future no one will be allowed to add or subtract from a recording of one of my songs without my permission."

He also admitted that he had considered orchestrating 'The Long And Winding Road' but had decided against it, and now wanted the Spector recording to be altered so that the strings, horns and voices were all lowered in volume, the vocals and Beatles instrumentation brought up in volume, and a harp removed completely from the end of the song and the original piano notes substituted.

He signed off with the warning to Klein – "Don't ever do it again" – and copied the letter to both Spector and John Eastman, McCartney's brother-in-law.

Discussing the draft accounts for 1970, which showed The Beatles' income to be around £4 million, with a potentially huge tax liability, Hirst claimed that the accounts obtained gave differing versions, which made it difficult to ascertain McCartney's financial position. "But this," he added, "has not prevented Mr Klein's company, ABKCO, drawing commission to the tune of £1,500,000 out of the business."

He added that EMI were holding £488,000 in royalties earned by McCartney's album *McCartney* until the courts decided whether they should go to the partnership or to the former Beatle himself.

McCartney did not give evidence from the witness box but had a prepared statement read to the court by Hirst. In it, he confirmed that

The Beatles had drifted apart after the death of their manager Brian Epstein and that, when Lennon urged Harrison and Starr to follow his lead and appoint Klein as their business manager, it appeared that for the first time there might be an irreconcilable difference between the group members.

Letting everyone in court know exactly how the ex-Beatle felt, McCartney's written brief went on: "As time went on I grew to distrust Klein on the grounds of his proneness to boast about his ability to make spectacular deals which he proved unable to fulfil; his tendency to sow discord; his untruthfulness; and his unscrupulous efforts to hold himself out as my manager and gain commission in other fields not covered by his agreement."

After explaining to the court that he and Lennon had criticised each other's music, that both Harrison and Starr had briefly left The Beatles and that his own efforts to get the group to perform again had been rebuffed, McCartney said he sent a note to Lennon in August 1970 suggesting that they should "let each other out of the trap".

According to McCartney's statement, Lennon replied with a photograph of himself and Yoko Ono with a balloon coming out of his mouth with the words: "How and why?" Paul's reply suggested they sign a piece of paper saying they dissolved the partnership because there *was* no partnership, to which Lennon sent another card, this time saying: "Get well soon. Get the other signatures and I will think about it."

The next day's proceedings centred around a number of disagreements between Hirst and his opposite number, Mr Morris Finer QC, acting for Lennon, Harrison, Starr and Apple Corps. Speaking on behalf of Klein, Finer said the American lawyer had "rescued The Beatles from almost total bankruptcy. His job was to get money for the group ... and in that he was very successful".

After Hirst claimed that newspaper cuttings showed that "Mr Klein has a bad reputation" and produced an affidavit from a lawyer that said, "I could not permit any client of mine to be represented by a person of the character shown in these cuttings", Finer said that the criticism of Klein was an attempt to "assassinate a man morally and commercially". He then added that Klein was not a party to the proceedings and would never have the opportunity of giving evidence.

Describing the finances of The Beatles, which Klein inherited in early 1969, as being in a "dreadful situation", Finer said that Klein took the view that the important thing to do "having regard to the total mess and almost total bankruptcy of their affairs" was to generate income as quickly as possible.

He read to the court a newspaper cutting in which Lennon was quoted as saying, "If Apple goes on losing money at the present rate we will all be broke in six months."

Explaining that the members of The Beatles, apart from McCartney, had always considered individual earnings as group assets, Finer admitted that Harrison's solo number one record, 'My Sweet Lord', was likely to earn over £1 million in royalties during 1971. "My clients have always treated these royalties from individual recordings as partnerships assets," he added.

He suggested that this would be no disadvantage to McCartney as Harrison's solo record royalties would be "twice as much as McCartney's in the current year".

Day three brought more written statements for the court to listen to, this time from the three Beatles named as defendants in the action brought by McCartney to dissolve their partnership. And it was apparent to all in the High Court that this was no longer a tale of peace, love, and understanding.

Harrison, dubbed by many as the "quiet one", admitted that there was an issue with McCartney about whose songs should go on The Beatles' albums. "To get a peaceful life I had always let him have his own way, even when it meant that songs I had composed were not being recorded. At the same time I was helping to record his songs and, into the bargain, I was having to put up with him telling me how to play my own musical instrument."

Harrison's written testimony went on to cover the day he quit the band during the filming of *Let It Be*, when he believed that Paul was criticising him in front of the cameras about the way he was playing. "I told the others I had had enough and was leaving the group. After a few days they asked me to return and, as Paul agreed that he would not try to interfere or teach me how to play, I went back."

To Starr it seemed that McCartney was both good and bad, as he described him as the greatest bass player in the world but also as some-one who was "very determined". "He goes on and on to see if he can get his own way," added the man who had been the last recruit to the group in 1962.

Things came to a head when it was decided at Apple that McCartney's first solo album should be delayed because of the group's pending *Let It Be* and Ringo's debut solo offering, *Sentimental Journey*. "He went completely out of control, shouting at me, prodding his fin-gers towards my face, saying, 'I'll finish you now' and 'You'll pay'," said Starr. "While I thought Paul had behaved like a spoilt child, I could see that the release date of his record had a gigantic emotional significance to him."

After Starr's album had been brought forward and the group's release put back to accommodate *McCartney*, Starr was "shocked and dis-mayed" to find that McCartney had issued a writ after he had promised a meeting of all four Beatles in January 1971. "I trust Paul and I know that he would not lightly disregard his promise. Something serious, about which I have no knowledge, must have happened between Paul's meeting with George in New York and the end of December." Starr's final statement to the court was one of hope despite the circumstances and surroundings. "My own view is that all four of us together could even yet work out everything satisfactorily."

The last statement read to the court came from McCartney's princi-pal rival in the battle to rule The Beatles. John Lennon began by claim-ing that the main cause of the rows in the group were musical and artistic differences. "Paul preferred pop-type music while George and I preferred what is now called 'underground'," he said. "This may have led to arguments, particularly between Paul and George. But the con-trast in our tastes I am sure did more good than harm and contributed to our success," added Lennon.

He also told of the time after the death of Epstein when "spongers and hustlers" descended on Apple while the staff were "lavish with money and hospitality".

His statement was confirmation of what the music industry had been writing and talking about for months – the totally disorganised state of affairs at Apple. "We have since discovered that around that time two of the company's cars had completely disappeared, and also that we owned a house which no one can remember buying."

Acknowledging that there had been a power struggle for control of The Beatles' affairs between Klein and Lee Eastman, Lennon, Harrison and Starr agreed that Klein was honest, hard-working and had their interests at heart, although he could be "rough, tough and blunt".

Counsel for Lennon, Harrison, Starr and Apple also suggested that any inference from McCartney's counsel that Mr Klein had "his fingers in the till" was completely untrue.

Explaining that after the death of their manager, he and McCartney had tried to be businesslike about the group's affairs, Lennon admitted that it had not been easy. "We were handicapped by our general ignorance of accountancy and business practice and preoccupied with musical activities," he said, before outlining some of the worthwhile things that Klein did soon after his appointment.

According to Lennon, Klein dismissed the incompetent staff, stopped the hustling and lavish hospitality, sent each of The Beatles accounts of their own personal spending, together with regular bank statements, and generally brought order back to Apple.

"My own experience of Klein," added Lennon, "has been that if I asked a straight question I would get a straight answer. If Paul is trying to break us up because of anything that happened before the Klein-Eastman power struggle, his reasoning does not make sense."

So in just one day, three Beatles had set about their old mate in an English court of law and shown once and for all that the chances of a Beatles comeback were lost in tales of acrimony and mistrust. They once sang that money can't buy you love – and now everybody knew it was true.

Allen Klein had risen to fame and fortune as manager of the singers Sam Cooke and Bobby Vinton and from representing the likes of The Animals, Herman's Hermits and The Rolling Stones, for whom he re-negotiated a record deal with Decca in 1965 that outstripped even The Beatles' EMI contract.

His ABKCO operation (the Allen and Betty Klein Company), set up in 1969, was born out of Cameo Parkway Records, in which he had a controlling interest, and his long-time ambition to look after The Beatles had been noted by EMI executives even before Epstein's death.

Having achieved his goal in 1969, Klein found himself in court on February 24, 1971 listening to counsel read out a sworn affidavit defending his actions.

After evidence claiming that in just 18 months Klein had boosted The Beatles' income from £850,000 to £4.3 million, the American accountant maintained that The Beatles had "greatly benefited" from the deals he had done.

Saying that McCartney had made attacks on his commercial integrity in general and in his dealings with The Beatles in particular, Klein gave details of his involvement with Cameo Parkway Records dating from 1967, a year before over-the-counter trading in the company's stock was suspended as its assets did not meet requirements for certain transactions.

"Since it has been suggested that the suspension and de-listing of the stock is an indication of lack of commercial integrity on my part, I stress that there is no allegation by the American Stock Exchange of any dishonest or improper conduct on my part," Klein stated, although he did confirm that he had been found guilty of tax offences in New York.

As his evidence ran into a second day, the court heard that since 1962 The Beatles had earned £17 million but that in the 19 months since Klein had been their manager, the group had made £9 million – more than they had made in the six years before he was appointed. "Truly remarkable figures," said Finer.

He added, "There is no question at all that they [The Beatles] are not merely solvent but very solvent indeed", and the court was told that The Beatles' assets currently amounted to over £8.5 million.

The details of The Beatles' finances were laid bare before the court as part of Klein's claim that the group had benefited from his period as their manager, with Finer pinpointing the periods and the earnings.

Between June 1962, when they signed their first one-year recording contract with EMI Records, and December 1968, The Beatles had earned a total of £7,864,000 from tours, films, record royalties and various other sources. "Just under £8 million in six and a half years," said Finer.

From May 1969 and December 1970, their earnings had increased to £9,142,000 and, of this, £8,100,000 came from record royalties and £704,000 from films, with no account of receipts from other writing, explained Finer, who confirmed that, as counsel for Apple, he was keeping a "watching brief" for Klein.

Dealing with McCartney's request for a receiver to be appointed to oversee The Beatles' assets, Finer stated, "It will be certain, as I see it, to undermine the financial and commercial status of The Beatles' companies. It will make it impossible to recruit new artists and it will create enormous confusion in the minds of companies and individuals having dealings with Apple as to whom they should account and with whom they should deal."

The man who started the action to break up the biggest band of all time gave his evidence, again in a written statement, on Friday February 26, immediately countering Klein's claims that The Beatles' assets were enormous and that the film *Let It Be* was "making an absolute fortune for all four of them".

His view was that the film – premiered in London on May 20, 1970 with not a single member of the group present – might have been more lucrative if the rights had not been transferred by Klein from Apple to United Artists without McCartney's approval.

The man who wrote 'Yesterday' – the world's most covered song – then told the court of a telephone conversation with Klein in which he alleged the group's manager told him, "The real trouble is Yoko. She is the one with ambition." McCartney said his reaction to this statement was, "I wonder what John Lennon would have said if he had heard that remark", and claimed that, in the same call, Klein also said, "John is angry with you because you came off better than him in *Let It Be*."

Covering the well-reported rows and walkouts in the group from 1968 onwards, McCartney accepted that, while he was partly to blame for the flare-up with Harrison, the guitarist had walked out because he "could not get on with Yoko".

He also admitted that in his row with Starr he had told the drummer, "If you drag me down I will drag you down." McCartney's counsel, Hirst, took time out to explain that what his client meant was that whatever the rest of the group did to him, he would do to them.

Three months after Klein's arrival, McCartney told the court, The Beatles had stopped recording together and had eventually broken up, because by then they had their own individual musical careers. "We have no idea of the financial position of the group," he said.

McCartney's counsel continued his client's argument when the court resumed on Monday, March 1. "Mr Klein has already drained assets to which he is not entitled to the tune of several hundred thousand pounds," he said, before adding that the group's American manager was claiming a further £200,000 commission on record sales.

"If a receiver is not appointed," said Hirst, "no doubt Mr Klein will collect the £200,000 and continue to collect the full 20% rate on all future payments, including the recent receipt in February of a further £800,000."

Hirst went on to claim that Klein had received £647,000 in commission on record royalties and this was nearly £400,000 too much.

Counsel for Lennon, Harrison, Starr and Apple Corps responded by telling the court that Beatles assets worth £1.5 million, at the time frozen in New York, could be brought to London as part of his client's plan to halt the appointment of a receiver to look into the multi-million pound affairs of The Beatles.

Finer denied that The Beatles' assets were in jeopardy and stated that under the proposals he had suggested, the accounts of Apple Corps could be produced for inspection within two weeks of the end of each month.

He added that it would be cheaper to keep the £1.5 million in America, but agreed that if they waited for the exchange rates to alter it could take several months. He also claimed that appointing a receiver would put a stop to transactions involving The Beatles.

At this point, Mr Justice Stamp jumped in to confirm what effect appointing a receiver would have: "It would not stop the business. I want to make that clear." Finer was still unconvinced and declared that a receiver "would be an absolute disaster" and lead to competing claims for the money earned by The Beatles.

Commenting on the judge's interruption, Finer went to some lengths to make clear that he did not intend to convey the impression that The Beatles' business would come to a full stop, but still argued that a

43

receiver would have a disrupting effect. "The business and commercial reputation of the company is likely to be very seriously affected," he claimed.

At this point, McCartney's counsel offered some small ray of hope to the other Beatles and their counsel by confirming that he was willing to consider proposals that did not involve a receiver being appointed.

The judge, however, appeared committed to his proposal of appointing a receiver with the authority to appoint sub-managers to look after the affairs of the individual Beatles. He also confirmed that if Lennon, Harrison and Starr wanted to propose Klein in this role while McCartney wanted to nominate somebody else, then that would be acceptable.

Then, just before lunch on the 11th day of the hearing, second counsel for the three Beatles and Apple, Mr William Forbes, requested an adjournment to take instructions on the judge's proposal.

After the adjournment, leading counsel Finer returned to the fold and asked permission to speak to the court. He then made clear his objections to Mr Justice's Stamp's proposals and offered an undertaking that, he stated, was designed to give McCartney complete control over his own affairs.

Not surprisingly, the judge seemed less than pleased with the defence counsel's take on events before the court and cut him off early. "What it amounts, to Mr Finer, is that you are not prepared to accept my suggestions and you are putting forward a counter-proposal." The judge then asked McCartney's counsel, Hirst, if he was prepared to accept this development.

"Certainly not," came the reply.

At this point, the judge brought the hearing to an abrupt end with the words, "In that case judgement will be reserved," before leaving the court.

Just over a week later, Mr Justice Stamp returned to the High Court to give his judgement. In his summing-up he confirmed that Klein had been appointed as manager of The Beatles by Lennon, Harrison and Starr, without McCartney's approval. "The document by which the appointment of ABKCO was effected was in truth a remarkable document," he concluded.

He added that the same three Beatles, again without telling McCartney, had agreed that Klein should take more commission than was specified under his agreement. He called that a "grave breach" of their responsibilities to their partner. "Had the agreement been brought to the attention of Mr McCartney there would have been a row which would have reverberated through the voluminous mass of papers which are before me."

Observing that The Beatles company was not "a Frankenstein set up to control the individual partners", Mr Justice Stamp added, "Apple, like the individual defendants, is the plaintiff's partner and if, as submitted, the defendants or any of them covertly made an oral agreement increasing ABKCO's commission in the way I have indicated, without the plaintiff's knowledge and consent, it in my judgement committed a grave breach of its duties as the plaintiff's partner."

While the arrangement that was kept secret from McCartney gave Klein's ABKCO more commission than it should have had, the judge stressed that Klein had not taken any of The Beatles' money, but he did agree that McCartney did have grounds for distrusting Klein. Klein's attempts to justify his actions were, according to the judge, the "irresponsible patter of a second-rate salesman", although, he added, Lennon, Harrison and Starr did attribute to the manager a "vast increase" in their income.

But it was their decision to exclude McCartney from his share in the management of their Beatles & Co partnership that, according to the judge, pointed strongly in favour of a receiver being appointed. "The controversy in this action has centred around the personality and activities of Mr Klein," said Mr Justice Stamp. "However successful Mr Klein may have been in generating income, I am satisfied that The Beatles' financial situation is confused, uncertain and confusing. A third party is needed not merely to secure the assets, but so that there may be a firm hand to manage the business fairly and produce order."

Before finishing the business of the court, and effectively agreeing to the end of The Beatles, the judge turned his attention to Klein and expressed some sympathy that he had been forced to sit and listen to "allegations regarding his conduct, with which he, not being party to the action, could not deal".

But Mr Justice Stamp then focused on the court action in America against Klein. "There is the unfortunate fact that he has been found guilty, and his evidence not believed, in a recent trial in New York on charges that he did unlawfully, wilfully and knowingly fail to make and file returns relating to the withholding of employees' taxes.

"It is right to add that the conviction is under appeal, but I find Mr Klein's description of the proceedings in his affidavit is somewhat disingenuous."

Naming chartered accountant James Douglas Spooner to be both manager and receiver of The Beatles' multi-million pound business empire until a full trial determined the long-term future of The Beatles and their companies, the judge then postponed the appointment for a week in case the other three Beatles decided to lodge an appeal.

This news came after he accepted the submission that it would be unreasonable to expect McCartney to submit to "ABKCO's continued management". He posed the question: "How can the plaintiff, in light of his commercial trust and having regard to the inevitable personal difficulties that would arise, be expected to go on dealing with Mr Klein?

"Nor do I believe that the appointment of a receiver will in the least degree discourage the purchase of Beatles records from which their income stems."

Not surprisingly, the reaction of the main players in the High Court drama reflected which side they were on in the dispute. McCartney's brother-in-law, John Eastman, was reported as commenting, "Round one for the good guys", before adding, "In my opinion Stamp's judgement was very lucid and accurate."

On the other hand, Klein was quoted as saying, "I couldn't understand the appointment of a receiver. If there hadn't been any money then I could understand it. But there was so much money."

McCartney's comments went along the lines of, "So I got my freedom out of that", before adding, "Funnily enough we couldn't get Klein, because what he'd done wasn't actually a crime."

He also acknowledged that breaking up the most popular music group the world had ever seen was never going to be the greatest PR move. "It certainly did not make me the most popular man in Britain. It was very, very traumatic and there was no great joy in winning, except I knew that justice had been done, although in my case, personally, justice hadn't been done because the others were continuing to slag me off."

In May 1971, the plans of Lennon, Harrison and Starr to launch an appeal against the final trial to dissolve The Beatles' partnership were formally abandoned.

Their counsel, Finer, found himself once again in the High Court, this time to admit that his clients thought it best, in the circumstances, to work out a way in which McCartney could "disengage" himself from the partnership – and The Beatles. Asking for their appeal to be dismissed, Finer admitted that the appeal would be hostile to the atmosphere best suited for negotiations.

As McCartney was allowed to continue his action to dissolve The Beatles, his three former partners had to find in the region of £100,000 to pay the legal costs the original judge had ordered them to pay at the end of the first hearing.

The five-minute hearing to abandon the appeal, which attracted none of The Beatles to the court, ended with Lord Justice Russell saying that he hoped the four Beatles would reach an amiable and sensible agreement, before adding, "My only disappointment is that I am not able to make a joke about preserving the Status Quo – which is the name of another pop group."

Within two years of these High Court actions – pitting Lennon, Harrison, Starr and Apple against McCartney in a public row over Klein – the three defendants themselves ended their management contracts with the American businessman and were immediately involved in litigation with Klein.

In June 1973, Klein sued Lennon for the alleged non-payment of a $500,000 loan, while his three former clients then sued him, alleging misrepresentation. Their ex-manager responded with a counter-charge claiming commission and expenses in excess of $42 million, plus damages of over $10 million.

Even after he lost the case in London, Klein pursued The Beatles through the courts in New York until the saga of litigation finally came to an end in January 1977. In a deal rumoured to have been brokered by Yoko Ono, the group paid Klein over $4 million to settle all outstanding differences.

Years later, Ringo conceded that getting rid of Klein was an expensive exercise. "It cost us a small fortune – but it's one of those things that we found all through life; two people sign a contract and I know exactly what it means and you know exactly what it means, but when we come to split up, magically it means something else entirely to one of you."

But, even in the light of their initial separation from Klein, the other three Beatles, according to McCartney, were reluctant to admit the error of their ways or recognise that McCartney's concerns over Klein were perhaps justified.

"In one meeting George did say, 'Well, you know, thanks for getting us out of that.' It was just one little sentence of recognition of that hell I'd been through," was how McCartney was quoted as feeling. "It was better than nothing. So they didn't actually ever thank me, and it would have been un-Beatle-like for them to thank me."

Harrison did, however, have the good humour to liken real life to fiction and compare life in The Beatles and Apple with the parody television documentary he encouraged featuring The Rutles and Rutle Corp. Premiered in 1978, *All You Need Is Cash* told the story of the four most successful musicians in the world and the people they met along the way.

"When Allen Klein came to Apple it was like that scene in *The Rutles*," said Harrison. "When Ron Decline comes into Rutle Corps and everybody jumps out of the window. He fired people, or some people ran away in fright, and then he installed a bunch of his men who then proceeded to control everything in the manner he wanted."

Finally, the long-awaited announcement formally dissolving the partnership of The Beatles & Co., which had bound together the best-loved musicians on the planet, came in January 1975. With the necessary documents signed, an application was made before a Master in the Chancery Court for the formal recognition of the fact that settlement had been reached and for the receiver, Mr Spooner, who had been supervising The Beatles' business empire since March 1971, to be withdrawn.

It was assumed that while all the ex-Beatles were free to function in their own right, they would retain their involvement with Apple, with all four of them becoming directors. Previously, only Lennon and Harrison had sat on the board.

While the four Beatles set about their solo recording careers with varying degrees of success, Klein once again found himself in court in America facing charges of tax fraud. These concerned failing to declare cash payments of close to $220,000, received from the unlawful sale of Beatles promotional records, which were considered to be free give-aways. He was fined and sentenced to two months in prison and, on his release, returned to the music business where he was involved in films, theatre and artist management.

Even if The Beatles were no more, Apple was very much still in business and, even after the deaths of Lennon and Harrison, the company they helped create has continued to represent the business and creative interests of the group.

Over the 30-plus years since The Beatles were formally and irrevocably separated, Apple has vigorously sought to protect The Beatles name and rights, and brought actions against photographers, record companies, sportswear manufacturers – plus a computer company with an almost identical name.

Chapter 4

GEORGE HARRISON

Why his first solo number one turned sour

The fact that George Harrison struggled to get his songs on Beatles albums is perhaps not surprising when you consider that he found himself up against two of the best contemporary songwriters of the 20th century.

However, he first got his chance in 1963 with a single track on the group's second album, *With The Beatles*, and, over the next seven years, contributed a further 19 solo compositions to the group's multi-million-selling albums.

In 1969, his song 'Something' became the first Beatles track not written by the esteemed team of John Lennon and Paul McCartney to be released as a single, but it was a song written for his first solo album, *All Things Must Pass*, that brought Harrison even more headlines as he was issued with a legal suit alleging plagiarism.

At just about the same time as the future of The Beatles became a matter for legal argument, Harrison released his triple album box-set in December 1970 and chose as the first single 'My Sweet Lord', which featured bass player Klaus Voormann, Ringo Starr on drums, pianist Gary Wright and members of the group Badfinger on guitars.

Co-produced by Harrison and the legendary Phil Spector, the single was released in America at the same time as the album and hit the top spot during Christmas week. Within a few weeks it had also reached number one in the UK.

By January 1971 the record had passed the 700,000 sales mark, with EMI allocating an impressive 20 record presses to meet demand for the single, which was selling at a rate of 11,000 copies a day. 'My Sweet Lord' became a massive worldwide hit, with sales of over five million – and made Harrison the first Beatle to make it to number one as a solo artist.

All this success came from a song that Harrison had originally given to recording artist Billy Preston, whom he had signed to The Beatles' own Apple record label. While it was claimed that Preston had contributed to the song's creation, the American gospel singer and pianist had, in fact, planned to release 'My Sweet Lord' as a single to go with his 1970 album *Encouraging Words*. However, these plans were shelved, presumably when Harrison decided to record and release the song himself.

While still an official member of The Beatles, Harrison had taken time out in December 1969 to tour with Delaney & Bonnie & Friends – a group led by US gospel artists Delaney and Bonnie Bramlett and featuring singer Rita Coolidge – and it was when the band were playing in Copenhagen, Denmark that 'My Sweet Lord' began to take shape.

Over 12 months later, the first inklings of a problem that was to haunt Harrison for years came to light. The February 27, 1971 issue of *New Musical Express* carried the story that Harrison, his Harrisongs publishing company and Apple Records were being sued by the owners and publishers of the million-selling hit 'He's So Fine'.

The song, recorded and released by the US girl group The Chiffons, reached the top spot in America in 1963 but failed to make it into the UK Top 10. However, the US music publisher Bright Tunes was certain that Harrison's composition owed more than a passing nod to the original song, written by Ronnie Mack, who also managed The Chiffons but tragically died just months after the group's success.

The action against Harrison, alleging copyright infringement, was brought in the UK by Keith Prowse Music (KPM), whose move was to instruct their affiliate companies plus other associated publishers around the world to stop all royalty payments on 'My Sweet Lord'.

A *Billboard* report from March 1971 said that unless Essex Music, which looked after Harrisongs on Harrison's behalf, "gives up their rights the matter will probably go to court".

A week later, the same US music industry magazine confirmed that Bright Tunes had made a legal claim that 'My Sweet Lord' plagiarised the song 'He's So Fine' written by their late client, Mack. The story also reported that Harrison claimed that his song in fact had been inspired by the song 'Oh Happy Day', a 1969 hit for the US gospel group Edwin Hawkins Singers.

After receiving the lawsuit, Allen Klein, who at the time was acting for Harrison (together with John Lennon and Ringo Starr) met with the head of Bright Tunes, Seymour Barash, in an attempt to resolve the dispute.

It was claimed that Klein's way of solving the issue was for Harrison to buy the entire Bright catalogue, including 'He's So Fine'. Barash's answer, it seems, was to suggest that Harrison surrender the copyright of 'My Sweet Lord' to Bright Tunes, which would then pay half the proceeds from the song to Harrison.

There was now an impasse, and things became even more complicated by the fact that Bright Tunes was placed in receivership while the case was waiting to go to court. As if this wasn't enough, Harrison also severed his contacts with Klein, which meant a further delay.

Once Bright Tunes was back on an even keel and its affairs were in order, Harrison was once again able to open negotiations in an attempt to achieve an out-of-court settlement.

Weeks before the trial was set to open in 1976 in New York, it seems that Harrison made an offer close to $150,000 – which represented a goodly portion of the royalties earned from 'My Sweet Lord' – with the proviso that he [Harrison] retained the copyright to his song.

Bright Tunes was seemingly disinclined to accept the offer, and apparently wanted a greater share of the royalties and also the copyright to 'My Sweet Lord', which had been given the accolade of Most Performed Work of the Year at the 1972 Ivor Novello Awards.

In fact, in a blatant effort to cash in on the publicity surrounding the lawsuit and the song, The Chiffons actually released their own version of 'My Sweet Lord' in August 1976. It failed to chart and the four girls, who had successfully sued Bright Tunes in 1964 to get out of their contract, were destined for revival tours and the US club circuit on the back of the single's release.

In the midst of all this activity, with offers and counter-offers bouncing back and forth, Klein was showing a great deal of interest in acquiring Bright Tunes for his own ABKCO company, which would mean that he would own the copyright to 'He's So Fine' and then, presumably, be up against Harrison in any subsequent lawsuit.

One man who was apparently unaware of this particular development was Harrison, who was still attempting to find some sort of settlement that would keep the issue out of court. It is unlikely Klein would have wanted to buy Bright Tunes had Harrison actually won the case, and would no doubt have insisted on some sort of get-out clause had the US music publisher lost.

In the end, neither Harrison nor his ex-manager were able to reach any sort of settlement with Bright Tunes and the case was set for trial before Federal Court Judge Richard Owen in February 1976.

At the heart of the trial concerning the alleged copyright infringement and accusation of plagiarism was an analysis of the music in both 'He's So Fine' and 'My Sweet Lord'. The two parties could not have found a more able arbiter than Judge Owen, who both composed music and conducted orchestras.

Arguments were waged about musical phrases identified as "motif A" and "motif B", both of which appeared in 'He's So Fine' and subsequently in 'My Sweet Lord', around seven years later.

Harrison recalled in court that he had begun writing 'My Sweet Lord' in Copenhagen during the tour with Delaney & Bonnie & Friends, and introduced the three-note motif A into the song alongside 'My Sweet Lord' and the words "Hallelujah" and "Hare Krishna". When he returned to London, he worked on the song with Billy Preston in the recording studio.

In fact, motif A appeared in Harrison's composition four times and was followed three times by the four-note motif B from 'He's So Fine', although there was a change in the fourth repetition. In addition, there was a "grace note" (defined as an extra note added as a non-essential embellishment), which appeared in Mack's original song and was also included in Preston's first version of Harrison's song, but which did not appear in Harrison's hit version of 'My Sweet Lord'.

Asked if he thought that motif A developed in that recording session, Harrison accepted that it was then that the notes were finalised as the beginning of the song, and, when asked if it was possible that Preston had hit on the notes, Harrison said: "Yes, it's possible also that I hit on that too, as far back as the dressing room, just scat singing."

Harrison agreed in court that motif B and the grace note probably came about in the same way as motif A – in the recording session with Preston who, he said, "might have put that there on every take, but I might just have been on one take, or he might have varied it on different takes at different places."

Experts called by Harrison attempted to persuade the court that there were differences in the two songs, and pointed out the omission of the grace note in the final released version of 'My Sweet Lord'.

Also called was Bonnie Bramlett, who gave evidence of the backstage get-together in Copenhagen, but Judge Owen ruled that her testimony was hearsay. Her husband, Delaney Bramlett, had been called as a witness but was apparently unavailable to give evidence. Had he testified he might have repeated what he subsequently told various writers about his own use of 'He's So Fine' as a blueprint for 'My Sweet Lord' during the 1969 tour. "I grabbed my guitar and started playing the Chiffons' melody from 'He's So Fine' and then sang, 'My Sweet Lord, oh my Lord, oh my Lord.'"

Later, when he heard Harrison's record on the radio, Bramlett called up George and said that he didn't mean for him to use the melody to 'He's So Fine'. "He said, 'Well, it's not exactly' and it really wasn't. He did put some curves in there but he did get sued."

In fact, Bramlett was more concerned when he discovered that Harrison was the only credited writer on the record. "I called George and he promised me that it would be on the next printing of the record. I was never given credit on that song but he did admit that the song, to a large extent, was mine, and I never saw any money from it."

The silver lining to that particular cloud was that the Mississippi-born musician never saw the inside of a New York courtroom as a co-defendant in the case brought by Bright Tunes against the only credited writer of 'My Sweet Lord' – George Harrison.

Meanwhile, as Harrison was forced to concede that he had heard 'He's So Fine' prior to writing 'My Sweet Lord', the court heard that it was a possibility that in his subconscious he knew the combination of the notes with his lyrics for 'My Sweet Lord', and this led to the similarity between the two songs.

On September 7, 1976, Judge Owen finally came to the conclusion that it was "perfectly obvious the two songs are virtually identical" but made his feelings clear in his summing up. "Did Harrison deliberately use the music of 'He's So Fine'? I do not believe so deliberately. Nevertheless it is clear that 'My Sweet Lord' is the very same song as 'He's So Fine' with different words and [that] Harrison had access to 'He's So Fine'.

"This is, under the law, infringement of copyright, and is no less so even though subconsciously accomplished."

At the same time, the judge was also called upon to decide the amount of damages due to Bright Tunes. This involved calculating the royalties earned by 'My Sweet Lord' both as a single and as a track on the *All Things Must Pass* album and a forthcoming *The Best Of George Harrison* collection.

The judge decided that Harrison owed the American music publisher a total of $1,599,987, the money earned by 'My Sweet Lord' that could be attributed to 'He's So Fine'. However, it was another five years before the question of damages was eventually settled.

The delay was caused in part by Klein's acquisition of Bright Tunes (including the copyright to 'He's So Fine') by his ABKCO company for $587,000, which led to Harrison's attorney claiming that Harrison's former manager could not buy the song *and* prosecute a former client.

While Klein requested full damages of over $1.5 million, it was made clear by the court that he had acted improperly by giving financial details about 'My Sweet Lord' to Bright Tunes, before Judge Owen found in the publisher's favour.

Concluding that the manager had breached his obligation to his former client, the judge decided that Klein could hold the copyright to 'He's So Fine' but would have to hand over the rights to Harrison in return for $587,000 plus interest, which could cover Klein's purchase of Bright Music.

This decision was met with disappointment and not a hint of cynicism by Harrison, who declared: "I don't even want to touch the guitar or piano in case I'm touching somebody's note. Somebody might own that note, so you'd better watch out."

He further showed his displeasure at the court's ruling by composing and releasing 'This Song', a satire on the legal issues, which also subtly mentioned the publisher of 'He's So Fine'. But the fact was that Harrison and Klein were destined to spend more time in front of Judge Owen as their attorneys disputed the settlements.

It was in November 1990 – nearly 20 years after Bright Tunes first issued a writ against Harrison – that the judge once again met up with the case involving the former Beatle and his ex-manager.

At the time, his decision was described in press reports as "a final judgement", which had supposedly been accepted by both parties, but the financial details were subject to a further appeal.

Judge Owen's judgement of November 5, 1990 was that Klein's ABKCO would own the song 'He's So Fine' for the world except the US, UK and Canada, where it would be owned by Harrison. At the same time, 'My Sweet Lord' would remain with Harrison for the world, although ABKCO would own an interest in all income earned by the song in all territories except the US, UK and Canada.

The New York Federal Court also decreed that in return for obtaining partial rights to 'He's So Fine', Harrison should pay ABKCO a net sum of $270,020.

At the end of the hearing, Harrison's attorney, Joseph Santora, reportedly told the media: "This is the only time I'm aware of where the defendant was found guilty of copyright infringement and wound up being awarded the song in question."

Klein, however, challenged a reduction in the price Harrison would be asked to pay for the US, UK and Canadian rights to 'He's So Fine' and, in October 1991, the case was back in court in New York.

The appeal judge sided with Harrison, and the court also denied Klein a 20% administration fee for overseeing the copyright of the song. Eventually, in March 1998, the two parties finally settled all the outstanding accounting differences relating to 'My Sweet Lord' and 'He's So Fine' – two songs that almost became one.

In the aftermath of the original lawsuit, Harrison's fellow Beatle John Lennon offered his own opinion of the alleged plagiarism. "He [Harrison] walked right into it. He knew what he was doing. He must have known. He's smarter than that. He could have changed a couple of bars in that song and nobody could ever have touched him."

In his book *I Me Mine*, Harrison, who died in November 2001, laid out his own recollections of 'My Sweet Lord' and the million-dollar lawsuit that ran for nearly 30 years.

"I wasn't consciously aware of the similarity between 'He's So Fine' and 'My Sweet Lord' when I wrote the song as it was more improvised and not so fixed although when my version came out and started to get airplay people started talking about it and it was then I thought, 'Why didn't I realise?'

"It would have been very easy to change a note here or there and not affect the feeling of the record."

In January 2002, 'My Sweet Lord' was re-issued as a single, complete with a new version recorded by Harrison in 2000 as a bonus track. Three months after his death and almost 31 years to the day after it first topped the British chart, 'My Sweet Lord' was again at number one. This time there were no arguments over money – all the proceeds went to the Material World Foundation set up by Harrison to aid poverty-stricken children around the world.

Chapter 5

APPLE

*A band and a corporation playing the name game with
each other*

"Excuse us, we've got the name Apple. You can't trade under that name." With these words, Paul McCartney outlined the basic facts behind the legal dispute between The Beatles' Apple Corps and the US corporation Apple Computer, an argument that spanned nearly 30 years and numerous court hearings.

The Beatles first registered Apple Music Ltd. in May 1967 as a vehicle through which the group could offset some of their top-rate income tax – rumoured to be around £3 million at the time – by investing in businesses related to their work as creative musicians.

Adopting the name Apple Corps – and its famous Granny Smith logo – in February 1968, the group and their advisers established Apple companies in businesses as diverse as fashion, electronics, films, records and music publishing.

The new Apple Corps – the name came from a pun devised by McCartney – bought 80% of the stock of the original Beatles Ltd. company, which had been established in June 1963, and set out on a sometimes successful but most often chaotic business programme.

Eventually, the operation focused on overseeing The Beatles' back catalogue while also acquiring photographs, film and TV footage of the group, protecting their name and copyright and giving its name and support to projects such as the *Anthology* book, CDs and documentary, and world-famous Cirque du Soleil's *Love* production.

In the late Sixties, the company was a haven for dropouts and freaks, its Savile Row offices permanently besieged by parasites seeking handouts from The Beatles. To a certain extent the group asked for it by placing adverts in the music magazines that suggested the doors were open to all and sundry with original music projects, with money for them being freely available. Inevitably, the company haemorrhaged money. "If it carries on like this we'll be broke in six months," John Lennon told *Disc*'s Ray Coleman in January 1969, a statement that prompted Allan Klein to fly to London to offer his services as business manager. When Klein's brief but eventful association with The Beatles was over, Apple was eventually put on an even keel under the watchful eye of former Beatles assistant Neil Aspinall.

The man who had hung around with McCartney and George Harrison at school in Liverpool became the group's most trusted employee and was named managing director of Apple Corps in 1968, a job he retained until he retired in 2007. One of the most important things Aspinall is credited with doing was copyrighting the name Apple worldwide, which, McCartney acknowledged, enabled them to face up to a growing computer company with a very similar name and logo.

"They [Apple Computer] said, 'We're very big now, we're going to be giants in the computer world.' We said, 'Well, we'll do a deal then', and we did a deal for a large amount of money. Probably that one deal made more than Apple Electronics cost."

That first deal followed Apple Corps filing an action in 1978 accusing Apple Computer of trademark infringement over its name and half-eaten apple logo, after Harrison had apparently spotted a magazine advert for the company.

Without the need for an expensive and lengthy court case, the American company handed over a reported £50,000 to the London-based music company and agreed not to enter the music business.

Ironically, the man who co-founded Apple Computer Inc. in 1976 and based it in Cupertino, California was an admitted Beatles fan. In fact, Steve Jobs has been described as a Beatles obsessive who "can talk your ear off about why Ringo is an under-appreciated drummer".

While neither he nor co-founder Steve Wozniak has ever publicly confirmed that they chose the word Apple as their company name as some sort of homage to The Beatles, their first logo was a long way from the band's fruit symbol.

Although it was only short-lived, the first design depicted Sir Isaac Newton sitting under an apple tree. However, it was soon replaced by a multi-coloured silhouette of an apple with a bite taken out of it, which stood the test of time – running from 1976 until 1999 – and became an instantly recognisable brand.

At the turn of the millennium, Apple adopted a monochrome version of the same logo, which used its shape to identify the company's wider range of goods as it expanded into a computer hardware, software and consumer electronics company.

In 2007, the company finally dropped the name Computer from its title to once again emphasise its wider range of goods and services. With over 20,000 full-time and part-time employees around the world, Apple Inc. posted third quarter results in July 2007 showing revenue of $5.4 billion and a profit of $818 million.

This healthy looking balance sheet reflected the success of the new businesses that Apple Inc. have expanded into over the past three decades, but there has remained one aspect of this multi-million dollar company's expansion that continues to rankle with The Beatles.

In 1989, The Beatles and Apple Corps took action against Apple Computer for the second time. On this occasion, the issue was the electronics company's decision to use the name Apple on a computer including a sound chip from synthesizer maker Ensoniq music.

The British music company claimed that this move breached part of the earlier 1981 agreement in which Apple Computer agreed to stay out of the music business. And for the second time The Beatles won and, in an expensive 1991 settlement, the Californians paid out $26 million to Apple Corps.

There was also further clarification of who could do what in business terms under the name of Apple. Apple Corps' "field of use" covered Apple music artists, catalogue and merchandising plus "current or future creative works whose principal content is music and/or musical performances".

The "field of use" for Apple Computer was defined to include electronic goods – not limited to computers – processors, computer software, data-processing equipment, plus broadcasting and telecommunication services.

Once again, McCartney had a few words to say when Apple Computer overstepped the mark and ventured into the business he and Apple Corps considered their domain. "Then Apple put a music chip in, so we went back to them because there was one proviso; they could use the name so long as they had nothing to do with music. They were Apple Computer, we were Apple Music.

"And then we settled for another very large amount of money, so actually the fact that we copyrighted the name Apple is one of the things that has made us the most amount of money."

With the latest settlement under their belts, Apple Corps and Apple Computer went about their various businesses for a further 12 years, until the day when Apple Computer came up with its online music downloading store iTunes, along with the iPod range of portable players.

Both these items were marketed under the Apple name and bearing the company's logo – the third outline version was introduced in 1999 – and they immediately set alarm bells ringing (again) in the London offices of Apple Corps.

This, Apple Corps argued, was a further breach of the 1991 agreement under which the computer giant agreed to stay out of the music business. But here the latter was offering music and music players under an Apple brand.

The next round of legal action began in late 2003, when Apple Corps once again sued Apple Computer for alleged breach of the Trade Mark Agreement. An action came to court in London in February 2004 when Mr Justice Edward was asked to consider an application from Apple Computer that the case should be heard in America rather than the UK.

There were arguments about whether the Trade Mark Agreement came under Californian or English law, which would impact directly on the location of the court case. Claims concerning the level of disruption to Apple Computer – their documents and witnesses were in California – and Apple Corps – their only executive officer would be heavily involved in the case – were made in favour of both the US and the UK.

It was also claimed that a trial in England would take only three days against a possible 10 days in California, but the judge believed that a trial was a trial was a trial, and that a hearing should last roughly the same time in either country.

He was also of the view that pre-trial preparation in California would be more disruptive and costly, and that a Californian trial date would not come around any quicker than one in London, and would quite possibly be much later.

At the end of a three-day hearing in the Chancery Division of the High Court, Mr Justice Mann decided that it was more appropriate for the trial to be heard in England. Apple Computer thus lost the first round in their latest dogfight with The Beatles.

Following the judge's February 2004 decision, the two adversaries finally lined up against each other in March 2006 to hear Apple Corps' case against Apple Computer for breach of the Trade Mark Agreement.

Mr Justice Mann was once again on the bench, although he had considered excusing himself on the grounds that he was an iPod owner, finally deciding that his impartiality would not be affected.

Opening for Apple Corps – the claimant in the case – Mr Geoffrey Vos QC announced that just before it launched its iTunes Music Store, the defendant, Apple Computer, had offered $1 million to buy the rights to the Apple brand from Apple Corps.

Confirming that The Beatles' company had rejected the offer, Vos claimed that "to suggest the use of the Apple mark is a part of the delivery mechanism is to look through one end of a two-ended telescope", and further stated that Apple Computer co-founder Steve Jobs had said publicly that downloading music from the internet was now no different from buying a record.

Vos argued that the US computer operation violated the 1991 trademark agreement by selling music online, and that the company's argument that it used the apple mark only in connection with a delivery system was "plainly wrong". Referring to iTunes as an electronic device was a "perversion" of the earlier deal, he said.

Explaining that the Apple logo was prominent on the iTunes website and the majority of the advertising, Vos added, "Computer was promoting a store at which to buy music, and more particularly, Computer's musical recordings – permanent downloads – with special characteristics. No objective onlooker could think otherwise."

For his in-court demonstration of how to download music, Vos chose the 1978 hit 'Le Freak' by the US soul group Chic, along with UK band Coldplay's track 'Speed Of Sound'. It was part of his case to show how many times the apple logo appeared on the website.

The question of the use of the apple logo in the computer firm's television advertising was also presented to the court. In an advert featuring The Who's 'My Generation', the final shot showed Apple Computer's apple logo over the word Applemusic.com.

In a commercial featuring U2, the same apple logo appeared for two seconds, it also featured briefly in an advert featuring Eminem, while Apple Computer gift cards carried the words "iTunes Music Store Card" above an apple logo. An accompanying leaflet had the slogan, "Remember – iTunes isn't just the #1 music download store. It's also the best jukebox around."

All these, according to Vos, showed the use of the "apple mark" in connection with recorded music, which, he claimed, was breach of the earlier agreement.

He explained that the agreement recognised the potential for future problems and made it clear that, in this situation, each party kept to their own field of use. This made it acceptable, he said, for Apple Computer to use their mark on a service delivering music content provided that the mark was not also used on or in connection with the content itself.

Vos also outlined to the court the success of Apple Computer's iTunes Music Store, saying that the public had been given access to 3.7 million tracks worldwide and that there had been more than one billion downloads through the website.

From the witness box, Neil Aspinall, the head of Apple Corps, told the court of his meeting with the Apple Computer chief in 2000 at the US tycoon's California home. Aspinall said he met with Jobs to discuss the setting up of a *Beatles 1* website to go with the group's best-selling

2000 compilation album of the same name, but there was no mention of placing the group's catalogue of recordings on iTunes.

"I am computer illiterate and don't even know how to turn one on," said Aspinall. "Steve drew me some simple diagrams to explain things on a blackboard... but the meeting came to nothing."

The judge was keen to know what sort of relationship existed between the record chief and the computer mogul. "I've got a very good personal relationship with Steve Jobs even now," said Aspinall, who told the court that the American executive had once told him that he loved The Beatles so much that he named his company after their record label.

Lord Anthony Grabiner QC, counsel for Apple Computer, wanted to know why, if Apple Corps was so concerned with the computer company's logo being associated with musical content, it chose Apple Computer's QuickTime software to host video clips on the *Beatles 1* website.

Explaining that he had not been involved in the building of the website, Aspinall confirmed that IT experts at EMI, The Beatles' record company, kept him up to date with the latest technological developments.

Grabiner suggested to the court that "even a moron in a hurry" could see the computer business was not purporting to represent the Apple record label.

During his evidence, Aspinall disclosed plans to make The Beatles' back catalogue available digitally, and revealed why he had resisted putting the music on iTunes Music Store. "We're re-mastering the whole Beatles catalogue, just to make it sound brighter and better, and getting proper booklets to go with each of the packages. I think it would be wrong to offer loads of the old masters when I am making new masters."

Arguing its version of "on or in connection with", Apple Computer's counsel explained that for the US company to cross into the music operation's territory with its mark it would have to have indicated, by use of its mark, that it was the source or origin of the music.

Giving evidence on behalf of Apple Computer, the company's head of iTunes, Eddie Cue, claimed that he did not think "any normal person would come to the conclusion that the computer giant was purporting to own the music it sells, which the record label is accusing it of having done".

After a hearing covering five days and ending on April 5, 2006, Mr Justice Mann retired to consider his verdict in this third legal spat between the two Apple companies.

His decision finally came on the morning of Monday, May 8, and in his summing-up the judge pointed out that one of Apple Computer's main points in the case had been that it was selling other people's music and not acting as a record label, although Apple Corps had suggested that this was irrelevant.

He pointed out that, while he found the evidence of Apple Corps executive Aspinall honest and straightforward, he had reservations about one aspect of his statement. "I think that he sought to portray himself as somewhat more naïve and ignorant about technological issues than is really the case."

The judge suggested that "it would require a serious distortion of fairly plain notions to say that files delivered by ITMS (iTunes Music Store) and stored somehow in digital form, and/or the hard disk which stores them, amount to 'physical media' which 'deliver' pre-recorded content."

At this stage things were not looking good for Apple Corps, and its worst fears were realised when Mr Justice Mann found in favour of Apple Computer and dismissed the claim from The Beatles' music company.

The judge ruled that iTunes was "a form of electronic shop" that was not involved in creating music and that the "use of the apple logo does not suggest a relevant connection with the creative work". He added, "I think that the use of the apple logo is a fair and reasonable use of the mark in connection with the service, which does not go further and unfairly or unreasonably suggest an additional association with the creative works themselves."

The only good news for Apple Corps was the judge's decision to refuse an interim costs payment of £1.5 million to Apple Computer, whose top man, Jobs, not surprisingly welcomed the ruling. "We are glad to put this agreement behind us. We have always loved The Beatles and hopefully we can now work together to get them on the iTunes Music Store."

On the other hand, Aspinall was far from happy with the outcome, and made his feelings clear in a brief statement. "With great respect to the trial judge, we consider he has reached the wrong conclusion.

"We felt that during the course of the five-day trial we clearly demonstrated just how extensively Apple Computer had broken the agreement. We will accordingly be filing an appeal and putting the case again to the Court of Appeal."

But an appeal never happened and, in February 2007, Apple Corps reached a quite surprising agreement with the computer giant, now called Apple Inc., covering the use of the name "Apple" and the apple logos.

Replacing the 1991 agreement, the new deal gave Apple Inc. ownership of all the trademarks related to "Apple", but they agreed to license certain trademarks back to Apple Corps for their continued use. While the financial details of the deal remained confidential, it signalled the end of all litigation between the two famous companies, as both sides viewed the prospect of huge sales from online sales as reason enough to settle.

As a result, Apple Corps – and its directors McCartney, Starr and the estates of Lennon and Harrison – decided to abandon its much-publicised plan to appeal against the 2006 ruling.

Industry insiders had suspected something was afoot a month earlier, when Jobs used The Beatles' song 'Lovely Rita' at the launch of the new Apple iPhone, and speculation has continued about when the first Beatles tracks will become available via Apple iTunes.

EMI Records was reported to be keen to get Apple Corps to do a deal for downloads of Beatles tracks as soon as possible in order to boost sales, and even help the company's then ailing share price. With downloads also figuring in the UK singles chart returns, there was the chance for The Beatles to once again dominate the hit parade, 45 years after their first number one hit.

The deal between Apple Inc. and Apple Corps unsurprisingly brought forth flattering statements from both parties, with Jobs telling the world, "We love The Beatles and it has been painful being at odds with them over these trademarks. It feels great to resolve this in a positive manner and in a way that should remove the potential of further disagreements in the future."

On the other hand, Aspinall made what would turn out to be one of his last official statements as head of The Beatles' corporation. "It is great to put this dispute behind us and move on. The years ahead are going to be very exciting times for us. We wish Apple Inc. every success and look forward to many years of peaceful co-operation with them," he said in early 2007 – but within three months he had left his post.

Amid speculation that he was unhappy with a reported new "cash cow" attitude within Apple Corps, the man who joined The Beatles as their roadie at the end of 1960 and went on to oversee their empire for nearly 40 years, departed the company that had been set up in the Swinging Sixties.

According to an official statement, his departure was amicable and "he decided to go in his own time".

As he left, with the sound of Apple Inc.'s final victory perhaps still ringing in his ears, Aspinall might have mulled over the news that book-maker William Hill – on the back of the new deal – was offering odds of 10/1 that The Beatles would have all top 10 tracks in the official UK charts sometime during 2007, with 'Hey Jude' being the 8/1 favourite to be the first Beatles number one of the digital era.

It didn't quite turn out that way and Aspinall would never find out as he died of cancer, aged 66, on March 24, 2008. As 2007 came to a close, Paul McCartney did predict that 2008 would be the year when The Beatles became available online. "It's all happening soon. It's down to fine-tuning but I'm pretty sure it'll be happening next year," said the now knighted Beatle, and it's worth betting that Apple Inc. will be involved.

Chapter 6

GILBERT O'SULLIVAN

Standing up to the man who made him

By the time Gilbert O'Sullivan and Gordon Mills met and forged what was to be a hugely successful but ultimately fraught business relationship, the two of them were two decades apart and at opposite ends of their musical careers.

For Mills, success first arrived in the early Sixties as a member of The Viscounts, a three-piece vocal group, and their hits 'Shortnin' Bread' and 'Who Put The Bomp'. The India-born son of a British Army worker followed this by turning his hand to songwriting. He came up with hit songs for Johnny Kidd ('I'll Never Get Over You' and 'Hungry For Love'), The Applejacks ('Three Little Words') and pop's ageless wonder Cliff Richard ('I'm The Lonely One'). ✗

Somewhere in the midst of all this he turned his hand to talent-spotting and, in 1964, signed up a young Welshman he saw on stage in Pontypridd supporting a curvaceous blonde named Mandy Rice-Davies, who, a year earlier, had been at the centre of the sex-and-politics Profumo scandal.

Tom Jones eventually hit the top of the charts in March 1965 with 'It's Not Unusual', a song co-written by Mills and Les Reed and originally

✗ CRAP

68

offered to Sandie Shaw. Within a year, Mills' management stable was further boosted by the arrival of a struggling young singer named Gerry Dorsey, who was persuaded by his new manager to adopt the name Engelbert Humperdinck.

In early 1969, Mills floated his Management Agency & Music (MAM) company on the London stock market. The company was valued at £1 million by the City and shares in the new MAM public business were launched at what was considered the high price of 13s 3d (66p) each. But, with Jones and Humperdinck among the industry's biggest earners and MAM's booking and promotion business also thriving, it was considered a reasonable investment.

By this time, Raymond O'Sullivan, a former graphic design student at Swindon Art College, had had two of his songs covered by The Tremeloes and released three unsuccessful solo singles on the CBS and Major Minor labels under the name Gilbert. O'Sullivan was not only interested in music but also imagery, and, with the demo tape he sent to Mills, he included a photograph of himself wearing short trousers, a sleeveless jumper and flat cap covering a pudding basin haircut, which brought back memories of the famous "Bisto kid" featured in five decades of advertising for a gravy mix.

The music caught Mills' attention and – even though the singer/songwriter turned record company boss and producer was not keen on using the image – the young Raymond was adamant that this was how he was going to appear under the new name suggested by Mills – Gilbert O'Sullivan.

The entrepreneur signed the young singer/songwriter to recording, publishing and agency deals with MAM, while also becoming the artist's personal manager – something O'Sullivan saw nothing wrong with. Indeed, around the end of 1970, he perhaps naively told the *Evening Standard*, "When I signed the contract I didn't even look at it. If you respect somebody and they're going to manage you, then you have to trust them. That's the most important thing."

Success came with O'Sullivan's first release on Mills' MAM label. 'Nothing Rhymed' hit the UK Top 10 in November 1970 and – together with an image change in 1972, when longer hair and a college sweater came into play – over the following six years the singer and his manager/producer/record company boss enjoyed a further 11 UK Top 20 hit singles. These included two chart toppers, four hit albums and four major US chart entries, including his number one American debut release 'Alone Again (Naturally)'.

Thanks to the success of Jones, Humperdinck, O'Sullivan and chart topper Dave Edmunds, MAM reported pre-tax profits of £2.5 million in 1971-2, and these increased further in the following year thanks to the arrival of new star Lynsey de Paul.

But, despite the international hit records, sell–out tours and prestigious Ivor Novello Awards, O'Sullivan was less than satisfied with his situation. He was beginning to have serious misgivings about the contracts he had signed with Mills, a man who had almost deliberately created a reputation for himself as a tough and occasionally uncompromising businessman.

Even though he had earlier reportedly been offered 50% of the copyright in the songs he wrote and recorded, O'Sullivan was far from happy with the situation covering ownership of his music, the royalties he received from Mills and MAM and his employment agreement with a company called Ebostrail, which was set up by MAM under the direction of company director and accountant Bill Smith to handle overseas earnings.

O'Sullivan's royalties took a long time to arrive and he was forced to live each day on a small salary seemingly provided by MAM, which also covered all his living expenses only to deduct them from his earnings. Initially, even with best-selling hit records under his belt, O'Sullivan received just £10 a week from his record company, although this rose to £150 after more success.

It seemed that despite sales of two million copies of 'Alone Again (Naturally)', three million of the album *Back To Front* and 1.5 million of the single 'Clair' (written about Mills' daughter, for whom O'Sullivan used to babysit), the performer received close to just £110,000 from gross earnings exceeding £2.2 million.

In the summer of 1979 – three years after his last UK hit – 32-year-old O'Sullivan finally decided, despite his millions of record sales, that he would have to turn to the law in an effort to gain satisfaction.

In a writ issued on June 8 against Mills and MAM, he demanded the return of all his copyrights, millions of pounds in back royalties and the cancellations of his agreement with Ebostrail and his recording contract with CBS in America.

Before the case came to court, O'Sullivan took a calculated risk and signed to CBS Records in the UK in late 1980. The danger was that Mills and MAM, who still had O'Sullivan signed to contracts that were in dispute, would seek an injunction to halt the new deal, rather than seeking damages or adding the issue to the agenda in the impending court case.

In court in early March 1982, O'Sullivan told Mr. Justice Mars-Jones that he was an "innocent unknown" when he was persuaded to sign the agreements, which he claimed deprived him of substantial royalties and of the copyright in his compositions.

The Irish-born singer added that in 1975 he asked to look at his accounts, which he then described to the court as "horrifying", saying that while his records were topping the charts, he was being told by his manager to tighten his belt.

Even when he was voted the world's most successful artist in 1972, O'Sullivan said he was told he could not afford a modest £95,000 house in Weybridge, Surrey, and that money would have to be borrowed in order to finance the purchase.

Explaining that he was reprimanded for spending £1,000 on a brass bed, the plaintiff said that he "had the impression that I was living beyond my means", and that when he queried his royalty statements Mills, "like a school master, gave me a good rollicking for going behind his back".

The singer's counsel told the judge that his client had been "served up, bound and packaged" to Mills' various MAM companies, which Mills, surprisingly, agreed was in fact the case, although he claimed there were good reasons for what happened.

Mills argued that all the contracts O'Sullivan signed were in his best interests, before adding, "What Mr O'Sullivan was due, I am sure was paid to him."

Mills and Bill Smith claimed in court that O'Sullivan's contracts with their companies had been fair and were normal for the time, and that without MAM's substantial efforts and huge resources, the singer might still be employed as a postal clerk. They further claimed that O'Sullivan was "hardly poor".

After considering all the evidence from music business executives, accountants and lawyers, Mr. Justice Mars-Jones returned to the High Court on May 5, 1982 to give his judgement. He referred to evidence showing that between 1970 and 1978, O'Sullivan's record sales had grossed approximately £14.5 million but the singer had received just £500,000 before tax.

"That," said the judge, "is some indication of the scale of the exploitation of this young man's talent."

Setting aside the agreements O'Sullivan made with Mills and his MAM companies, the judge ruled they were illegal because they were "oppressive and inequality of bargaining power and an unreasonable restraint of trade".

Going further, Mars-Jones told the court that O'Sullivan had hero-worshipped Mills and signed agreements without question. "Completely trusting his hero, he had only the vaguest notion of what he was signing. He was shown where to sign and did so without murmur."

Expressing the view that O'Sullivan was being treated "as a company asset" by Mills and his fellow MAM director Smith, the judge accepted that at one point the plaintiff had been promised a joint publishing agreement. "But despite a variety of excuses and explanations, I consider the defendants deliberately dragged their feet over this matter to the financial detriment of Mr. O'Sullivan."

Accepting that during the time of his MAM contracts, O'Sullivan was not interested in making money as much as making music, the judge noted, "He was happy as long as he earned enough to eat, rent a television set, write his songs and play his piano."

Describing the million-selling performer as "very talented", the judge also declared, "I was impressed with him as a witness. He was a patently honest and sincere young man. I regret the same cannot be said about Mr. Gordon Mills and Mr. William Smith, chief witnesses for the defence. In so far as their evidence conflicts in any respect with that of the plaintiff, I prefer the plaintiff's testimony."

In addition to awarding costs estimated at £100,000 to O'Sullivan, who reportedly sold his Surrey house to fund his case, the judge also ordered an inquiry into how much profit was made out of the various agreements, with the eventual sum, expected to run into millions, going to O'Sullivan.

The singer also won the copyright to all his songs and the master tapes of his recordings. He was suitably delighted after his court victory. "I didn't do this for the money. To a songwriter, his songs are like a pension. I really wanted the tapes back and the copyright."

He added that the decision to sue Mills had made him "very sad" but, "I had been hurt and I felt I had been wronged by him".

Equally delighted was O'Sullivan's personal and business manager, Charles Negus-Fancey, who had been appointed ahead of the history-making trial, which set new parameters in dealings between artists and managers and earned his client an amount estimated in newspaper headlines to be close to £7 million

"It is a fantastic result and an important one. I think it is the first time a writer/recording artist has won back copyright and masters in this way. It is a very important decision," said the man who previously worked for music entrepreneur Robert Stigwood and film-maker Alan Carr.

Mills did not appear for the day of judgement. Former Decca Records A&R chief Dick Rowe, who appeared as a witness for the music manager, said later that it was "very sad" for the man who had so successfully delivered both Jones and Humperdinck to Decca in the Sixties.

"He [Mills] didn't know what to say. The opposing counsel just tied him up in knots and made him look like a fool. It must have been sad for Gilbert's people to see this man, the managing director of MAM, made to look like an ignorant office boy," added the record company executive.

Saddened or not by the events in May 1982, Mills bounced back to launch an appeal against Mr. Justice Mar-Jones' decision and, almost two years later, a Court of Appeal ruling softened the blow for the manager and his company.

While the three Appeal Court judges – Lord Justice Dunn, Lord Justice Fox and Lord Justice Waller – did not change the ruling giving O'Sullivan the copyright in his songs and the master tapes of his recordings, they did acknowledge the work done by Mills and MAM in breaking the singer.

Giving judgement, Lord Justice Dunn acknowledged that, "Until Mr. O'Sullivan had met Mr. Mills he had achieved no success and after they parted company in 1976 he achieved no success."

This, according to the three judges, meant that Mills and MAM were entitled to an allowance for "reasonable remuneration, including a profit element for all work done in promoting and exploiting Mr. O'Sullivan and his compositions."

Out-of-court calculations put the amount of money that the singer would now receive from his ex-manager and former record company at closer to £5 million than the original 1982 estimates of £7 million, while a statement from MAM after the decision put the figure at £3 million.

But, despite the court hearings, the dispute about the amount of money O'Sullivan should receive in royalties and interest dragged on, as the two parties and their lawyers prepared themselves for a referee's assessment of the exact amount owing.

However, after the expensive High Court and Appeal Court hearings in 1982 and 1984, and with the likelihood of a further two years of legal wrangling in the pipeline, it was all finally agreed in an out-of-court settlement announced in March 1985.

Seven years after the initial writ was issued and three years after the original High Court hearing, it was decided that O'Sullivan would receive £1.9 million but, for the singer with a total of 15 UK hit singles and six chart albums, things would never be the same again.

While continuing to draw a healthy six-figure annual income from his copyrights, O'Sullivan's chart career stalled, with a minor hit single in 1990 and a Top 20 compilation album in 2004.

The absence of any new material between 1982 and 1987 – the court years and beyond – made O'Sullivan a decidedly non-commercial proposition. While he continues to write and record new material, the singer can also still be seen in concert performing the songs he won back over 20 years ago in a landmark court case.

For Mills, the fight with O'Sullivan cost him his empire. The City was wary of investing in the company while the case dragged on and the company's premier position in the music, jukebox, slot machine and leisure industries began to crumble.

In 1985, MAM was taken over by the Chrysalis Group, run by Chris Wright, and Mills was left to focus his attention on the one artist he still managed – Tom Jones – until his sudden death from cancer in July 1986, aged just 51.

Chapter 7

RAY JACKSON

Claimed his record company didn't try hard enough

After six years as a member of a successful chart-topping band, Ray Jackson, like so many before him, went in search of fame and fortune as a solo artist – only to find himself defending his career in a court of law.

Born in Newcastle-upon-Tyne, Jackson was a founding member of the good-time folk-rock band Lindisfarne, who, between 1970 and 1973, racked up three hit singles and the same number of hit albums including the number one *Fog On The Tyne*, which was also listed as the best-selling album by a British act in 1971.

Named after the historic island off the Northumbrian coast, the original five-piece band signed to Charisma Records in 1970, and pretty soon Jackson, singer/songwriter/guitarist Alan Hull, lead guitarist Simon Cowe, bass player Rod Clements and drummer Ray Laidlaw became favourites with both music fans and the music media.

But in 1973 there were disagreements in the ranks and the band split in two, with Cowe, Clements and Laidlaw leaving to form Jack The Lad. This left Hull and Jackson as Lindisfarne but, even though they recruited new members and continued recording and touring, the group's days were numbered.

Hull, who died in 1995, achieved limited solo success, becoming a hard-working, hard-living favourite on the club circuit as well as a committed, conscientious left-wing political activist. Jackson also sought new horizons after the band finally split in 1975 and came into contact with arguably Britain's largest music company. He signed a deal with EMI Records in early 1976 and, nine years later – without a single hit record to his name – found himself taking the major label to court, claiming damages for alleged breach of contract.

Jackson and his management, Barry McKay International Music (UK), faced EMI in the Newcastle High Court on January 15, 1985 before Mr. Justice Michael Davies, in a case that was to test the rules as to how much effort record companies were obliged to put behind into artists' careers.

Opening the case for the plaintiffs, Mr. Jeffrey Gruder QC said, "The conduct of EMI in this case is absolutely appalling. They did, by their complete neglect of Jackson, stifle any chance of a solo career.

"They were a shambles. They had him on their books for two years and really did absolutely nothing for him." Counsel further claimed that EMI failed to pay £10,000 for the extension of Jackson's recording contract into a second year.

The court heard that after Lindisfarne first separated in 1973, Jackson had taken a demo tape to McKay who, at the time, was a Newcastle record store owner and budding manager. McKay signed Jackson and took the tape exclusively to EMI. Despite the company's enthusiasm for the songs, only one record was ever released, and the sales of 'Take Some Time' were just over 250, with 50 of those coming from one of the shops owned by McKay. Suggesting that EMI was in "absolute chaos", Gruder maintained that had the record company made any effort to push the single, thousands of copies would have been sold in the north east of England.

"They were willing to keep Ray Jackson and his manager like a puppet on a string – keep them dangling just in case there might be a reformation of Lindisfarne but not really doing anything for him."

In his evidence, McKay said he had chosen to take Jackson to EMI because it was a British company and had promoted The Beatles. He admitted that he did not have a great knowledge of recording contracts at the time but had read the UK music industry magazine *Music Week* and believed EMI was a professional company.

"I worked very hard for Ray Jackson and to the best of my ability at the time," added McKay. "But with the experience I have now I would have dropped the EMI contract in the bin. All the clauses were heavily in their favour."

Describing Jackson as a "superb performer", McKay said he took six recordings to EMI. The company advanced him £1,800 and said the music was "absolutely superb and thought there were three singles on the tape".

McKay explained, "I was told Ray Jackson's recordings were going to be priorities. Had they not been, I would not have been interested in signing." After the release of the first single, according to the manager, EMI did little to promote the record and seemed to lose interest in his client. When they ignored numerous telegrams, letters and phone calls, McKay became disenchanted and began to approach rival record companies.

McKay acknowledged that when Jackson's solo singles and an album were finally released by rival company Phonogram in 1979 it was three years too late. They failed because the music market had changed dramatically.

On the third day of the hearing, Howard Shaw, counsel for EMI, questioned McKay about a tape he made of a telephone conversation he'd had with EMI, which was only brought to the court's attention a day earlier.

McKay denied being "devious" in making the tape and claimed that he had only found it on the day the hearing began. The manager also told the court that he thought the whole matter would have been settled before it came to court, at which point Judge Davies remarked, "This is one of the most absurd cases that has come to court in the 12 years that I have been a judge."

He added that if EMI lost the company could be made to look "as if they couldn't run a candy store", while if Jackson lost it would affect his reputation.

Called by the plaintiffs as an expert on the music business, record producer Gus Dudgeon told the court that he thought Jackson had a high chance of making it as a solo artist in 1976. "I would have considered them to be very good tracks and possibly made singles. I think Ray Jackson is a very good singer."

The man who made records for Elton John, Kiki Dee, Chris Rea and XTC, and who died in 2002, added, "This has always been a chancy business but with the right promotion I think he could have made it."

Called to give evidence on the fifth day, Jackson claimed that both he and his manager "just seemed to be completely ignored" by EMI. "I thought that I had completely wasted my time. I could have been recording elsewhere and been successful as a solo artist.

"The treatment I was given by EMI disillusioned me and I didn't feel like writing after that," said the singer, harmonica and mandolin player, who was supported by Steve Weltman, the managing director of Charisma Records, for whom Lindisfarne recorded. "He is a great communicator. He can sing and is an accomplished musician," Weltman told the court.

In light of the possible repercussions, it was no surprise that EMI fiercely denied the claims made by Jackson and McKay. The company suggested it had shown great faith and support for Jackson. However, it did admit to putting him on "hold" for some months after his one-year deal had expired, in order to complete the minimum contract commitment of three single releases.

One of the record company's string of witnesses was former contracts manager Chris John, who told the court that EMI had exercised an extension clause in order to keep Jackson at the company. This was described as a gentleman's agreement that was not uncommon in the music industry, and John explained that no written confirmation of the "hold" situation existed.

The ex-head of EMI's A&R (artists and repertoire) department, Nick Mobbs – the man who signed The Sex Pistols to the company – told the court that making an album with Jackson was "totally out of the question", and the company would have been foolish to even think about an album without the artist having any singles success.

"We genuinely believed in Ray Jackson and we didn't want to release sub-standard material that would fail and damage the artist's career," he explained.

Mobbs said that "we were deflated and surprised" after the relative failure of the first and only Jackson single, adding that he was "surprised that it didn't get more airplay and exposure".

While Mobbs claimed that major efforts were made to promote the record, he also stated that Jackson's contract did not contain a guarantee release clause, and that he had never promised the ex-Lindisfarne star priority status in the company. "It would be pointless putting something in the shops that you didn't believe in. We showed great faith and support, but I certainly didn't say we would treat him as a priority."

Mobbs also told the court that he'd had no plans to exercise the option for the second year of the singer's contract.

Two other former EMI A&R men were also called to give evidence on behalf of their previous employer. John Darnley, who had looked after Jackson in 1976, told the court, "I was certainly searching for a producer and songs for Ray Jackson. I tried my best for him and the artists on the roster." He dened that EMI, was "a shambles" in the mid-Seventies, asserting that it was regimented and better organised than other music companies.

His former colleague Mark Rye said that Jackson was a "very difficult artist to work with at the time because musical trends were changing", as punk was a fast-emerging trend.

"Artists from a slightly different generation were difficult to work with," Rye stated, adding that Jackson went "out of focus" when it became hard to find him suitable songs to record.

The final EMI witness was Paul Watts, the general manager of the company's Pop Division at the time that Jackson was signed. He assured the court that Jackson's single 'Take Some Time', "was a top priority in the company's promotion department, and they were put under pressure for a number of weeks to get airplay."

Following eight days of evidence, Mr. Justice Davies adjourned the hearing for a month and set February 25 as the date when he would give judgement in London's High Court. However, on that day, the judge delayed his decision further, saying that he would take "about 10 days" to consider his verdict.

Finally, on March 15, the judge gave his ruling and he came down on the side of Jackson and his manager, explaining that EMI had broken their contract to launch Jackson as a solo artist and that EMI had not given the singer "a fair crack of the whip".

Jackson and McKay were awarded damages of £12,500 to compensate for loss of royalties, publicity and opportunities, which, with interest of 12% payable since 1980, brought the total to £24,000. The judge also awarded them costs estimated to be between £40,000 and £50,000.

Beginning his judgement, Judge Davies said, "Ray Jackson was a very impressive and fair witness with a burning conviction that he had been let down by a great company which he trusted."

Commenting on the evidence of ex–EMI contracts manager John, the judge said it supported Jackson's case and his argument that at the time EMI's organisation was "a shambles". He added that EMI reached a "point of despair" when its barrister asked him to reject John's evidence.

Dealing with EMI's argument that the right material for a hit single was not available for Jackson, Mr. Justice Davies pointed out that it should have been found from another source.

In his concluding address, the judge said, "The plaintiffs are entitled to argue that Jackson did not have a fair crack of the whip by reason of only one and not three singles being made in the initial one-year period of his contract.

"I am satisfied that if the defendants had played fair there was a real possibility that Jackson would have succeeded. He would not have been a megastar but he would have achieved success that would have brought in substantial sums of money."

Despite these comments, the judge found against Jackson and McKay in their claim that EMI had not taken up an album option, saying that the required written notification was never given.

While Jackson declared himself "delighted" to have won, adding, "There are many other musicians in the same position as I was in and I think this decision could open the floodgates", the lawyers came up with contrasting opinions.

Richard Hart-Jackson, solicitor for Jackson, said that in the light of the judge's decision it would be impossible for a record company to sign a band and then sit back and do nothing with them. He suggested that there would be industry-wide repercussions for a large number of acts.

On the other hand, EMI's business affairs executive, Garth Hopkins, claimed, "This case does not create a general precedent in the industry and should be regarded as a decision relating to this case and its particular circumstances."

At the same he admitted that EMI was "disappointed and surprised" at the judgement. "The judge's remarks over the capabilities of EMI personnel relate to a past era and bear no relation to EMI Records and its business procedures in 1985."

While McKay was happy that "justice has been done and been seen to be done", he was disappointed that the issue ended up in court. "During 1979 and 1980 we made continuous efforts to avoid court proceedings. EMI's uncompromising attitude throughout left us with no alternative but to commence litigation, but we always hoped that good sense would prevail and a reasonable settlement could be achieved before the action came to court."

With Jackson's solo career effectively at an end by virtue of his unsuccessful stints with EMI and Phonogram, he turned to working with a selection of his old mates in various Lindisfarne line-ups and developed his talent as a painter of vintage buses.

In 1990, Lindisfarne teamed up with local football hero Paul Gascoigne to record 'Fog On The Tyne Revisited', a rap version of their hit single, which peaked at number two in the charts. Jackson left again after this brief success and the band played a final show in 2003, although band members, friends and colleagues got together in 2005 for an Alan Hull memorial concert in aid of the North East Young Musicians Fund.

Two years earlier, Jackson had considered further legal action – this time for a composer's credit and royalties from Rod Stewart's million-selling 1971 hit, 'Maggie May'.

Despite claiming he composed the song's mandolin hook on the superstar singer's record, Jackson received the standard £15 session fee for his efforts and a note from Stewart on the sleeve of the album *Every Picture Tells A Story* that read, "The mandolin was played by the mandolin player in Lindisfarne. The name slips my mind."

Jackson alleged that executives at Warner Chappell music publishing, which published the song, deliberately misled him and his manager McKay over the possibility of a composer's credit and subsequent share in the royalties.

A spokesman for Stewart dismissed the claim as "mind-boggling", saying that it was first brought up in the mid-Eighties, 14 years after the song was recorded. "Any contributions he [Jackson] may have made were fully paid for at the time as 'work-for-hire'."

By 2005, Jackson was forced to abandon any legal action against either Stewart or Warner Chappell when he learnt that the cost of an insurance policy to cover him against losing in court (estimated to be over £100,000) was going to be as much as any award for damages.

His loyal manager McKay commented, "We should have started pro-ceedings 30 years ago when the song was a worldwide smash. Ray could have royalties for three decades, which would have been a considerable sum."

At the same time, Jackson accepted defeat and said, "I am drawing a line under the 'Maggie May' story. I wrote the hook to one of the most successful songs ever recorded – not bad for a lad from Wallsend."

So the former Newcastle College art student, who now specialises in painting transport from a bygone age in addition to performing with ex-members of Fairport Convention, Steeleye Span and Pentangle in The Gathering Legends, has had to content himself with just one unexpect-edly successful day in court.

Chapter 8

ELTON JOHN &
BERNIE TAUPIN

Pop writers search for their "missing millions"

E lton John's success was not what you would call overnight. After winning a scholarship, aged just 11, to attend the Royal Academy of Music, he played on the British club and pub circuit in the mid-Sixties as pianist with the R&B group Bluesology.

In 1967, at the age of 20, he underwent a series of life-changing events beginning with a chance introduction – as a sort of consolation prize – to a set of lyrics sent by an aspiring songwriter's mother to the record company that had just turned John down.

Impressed with what he read, Elton began to create songs by post with the wordsmith, named Bernie Taupin, who was living with his parents in Lincolnshire. They didn't meet for months, but then an out-of-hours demo session in a recording studio in the heart of London's West End put them on the first rungs of the ladder to success.

The unapproved session was in DJM's studio on New Oxford Street, but company executive Stephen James still decided to give the songs a listen and subsequently took them to his father, the company's founder, Dick James. Between them they decided there was something in the compositions created by correspondence between the young artists.

The two ambitious songwriters, who had in fact finally met in the reception area of Dick James House – when Elton reportedly shouted, "Is there a lyricist here?" – were now summoned to meet James. In 1968 they were assigned to Gralto, the publishing company within DJM that looked after songs composed by members of The Hollies.

Over the next four decades, the careers of John and Taupin would scale previously unimagined heights. The piano-player, music-writer and singer helped turn the lyrics of the reluctant backroom boy into million-selling global hits, and the pair achieved great fame and fortune, which in turn would become the subject of a major court battle.

Born Richard Leon Isaac Vapnick, the son of Polish immigrants, Dick James began his own career in the music business as a singer – being the first British artist to enter the US charts, with 'You Can't Be True, Dear' in 1948, before venturing into music publishing, starting up Dick James Music in 1961. After struggling for a year, James was recommended by record producer George Martin – who had produced James' million-selling 'The Ballad Of Robin Hood' – to Brian Epstein as a prospective publisher for the songs of two Liverpudlian songwriters, John Lennon and Paul McCartney.

Through Northern Songs, the company he set up with Epstein, James handled the music publishing business of The Beatles over the next six years. While the company made him extremely wealthy and highly successful, James endured a rocky relationship with The Beatles after Epstein's death in 1967. Sensing that the group was in disarray, in 1969, without telling either Lennon or McCartney, he decided to sell his share of Northern Songs to ATV, which was run by Sir Lew Grade, who had been involved as an agent in James' earlier singing career.

By discovering and developing John and Taupin as a songwriting team, with the added bonus that the former was showing signs of becoming an accomplished artist in his own right, James and his son could switch their attention to a new talent and a potential new source of income for their company.

There were signs of discord brewing as early as January 1973, when John publicly claimed that DJM Records did not want his new single, 'Daniel', to be released. "Dick James said he did not want another single released to detract from the sales of the next album," John explained, adding, "So I've more or less forced him to put it out but he says he'll pay for the advertising if it makes the UK Top 10. Isn't that nice?" It reached number five, so presumably John got his ad money back.

Just three months later, John seemed happy enough to receive three gold records from DJM for two albums that sold 100,000 copies in the UK, and for a million sales in the US of *Don't Shoot Me, I'm Only The Piano Player*.

By 1976, John had switched from DJM Records to his own Rocket label, which he'd started in 1973, and was being managed by John Reid, a sharp-witted, hot-tempered Scot and a former label manager of Tamla Motown, whom DJM had initially employed to handle John's day-to-day affairs. Reid soon established his own company to manage his client, who in 1976 ended his songwriting partnership with Taupin – albeit temporarily.

At the time it was calculated that Elton John albums accounted for 2% of all records sold around the world in 1975, while the 1974 accounts for Dick James Music showed an annual turnover of £5 million.

However, in 1972, while working for DJM, Reid launched inquiries into the sub-publishing arrangements for John and Taupin and found that the US subsidiary, Dick James Music Inc., was retaining an unusually high percentage of royalties. Reid hired accountants to investigate and consulted with leading US attorneys; this carried on until 1981, long after the expiry of John's management contract with DJM. Reid was also concerned about the duo's 1967 publishing agreement, and John's 1968 and 1970 recording deals and sub-publishing agreements. A total of 144 songs written by John and Taupin and published by DJM, plus 36 unpublished compositions, and 24 unreleased recordings.

Under the guidance of Reid, a first writ was issued in 1981 suing James and his companies for the return of song copyrights, asking for their original publishing and recording agreements to be set aside and claiming damages for underpayment of royalties. It would be a further four years before the case of Elton John and Bernie Taupin versus Dick

James, Dick James Music and This Record Company finally made it to the London High Court.

As the music business readied itself for what many insiders saw as the industry's most important court case ever, there was speculation as to what it might all mean to Elton John in particular.

The view was that if he won, he could take back assets worth over £30 million but, if he lost, he could face substantial costs, close to £1.5 million. More importantly, for the men who ran music publishing, a win for the plaintiff could unleash a pack of writs from similarly disgruntled artists. It was no surprise to hear Stephen James predict that if this was the case then "the music business [was] finished".

John and Taupin's combined action opened on June 4, 1985 with their counsel, Mark Littman QC, telling the judge, Mr. Justice Nicholls, that thousands of pounds in royalties were "unjustifiably" poured into a worldwide network of "shell" companies operated under the umbrella of Dick James Music.

He told the court that these companies retained 50% of the royalties from sales in their territories, with the rest of the money being sent to the parent DJM company in the UK.

According to Littman, who was described as the "cleverest lawyer alive", independent publishers who handled the John and Taupin catalogue in various territories and were not under the control of DJM retained as little as 10%. "The difference in the amount received from the subsidiaries and the amount received from the independent publishers was quite unjustifiable."

Littman also told the court that originally there were DJM subpublishing subsidiaries in Australia, France and the US but, in the mid-Seventies, more companies were established in countries such as Germany, Holland, Italy, Japan and in Scandinavia. He alleged that with the exception of the US subsidiary these were "shell" companies. "They had no premises, no staff, nothing."

Among the songs in dispute were some of John and Taupin's most successful compositions – including 'Your Song', 'Rocket Man', 'Daniel', 'Crocodile Rock', 'Saturday Night's Alright For Fighting' and 'Candle In The Wind' – which were recorded and released under John's DJM recording agreement.

The two composers' action in suing Dick James and DJM for the return of their copyrights, missing royalties and the overturning of two agreements was because, according to Littman, the original agreements were obtained by "undue influence" and amounted to "an unreasonable restraint of trade".

As both John and Taupin were under 21 when these deals were struck, they had been countersigned by their parents and put in place by DJM. Clarifying the situation, Littman detailed that John was in fact 20 and Taupin just 17 at the time, and that over the next six years the pair wrote 136 songs, the copyrights to which all belonged to DJM, a company totally owned by Dick James and members of his family.

Littman also informed the court that the master tapes and discs were permanently owned by This Records, a DJM subsidiary. "The value of copyrights and master recordings is considerable. I am told the total retail value of recordings made of these master recordings up to now probably exceeds £200 million."

In the light of the huge potential earnings from these songs, plus John's single and album releases, Littman was keen to point out the low level of the pair's original deals. In their statements of claim, John and Taupin said they were given an advance of £100 when they were signed and, over the next three years, John received £15 a week and Taupin £10 a week in advance of royalties.

This, according to Littman, was proof that the two were taken advantage of because of their inexperience, while James' position in the music industry enabled him to persuade the pair to sign agreements that were "unduly onerous and one-sided".

Littman chose to take the court back in time to 1967, when John and Taupin were summoned to James' office where, as employees of the DJM subsidiary, they were caught using a recording studio to make demo recordings without permission. "While they were waiting in reception, quaking in their boots, a sound engineer told Dick James that he was impressed with what he heard and that James ought to sign them up."

So, with the encouragement of the anonymous sound engineer and, despite an earlier warning from guitarist Caleb Quaye, who had played on the session, that the songs were "not very good", James signed the songwriters to DJM.

Littman described the pair's reaction to the news that they were being signed rather than sacked. "When they came out of the office they were absolutely elated, breathing sighs of relief. In effect Dick James was their superior in this agreement. There were no negotiations. Elton John and Bernie Taupin say they didn't read their agreements. They were only delighted they had an agreement and they trusted Dick James."

Their appreciation and trust in James was made clear in 1971 when John remarked: "Dick is a straight, right–down–the–middle Jewish publisher. To me, he has been like a father. If there's any problem, Dick will sort it out for me. Dick's very, very aware of money but I'd rather have him on my side than anyone else, because Dick is honest."

But, 14 years after publicly praising James' business acumen and honesty, he and Taupin were sitting on the opposite side of a courtroom as they sued their "right–down–the–middle publisher".

James had built himself a reputation as an honest and traditional music publisher. He was brought up in an era when 50/50 deals, splitting earnings from songs equally between publishers and composers, were the norm. During the Sixties, aspiring writers such as Mitch Murray and Bill Martin welcomed his open door policy.

Whereas today, writers can earn as much as 85% of the income from a song, these 50/50 deals were accepted quite happily in the Sixties, if only because music publishers were expected to do a lot more for their money. They were required to plug songs to record companies and, if they got a song released, they were then required to promote it to radio and television while also setting up sub-publishing deals around the world to exploit it internationally – and collect the royalties.

This is what Dick James and his companies did successfully for many years, and it wasn't until John and Taupin took action that the question of overseas royalties in particular was investigated.

The practice of taking money from both the home-based publishing company and also from overseas sub-publishers – which sometimes existed in name only – was known in the business as "double dipping". Another arrangement, which involved monies from central European countries all being paid back through Switzerland, with its various tax advantages, was known as "the Swiss twist".

While James not surprisingly maintained there was no case against him, he vigorously contested the suggestion that the agreements he signed with the duo were one-sided, and denied having anything to do with the contracts on a personal basis.

However, as the trial continued, Littman claimed that James personally oversaw the diversion of funds, and left the judge to hear and analyse complex and detailed evidence covering royalty payments and sub-publishing arrangements.

It was revealed in the figures laid out before the court that, up to the time the legal action was launched, John had earned £13.4 million from record sales and £1.16 million from publishing royalties. During the same period, Taupin collected just over £1 million in publishing royalties.

In contrast, DJM's record label, This Record Co., made just over £7 million profit and DJM Records made £1.5 million, while the profits made by the entire DJM group on worldwide publishing, including the UK, amounted to around £2.6 million.

Muff Winwood, brother of Stevie Winwood and a former A&R man at Island Records, was called as a witness for the plaintiffs. He confirmed that Island Records' owner, Chris Blackwell, had looked over the DJM contracts, observed that they "had holes in them", and subsequently offered the songwriters a £10,000 advance.

John and Taupin turned down this offer but, when giving evidence to the court, John confirmed to the judge that he had not read the DJM agreements he signed, adding, "I still don't read contracts." He also acknowledged that, while his mother had signed as guarantor because he was only 20 years old, "I don't think she understood it, she wasn't an expert in publishing contracts."

The singer also confirmed to the court that the £50 he and Taupin were given as an advance was "a substantial amount of money" in 1967, and that the deal he signed seemed "very fair" at the time. Confirming that the pair of them never considered seeking legal advice and that neither of them had any sort of understanding of their legal obligations under the contract, John told the court, "I did not think about getting a solicitor. I trusted Mr. James. Anything anyone told me I believed."

Answering the claim that the Dick James organisation "whittled away vast sums of money" that John was entitled to, DJM's counsel, George Newman QC, later to become a High Court judge, asked the award-winning composer and performer to comment on the figures that showed his own earnings to be over £14 million and DJM's in excess of £8 million.

"I can't comment on them," said John. "I'm not a chartered accountant. My lawyers told me there had been mishandling of money and I just told them to get on with it. I was led to believe that vast sums were involved."

On the subject of the world's largest music market, Newman put it to John that DJM's US subsidiary was fully justified in retaining half the royalties it collected. "The American subsidiary incurred expense and costs and did a very good job, and there is simply nothing unreasonable at all about it retaining 50%."

The biggest-selling pop artist of the Seventies was seemingly out of his depth, and replied that he could not comment on the performance of DJM's American operation.

Following John into the witness box was his manager, John Reid, who confirmed that it was his suspicion that DJM's American subsidiary was retaining too much from royalties that started the investigation leading to the court action.

One of Reid's advisers was John Eastman, brother-in-law of Paul McCartney, who acted as legal adviser to the former Beatle. Eastman was seemingly of the view that there was a case for saying that James had not accounted properly, and had used sub-publishing companies as a device for diverting money.

American music publisher David Rosner, who had been employed by Dick James Music in New York in the early Seventies, told the court that it was usual practice for sub-publishers to retain 15% to 25% of mechanical royalties. Asked if 50% could be justified – as in the case of John and Taupin – he replied: "Not in the normal course of business."

As the case entered its sixth week, the first witness for the defence was James himself, who recalled his first meeting with the budding singer/songwriter, when John had complained to him that he was getting nowhere writing songs for small publishers. After that meeting,

James said he had listened to some of the songs written by John and Taupin and been impressed.

Denying that he had reprimanded the pair about using the studio without permission, James added: "As far as I'm concerned, if I was going to hear a good song out of it, it was worthwhile."

After James told John that he would consider putting him under contract, the pianist asked for a subsidy to allow him to give up working as a session musician and concentrate on writing, and requested one for Taupin as well. The agreed advance was £100 between them – described by James in court as "the right side of generous" – with a retainer of £10 per week for each, although John's was later put up to £15.

It was also disclosed at the hearing that Charles Levinson, then a music industry lawyer, had been retained to advise John in relation to his 1973 management agreement with Reid, which entitled the latter to 10% of John's recording activities.

This, as Reid agreed, meant that he received £579,000 between May 1973 and May 1976, plus a further £676,000 from May 1976 to December 1982, although Levinson claimed in court that he had no recollection of ever advising the superstar. However, when cross-examined, he was shown a letter that Levinson accepted "clearly shows that I did advise Elton John".

After nearly two months of witness statements, cross-examination and a plethora of evidence covering royalties and sub-publishing, the court adjourned at the end of July 1985 when the legal term came to an end.

John kept a fairly low profile during the recess, while James, who was deeply offended that he had been named personally in the writ, was left to sweat it out.

When the action returned to the High Court in October it entered its 50th day, and legal costs were already estimated to be at over £1 million.

First up was Newman, counsel for Dick James and DJM. In his view there was "not a scintilla of evidence" that the songwriters had been under undue influence when they signed with James in 1967. "There is no evidence of browbeating, persuasion or use of muscle in any way," said Newman, adding, "The fact that they might have been in awe of Dick James and his position is neither here nor there. You might be in awe of your bank manager.

"Elton John simply has never had a complaint about his career and about what was done for him in the way of exploitation and promotion. In fact he is very fond of Dick James. He's grateful to him in many ways. He has amassed a considerable fortune because of what Dick James has done for him."

With Newman's closing speech over, it was time for Littman to conclude the case for John and Taupin, and he immediately refuted the argument that the pair had brought their case at the suggestion of lawyers. "So long as these arrangements remain in respect of this very large body of master recordings and songs – a third of them unpublished – it is very reasonable to bring such a claim."

Counsel added that it was "inevitable" that John's confidence and trust in James would be undermined after his alleged discovery that royalties he should have received had been "siphoned off" into subsidiary companies.

While John was off on a five-month European tour, Mr. Justice Nicholls delivered his four-hour judgement (with Taupin present in court) in early December 1985. In a landmark decision, the judge rejected the bid by John and Taupin for the return of the copyright to their songs and the setting aside of early publishing and recording contracts. However, he did accept that they been signed under undue influence and that John had suffered under the "dominating influence" of James, but the problem for the judge was the length of time between the signing of the contracts and the issuing of the writ.

He also raised the point that no complaints had ever been raised against James while DJM had spent "substantial effort and money" exploiting the recordings and it would, he figured, be "unjust to return the copyrights now".

While his company may have kept the copyrights, Dick James still had to sit and listen to the judge's opinion of his business practices. "To have tied two young men at the beginning of their careers to a publishing agreement for six years on the terms in question represented an acceptably hard bargain."

The judge added, "It was clear on the facts that the first defendant [James] had assumed a dominating role over the plaintiffs and the 1967 publishing agreement was thus unfair. However, given the significant increase in the plaintiff's experience and commercial awareness at the time of conclusion of the 1970 agreement and the improved escalating royalty rates contained in it, that agreement was not an unfair transaction."

Nicholls sympathised with the question of John's UK record royalties and ruled that instead of the 4.5% of the retail price he had received, he should have been paid 12%. DJM was to make up the difference with interest.

Having lost their claim over the copyrights and agreements but having won on the issue of the recording royalties, the plaintiffs found further solace in the judge's decision regarding foreign royalties and DJM's sub-publishing arrangements. He found the company guilty of "deliberate concealment" of the agreements, which substantially decreased the two plaintiffs' incomes.

"Apparently, a 50% retention by the subsidiaries was normal in the business. Whatever might be the rights or wrongs of this as far as other writers with their own publishing contracts with DJM or other companies are concerned, the terms of which may be materially different, I am in no doubt that in this case DJM was in breach of its fiduciary duty," was the judge's summing up of the situation.

Excluding DJM's US company, Nicholls said that while DJM subsidiaries without staff or premises had withheld royalties at the rate of 50%, a normal rate for a foreign sub-publisher would be between 15% and 25%.

Setting a rate of 25%, the judge ruled that DJM should pay John and Taupin the backdated difference. Without the benefit of a lengthy audit, however, the final figure due to John and Taupin remained unclear, although the two sides tried their best to outspin each other. It could be as much as £5 million, said the plaintiffs' camp, while DJM reckoned it would not exceed £500,000. The division of costs – rumoured to be as high as £1.5 million – was another issue that was not decided at the end of the marathon trial.

However, the 1986 accounts for Dick James Music included extraordinary "provisions for the costs of settlement of a legal action and related professional charges", which were listed as totalling £2,762,000.

Stephen James claimed the upper hand and told reporters, "We're very relieved we did not lose on the main claim and we are treating it as a victory."

Not surprisingly, Taupin also saw the positive side of things. "I'm happy with everything. We may not have regained the copyrights but we did prove we were morally right."

The general consensus was that by ordering the payment of substantial backdated royalties but rejecting the allegations of fraud against James and DJM, and refusing John and Taupin the copyrights to their songs, the judge's decision smacked of compromise.

It was clear that while the two songwriters gained their rewards, John in particular lost an old friend in Dick James. "I really didn't want to go to court," he told Q. "It was unfortunate. It means a soured relationship between the James family and me, which I didn't have before.

"Before we went to court I had tried to have lunch with Dick. I tried to say, 'Let's settle this'. He wouldn't. I stood in that box and I didn't hate him at all. I didn't enjoy the experience very much and we got a very big financial settlement. It was shame because I did have a good relationship with Dick James and it spoiled it."

Speaking more than 20 years after the case, Stephen James acknowledged the judge's ruling. "Where we opened a subsidiary in a foreign country and had not employed our own people but had taken 50%, he felt that was an artificial dilution of the royalties."

For James' father, the important thing was that he had been cleared of all suggestions of fraudulent behaviour on his part, which came as a great relief to the James family. Sadly, the stress of the trial still took its toll and, in February 1986, just two months after his name had been cleared, Dick James died of a heart attack, aged just 65.

Later the same year, Stephen James sold the whole DJM company, made up of over 14,000 titles including the John and Taupin copyrights, to Polygram (now Universal Music). The price – rumoured to be around £12 million – reflected the value of the John and Taupin catalogue.

Among the songs included in that deal was 'Candle In The Wind', which Elton memorably sang at the funeral of Diana, Princess of Wales, in September 1997, before it was released as a single with all profits and royalties going to charity. In less than 40 days it became the biggest-selling record of all time, with worldwide sales in excess of £33 million.

More than two decades on from the trial, Elton John continues to thrive as one of the world's most popular and successful artists, despite well-publicised problems with drugs, depression and lawsuits. His charity work through the Elton John Aids Foundation has raised millions of pounds and, in 1998, the man born plain Reginald Dwight became Sir Elton John.

Chapter 9

OZZY OSBOURNE

Forced to defend his lyrics after three suicides

O zzy Osbourne's debut solo album, released two years after he left Black Sabbath, brought the Birmingham-born ex-jailbird much-needed success in his own right.

The wittily titled 1981 *Blizzard Of Ozz* represented Osbourne's arrival as master of his own destiny, while songs such as 'Crazy Train', 'Mr Crowley' (written about famed occultist Aleister Crowley) and 'Suicide Solution' were an indication of the direction in which the self-proclaimed frontman of heavy metal was headed.

The albums *Diary Of A Madman*, *Talk Of The Devil* (issued as *Speak Of The Devil* in America) and *Bark At The Moon*, released between 1981 and 1983, added to Osbourne's growing reputation and his obsession with the "dark side". Biting off the head of a live dove at a record company convention and doing the same thing to a bat on stage in Iowa only served to enhance his standing as the "wild man of rock".

While all this activity was adding considerable weight to both Osbourne's kudos and bank balance, serious allegations about the effect his music was having on some of his fans were making headlines in the US.

John McCollum was a teenager from Riverside, California who reportedly had drinking and emotional problems. He found some consolation and satisfaction in the music of Osbourne but, on October 26, 1984, tragedy struck when the 19-year-old killed himself with a handgun while listening to Osbourne's songs through his headphones.

Just over a year after the shooting, McCollum's family filed their suit against Osbourne, his band and his record label, CBS Records, in the Los Angeles Superior Court. In the lawsuit they alleged that, "It is not just the words of Ozzy Osbourne's music which incited John but his entire presence. Ozzy Osbourne's entire attitude and even his album covers demonstrate a preoccupation with death."

The January 1986 suit also described *Blizzard Of Ozz* as a "progression of songs which lead down the path of emptiness to suicide", and the track 'Suicide Solution' was picked out for special attention.

While the covers of Osbourne's albums featured all sorts of demonic imagery, it was the lyrics to 'Suicide Solution' that were highlighted, even though it was accepted that it was not the track that young McCollum had been listening to at the time of his death.

Lines such as, "Get the gun and try it/shoot, shoot, shoot" and, "Where to hide? Suicide is the only way out" were held up as examples of the lyrics that encouraged McCollum to shoot himself. In their suit, the teenager's estate sought court-determined property, exemplary and punitive damages.

In August 1986, Superior Court Judge John Cole upheld Osbourne's pre-trial challenge to the complaint, and subsequently also allowed the McCollum family to change the nature of their complaint. They now alleged that the song 'Suicide Solution' contained masked words that became audible after repeated listenings.

Finally, at a Los Angeles Superior Court hearing in December 1986, evidence came from the McCollums' attorney, Thomas Anderson that close to $40,000 had been spent on discovering the masked words. "You can hear it once you know it's there but even if you didn't know, your mind would pick it up," he claimed.

The Institute for Bio Acoustics Research was asked to evaluate the song and claimed to have discovered subliminal lyrics sung at one and a half times the normal rate of speech. These could not be recognised by a first-time listener but "are audible enough that their meaning and true intent becomes clear after being listened to over and over again".

The Institute also testified that the song included Hemi-Sync tones, which result from a process that uses sound waves to influence an individual's mental state, and these made McCollum vulnerable to suggestive lyrics.

In court the singer's counsel, Howard Weitzman, dismissed these claims and argued that the First Amendment of the American Constitution allowed Osbourne to write about anything he wanted. He said that the additional noises on the record were not subliminal but simply his client fooling around on the mixing desk.

For his part, Osbourne claimed that the song 'Suicide Solution' had been written as a warning about alcoholism, based on his own problems and the alcohol-related death of AC/DC singer Bon Scott in 1980.

However, Osbourne's case was perhaps not helped by reports that, in Canada on New Year's Eve, 1983, a young Canadian named James Jollimore had killed a woman and her two sons after allegedly listening to Osbourne's *Bark At The Moon*. There were also reports of another teenage suicide, this time in Fitzgerald, Georgia, and once again the victim's family were claiming that 16-year-old Michael Waller shot himself as a result of listening to 'Suicide Solution'.

But despite these tragic developments, Judge Cole denied a motion to reinstate the McCollums' lawsuit from January 1986. Just to make things clear, the judge sat again in early January 1987 and reaffirmed his decision not to reinstate the case against Osbourne, explaining that it involved areas "clearly protected by the First Amendment". He added that the August amended complaint "read more like a novel than a legal pleading".

The First Amendment to the American Constitution, which was adopted between 1789 and 1791, covers the rights of US citizens to the freedom of religion, freedom of speech, freedom of the press, freedom of assembly and freedom of petition.

Confirming his view that neither Osbourne nor his lyrics could be held responsible for the teenager's suicide, the judge said, "The words on a phonograph record cannot be distinguished from the same language appearing in a book or magazine. It could not be argued that the language would be actionable if in a book or magazine. Neither can it be so argued here."

While Osbourne and his fellow defendants hoped that Judge Cole's ruling would bring the case to an end, they were wrong. The McCollum estate continued with an appeal against the January 1987 ruling, and the issue was back in court in July 1988. Once again Osbourne was victorious, when the California 2nd District Court of Appeal affirmed Judge Cole's decision, saying that the singer would have to have engaged in an immediate incitement to violence to lose the right to his freedom of speech.

The Appeal Court judges concluded that the alleged masked lyrics on the album *Blizzard of Ozz* were "unintelligible" and added, "Reasonable persons understand musical lyric and poetic conventions as the figurative expressions which they are."

Weitzman unsurprisingly welcomed the ruling, saying that the appeal court made it "clear that a situation in which a fan commits suicide cannot be the catalyst for censorship in the creative world of entertainment". On the other hand, Anderson concluded, "I don't see this as a freedom of speech case any more than is running a red light."

On Osbourne's album *No Rest For The Wicked*, released three months after the California ruling, the heavy metal singer decided to reveal what he thought about the whole issue of subliminal lyrics. On the track 'Bloodbath In Paradise' he inserted a hidden message as a form of protest about the whole argument. "I got so fed up I did put a stupid fucking message on a track backwards. It said, 'Your mother sells whelks in Hull' and someone did come up to me and ask, 'What's a fucking whelk?'"

While the case in California was coming to an end, a new one was opening up in Georgia where, in April 1988, the family of Michael Waller filed a $9 million suit against Osbourne and CBS Records.

This time, the allegation was that a tape of 'Suicide Solution' was in the cassette deck of the youngster's truck when his body was found, and that the lyrics and subliminal messages allegedly buried in the track had prompted him to shoot himself.

While this case was awaiting a court hearing, another action was filed by the family of another Georgia teenager, Harold Hamilton, who killed himself in a separate incident in March 1988, supposedly, according to his family, after listening to a live version of 'Suicide Solution' on Osbourne's *Tribute* album.

This album was, in fact, dedicated to the memory of Ozzy's former guitarist Randy Rhoads, who had been named among the defendants in the original McCollum case but was killed in a plane crash in May 1982.

On the heels of the two Georgia families filing their suits, Osbourne was moved to observe, "If I wrote music for people who shot themselves after listening to my music, I wouldn't have much of a following."

Three years after the Waller family filed their lawsuit, the case came up in Atlanta before United States District Judge Duross Fitzpatrick, who gave his ruling on May 6, 1991:

"In a world full of traps for the unwary teenager, such as rampant drug and alcohol abuse and a new morality that stresses the importance of doing anything that feels good, an addiction to music of this sort could be another step in a path to self-destruction."

The judge made the point that, "Whether the defendants' album *Blizzard Of Ozz* could fit this description, or whether the court approves of rock music in general or of this particular brand of it, is irrelevant."

Judge Fitzpatrick ruled that since the lyrics of the song 'Suicide Solution' discussed the phenomenon in a "philosophical" sense rather than personally recommending that Waller take his own life, the defendants did not engage in "culpable excitement", which would have negated First Amendment protection.

Deciding that the existence of a subliminal message on the track was unproven, and that a ruling in favour of the plaintiffs "would open the floodgate of litigation", the judge's summary also defined, "An abstract discussion of the mortal propriety or even moral necessity for a resort to suicide is not the same as indicating to someone that he should commit suicide and encouraging him to take such action.

"Plaintiffs have made no such showing and have failed to demonstrate any manner in which the defendants' music can be categorised as speech which incites imminent lawless activity."

With that he dismissed the lawsuit brought by the Waller family and, in effect, also ended the case that the Hamilton family were preparing.

Some 18 months later – in October 1992 – a US Supreme Court finally refused to reinstate the lawsuits concerning the suicides of the two Georgia teenagers, confirming the ruling that Osbourne's songs were constitutionally protected speech.

Kenneth McKenna, counsel for the families of two other teenagers whose suicides prompted a similar case brought against the band Judas Priest in 1986, acted as a consultant to the two families of the Georgia suicide victims. After the decision in Osbourne's favour in the case of the California youth, he reflected, "That lyrics were protected by the First Amendment wasn't earth-shattering, but we were hoping the Osbourne case would recognise there was a line you could cross."

After nearly eight years of claims and counterclaims, Osbourne declared, "I never sat down to write lyrics with the intent that anyone should kill themselves. I feel very sorry for those kids. But why can't you sing about suicide? It's a thing that really happens."

The irony of the Osbourne lawsuits – where each of the victims was presented as a troubled teenager – was that the British rock singer was also a troubled soul. He had been charged with threatening to kill his wife, and had undergone long-term rehabilitation for drink and drug problems.

In November 1992, the final show of his US tour was billed as Osbourne's last ever performance, but the reaction was so great that he resurrected his career with the Retirement Sucks tour in 1995 and then launched the highly successful Ozzfest concerts dedicated to breaking new acts.

In 2002, Osbourne and his family became major international television stars thanks to the fly-on-the-wall documentary series on their home life entitled simply *The Osbournes*. In June of the same year, Ozzy appeared in the concert at Buckingham Palace to celebrate Queen Elizabeth II's 50 years as British monarch. In a bizarre rock'n'roll moment, the former hellraiser performed 'Paranoid'.

Chapter 10

ELVIS PRESLEY

Taking the King's name turned into a "soap" opera

Over 30 years after his death, the music of Elvis Presley lives on in the hearts and minds of millions of fans around the world.

But the plethora of hit records made by the great man during his long singing career is not the only thing to have survived the test of time. Other things have helped to keep "the King" in the public eye and among the music industry's highest earners.

Since his death in August 1977, Presley has regularly topped the rather macabre Top Earning Dead Celebrities' list in *Forbes* magazine. Back in 2005, his annual earnings were calculated at a mighty $45 million, which is considerably more than he had in the bank at the time of his passing.

The question of Presley's financial affairs was always something of a closed book until his death, it being assumed that an entertainer of his stature was immensely wealthy. Only after his death did his finances come under any real scrutiny, and there was a sharp intake of breath among industry insiders when it became apparent that Elvis hadn't left behind the colossal fortune that he was assumed to have amassed.

Elvis' father, Vernon, was named as head of the estate. However, when Presley Snr died in June 1979, his nominated executors – Elvis' first wife, Priscilla, family accountant Joseph Hanks and, on behalf of Elvis' daughter, Lisa Marie, the National Bank of Commerce - went to the Memphis Probate Court for approval of their appointment.

Judge Joseph Evans duly authorised their appointment but was concerned that they intended to extend the management contract of Colonel Tom Parker, who had managed Elvis since 1955. Under a deal agreed with Vernon after Elvis died, Parker continued to receive 50% of all income from the estate.

Concerned that Lisa Marie's inheritance was in jeopardy, Judge Evans appointed Memphis attorney Blanchard Tual to investigate the estate's affairs, and also named him as Lisa Marie's financial guardian. This was the first time that anyone other than Colonel Parker had real access to Presley's financial affairs.

In December 1980, Tual was granted the authority to secure tax information from the previous three years relating to Parker and his merchandising company, Boxcar. The lawyer also uncovered information regarding Parker's deal with RCA, which showed that Presley's royalty rate rose by only 5% between 1955 and 1973, while record prices in the same period had doubled.

He also discovered "questionable" payments of over $2 million to Parker from RCA, and that Parker had sold Elvis' royalty rights to RCA in 1973 for $5.4 million, taking over $2.5 million for himself along with future guaranteed payments.

In his 300 page report – delivered in July 1981 – Tual concluded that Parker's 50% contract was indefensible, describing it as "excessive, imprudent and unfair to the estate". He added that he believed Parker had gained his 50% because "Elvis was naive, shy and unassertive", while Parker was "aggressive, shrewd and tough".

Stating that Lisa Marie "should not be deprived of benefits of her father's talents due to self-dealing of her father's manager and record company", Tual recommended that the executors should not approve any compensation to Parker; enter into any further deals with him; and that they should file a complaint against both Parker and RCA. He concluded that Parker's agreement with Elvis ended when the singer died.

Returning to court in August 1981, Judge Evans ordered the cessation of all payments to Parker by the estate and ordered them to bring a lawsuit against the latter for improper activities. They were also to name RCA in the suit as Parker's accomplices. When the estate filed suit accordingly, the record company – anxious not to be listed as co-defendants with Parker – sued the Colonel and countersued the Elvis Presley estate.

Parker's response was also to file a countersuit against the estate, claiming that, as he had been Elvis' long-time business partner, he was entitled to half the entertainer's assets. This was the start of a lengthy course of delaying tactics, the most interesting of which was Parker's admission that his real name was, in fact, Andreas Van Kuijk, and that he had been born in Holland and entered the US as an illegal immigrant. He claimed that this threw into doubt US jurisdiction over him in the lawsuits.

With the prospect of facing a long, drawn-out legal battle, the Presley estate agreed an out-of-court settlement in November 1982, agreeing to pay Parker $2 million in exchange for his giving up all rights and claims on income from the estate. The money was, in fact, paid by RCA in return for the exclusive rights to Elvis Presley's recordings. The record giant also paid over to the estate a further $1.2 million for unpaid royalties dating back to 1973.

Thereafter, since early 1981, the business empire of the deceased rock legend has been looked after by Elvis Presley Enterprises (EPE), which has promoted, protected, publicised and profited from the name and likeness of the singer from Tupelo, Mississippi who became the most famous entertainer on the planet.

They have registered names and titles, images and products in Elvis' name – including controlling his re-releases and the singer's legendary Graceland mansion – and along the way have reportedly pocketed close to $100 million per annum. They managed to register as trademarks the words "Elvis", "Elvis Presley", "Elvis In Concert" and "Graceland", but failed when it came to getting a legal stranglehold over the words "The King".

With input from Priscilla, who served as president of the business for over a decade, and daughter Lisa-Marie, who became co-executor on her 25th birthday in 1993, EPE launched and sold hundreds of Elvis items and goods as part of a hugely successful merchandising exercise. The business registered T-shirts, posters, jackets, dolls, key rings, spoons, postcards, soaps and colognes, and entered into licensing deals that allowed a host of American stores and shops to sell official Elvis merchandise. They also sued those who tried to palm off unauthorised Presley trinkets, and were prepared to go to court to protect their multi-million dollar investment.

In England, a year after Presley's death, a former street-trader with a degree in economics saw an opportunity for a business based on the life and times of Presley. Sid Shaw published the *Elvisly Yours* fanzine and then went through the right channels to register the name *Elvisly Yours* as a trademark.

In addition, he ran an Elvis Presley fan club and made regular visits to Graceland, where he met up with key executives from the Presley estate. Between them they agreed a deal whereby Shaw sold *Elvisly Yours* goods to the estate for sale at Graceland. However, as Elvis Presley Enterprises came to terms with the huge opportunities for Presley merchandising, it decided to strike out on its own, producing its own products under its own trademarks and licenses. This move included registering the words "Elvis" and "Elvis Presley", plus the signature "Elvis A Presley" as UK trademarks in 1983 for a range of souvenirs.

Naturally, this new spirit of entrepreneurship didn't include Shaw's London operation and, before long, the once cosy relationship between Shaw and the Presley estate boiled over into a lawsuit, with EPE filing a writ charging Shaw with trademark infringement and unfair competition.

In April 1987, the US Sixth Circuit Federal Court ruled for EPE, saying, "Shaw admitted using the same marks on the same goods in the same trade channels to the same consumers as did EPE. From this alone one must infer confusion."

In response, Shaw requested details of suppliers of merchandise to EPE, plus copies of the estate's licensing agreements and tax returns. In October 1990, however, a US District Court, to where the case had been referred, issued a permanent injunction stopping Shaw from using Elvis Presley's name or likeness in any circumstances.

When the case went back to the Sixth Circuit Court, the injunction was limited to just the US, and Shaw was allowed to write about Elvis and sell licensed merchandise.

While all this was going on in America, EPE decided it was time to register its UK marks across a wider range of products, including those covered by Class 3 of the 1938 UK Trademarks Act, which included such un-rock'n'roll items as toilet preparations, perfumes, soap, deodorants and cosmetics, plus bath and shower preparations.

EPE made its application in 1989, only to find that Shaw had beaten them to the punch and already extended his Elvisly Yours mark to cover goods in Class 3. Even so, EPE's formal trademark applications were initially approved by the Patent Office, which advertised them in its official journal between March and May 1991.

On Boxing Day 1991, Shaw put in notices of opposition with the Patent Office to all three of EPE's applications, citing six reasons for opposing them including lack of distinctiveness and conflict with his own mark.

This took the whole matter to a hearing before the Registrar, Mr. J. Tuck, who, in a written decision dated January 31, 1996 – over four years after the original request and subsequent opposition – found against Shaw, commenting that, "the grounds for opposition were not made out", and allowing EPE to register their marks for Class 3 goods.

Undaunted, Shaw's next move was to appeal to the English High Court. In the spring of 1997, the case came before Mr. Justice Hugh Laddie, who was asked to consider issues relating to the words "Elvis", "Elvis Presley" and the signature "Elvis A Presley" alongside the title "Elvisly Yours".

Making it clear that he knew the extent of Presley's career, the judge added his own assessment: "His abilities as an actor did not match his abilities as a rock'n'roll singer. Nevertheless, the films contributed to the enormous fame which he had acquired by the time of his death."

He went on to define Presley's famous home in Memphis, Tennessee as "something of a shrine visited by large numbers of his fans together with inquisitive members of the public", and rightly concluded, "He must be counted amongst the most well-known popular musicians this century."

During the two-day hearing in the first week of March 1997, the court also heard that EPE had "as its principal object the exploitation of the name and the likeness" of the late Elvis Presley.

The judge added that in view of Elvis' fame, the marks would serve as a reminder of the deceased star and not as an indication of any specific trade source. "The more a proposed mark alludes to the character, quality or non-original attributes of the goods on which it is used or proposed to be used, the lower its inherent distinctiveness," was his formal wording.

At the same time, he outlined a less formal scenario. "Even if Elvis Presley was still alive, he would not be entitled to stop a fan from naming his song, dog or goldfish, his car or his house Elvis or Elvis Presley."

In the case of the names "Elvis" and "Elvis Presley", while the judge concluded that the two marks had very little inherent distinctiveness, he was faced with an argument that the public's awareness of merchandising practice meant that they would always assume that products of famous personalities or fictitious characters came from a particular "genuine" source.

Rejecting this suggestion, the judge said that in his experience such an assumption would be wrong. "When people buy a toy of a well-known character because it depicts that character, I have no reason to believe that they care one way or another who made, sold or licensed it.

"Similarly, when a fan buys a poster or a cup bearing an image of his star, he is buying the likeness, not a product from a particular source.

"Although Mr. Shaw has sold millions of pounds' worth of memorabilia bearing the name 'Elvis' or 'Elvis Presley' over the last 18 or so years, it has not been suggested that anyone has ever thought they emanated from [Elvis Presley] Enterprises."

On the subject of the signature "Elvis A Presley", the judge reminded the court that, as far as possible, the register of trademarks had to be kept clean of marks that ran the risk of causing confusion. While he took the view that EPE's proposed signature was not particularly distinctive, Laddie added that Shaw's already registered "Elvisly Yours" mark, written in a cursive script with a Greek E, bore some resemblance to the Greek E at the beginning of the "Elvis A Presley" signature.

He concluded that if adopted as a trademark, EPE's signature would "be likely to give rise to deception and confusion". In the circumstances, the judge said he saw no reason to even consider Shaw's additional point that there was no evidence to prove that the signature was in fact the signature of Elvis Presley.

On March 18, Mr. Justice Laddie returned to court to rule in favour of Shaw and reverse the decision to approve EPE's trademarks request made by the Registrar a year earlier.

Refusing to be outgunned by the London trader, the mighty EPE turned to the Court of Appeal, where their case was heard, two years later, before Lord Justices Brown, Morritt and Walker. Peter Prescott QC represented the appellants Elvis Presley Enterprises Inc and Richard Meade acted for the respondent, Sid Shaw's Elvisly Yours.

The court heard that under the more recent 1968 Trademarks Act, the definition of a "mark" included a device, brand, heading, label, ticket, name, signature, word, letter, numeral or any combination thereof.

EPE was deemed to carry out the merchandising activities previously operated by or on behalf of Elvis Presley, and it was pointed out that Shaw did not dispute that EPE should be regarded as the successor to Presley's merchandising business. The court accepted that Shaw, using as evidence a newspaper article that described him as "first and foremost the consummate salesman", had for 20 years made and supplied a range of goods "all somehow related to Elvis Presley".

The court also heard of the previous litigation between Shaw and EPE in America, which resulted in the injunction against the British trader, and accepted that the two parties "no longer enjoy an amicable relationship".

On behalf of EPE, Prescott argued that the law had moved on to the stage where the general rule is that a trader may not make unauthorised use of the name of a celebrity in order to sell his own goods. Acknowledging that this rule primarily referred to living celebrities, he suggested, "the death of Elvis Presley does not matter in view of his abiding fame and Enterprises' unchallenged status as his successor".

On behalf of Shaw, Meade told the Appeals Court that Elvis Presley had become an important part of popular culture whose name and image other traders might legitimately wish to make use of. This prompted Prescott to ask, "Can it be the law that the more famous a man becomes, the harder it will be for him to register his name as a trademark in respect of goods in which he intends to trade?"

Meade said it would be, subject to the qualification that the answer applied to goods sold as "memorabilia or mementoes" of Presley, and in circumstances where the average buyer "is buying a likeness, not a product from a particular source".

He added that in his view, EPE had failed to educate the British public that "Elvis" and "Elvis Presley" were "being used by Enterprises and its licensees in a trademark sense".

In reaching their final decision in the case, the three judges each gave their own summary. Early on, Lord Justice Walker raised his concern over the signature mark "Elvis A Presley" and its authenticity, even though Shaw never raised the question of authenticity to the Appeals Court.

In a statement, EPE claimed, "The mark is the signature of the late Elvis A Presley and fully satisfied the distinctiveness and other requirements of the Act". The judge, however, pointed out that it bore no close resemblance to any of the different signatures on the range of products shown to the court. "Indeed, none of the signatures on products appears in the form 'Elvis A Presley'."

Lord Justice Walker's concern was echoed by Lord Justice Morritt, who, in his summing up, simply said that he did not accept that the authenticity of the signature had been established beyond doubt. "The difference lies not merely in the variations in the script, which may occur with all signatures, but in the fact that there is no evidence of any signature with the initial 'A' interposed between the Christian name and the surname."

The Court of Appeal finally took the view that the signature was "distinctive", which was in direct conflict with Judge Laddie's earlier verdict but in agreement with his opinion that it was confusingly similar in writing style – with the Greek E – to Shaw's original "Elvisly Yours" mark.

On the subject of the words "Elvis" and "Elvis Presley" against the name "Elvisly Yours", Justice Walker said that there was no positive evidence of any confusion during the 20-year period when both sides in the case were trading.

Pointing out that the names "Elvis" and "Elvis Presley" differed by the addition of a not very common surname, the judge showed off his knowledge of modern popular music by adding, "Had it been almost any other surname – I except Costello – it would have made the mark more distinctive in the trademark sense. But in this case it simply confirmed the descriptive character of the mark."

Justice Morritt dealt with the question of "character merchandising" and the suggestion that by lending their name to a product or range of goods, a public figure is assumed to endorse it. "The consequence relied on is that the consumer comes to regard goods bearing that name as having the approbation or licence of his or her 'idol'."

Rejecting that submission, the judge felt that Shaw had sold goods with reference to Elvis that the public would assume to be a reference to Elvis Presley. "For example, his soap was called Elvis Soap because it was impregnated with an 'image [of Elvis] which remains right to the end'.

"It is not suggested that Mr. Shaw has ever claimed any connection with EPE and the fame of Elvis Presley as a singer. He was not a producer of soap. There is no reason why he or any organisation of his should be concerned with toiletries so as to give some perceived connection between his name and the product."

Finally, Lord Justice Brown made three points. He stated that there was no connection between the class of products in question (toiletries) and what made Presley famous and added that the sale of these products in the UK since Presley's death was done by Shaw, who had never claimed any endorsement from EPE.

In concluding he said, "The Elvis Presley legend is such as would inevitably attract a wide demand for memorabilia, little of which, in the UK and following his death, would the general public suppose to be officially licensed or approved."

With that, the three Appeal Court Judges dismissed the appeal by Elvis Presley Enterprises Inc. In the eyes of the law at least, EPE had failed to prove that any use of the marks in the UK had become distinctive of EPE in the eyes of the public. Therefore, according to the court, there was no reason why they should be registered. Justices Walker, Morritt and Brown added a further ruling that denied EPE leave to appeal to the House of Lords.

The court's ruling that there should not be "an assumption that only a celebrity or his successor may ever market his own character" brought to an end the 25-year dispute. A triumphant Shaw said after the case, "I've proved that Elvis belongs to all of us – Elvis is part of our history, part of our culture. They tried to put me out of business and they haven't succeeded. It's been an enormous struggle but I've always believed in justice and believed I would win."

However, just a month before his famous High Court victory, Shaw was forced to close his original Elvisly Yours shop, which was based in a terraced house in London's East End, following a dispute with Hackney council over non-payment of £18,000 business rates. The man who opened a supermarket in Russia in 1992 was quoted at the time as saying, "I have fought the Graceland mafia, the Russian mafia and now I'm fighting the Hackney mafia." He went on to continue running the business from a new shop in the much more upmarket Baker Street, in the capital's West End.

While there were press reports that he was willing to sell a stake in his Elvisly Yours enterprise to a potential new partner, Shaw continued to expand his Elvis memorabilia business to cover over 300 trademarks and licences, including an Elvis credit card.

At the same time, EPE saw a drop in revenues, with only $40 million coming through the door in 2004. However, the 30th anniversary of Presley's death in 2007 boosted the figure back to its previous higher levels.

Presley's daughter, Lisa Marie, ultimately became owner and chairperson of the board of EPE, with her mother taking an advisory role, and in 2005 she sold 85% of the company to the CFX Inc. Corporation for a reported $100 million. While retaining sole ownership of Graceland, Lisa Marie supposedly took $53 million in cash, but kept a reported 15% share and an active role in the business of promoting and remembering her late father.

Chapter 11

HOLLY JOHNSON

The problems of trying to go solo

Tagging themselves a "post-punk S&M gay cabaret act", Frankie Goes To Hollywood (a name inspired by a headline about Frank Sinatra moving into movies) burst onto the British music scene on the back of an appearance on Channel 4's music series *The Tube* in November 1982.

Spotted by producer Trevor Horn, composer of the show's theme tune and a former member of the hit act Buggles, the Liverpudlian group consisting of Holly Johnson, Paul Rutherford, Brian Nash, Mark O'Toole and Peter Gill were signed to ZTT (Zang Tuum Tumb), the label started by Horn and his wife, Jill Sinclair, in 1983 with financial support from Island Records. With a name taken from the description in an Italian war poem of the noise made by a machine gun, Horn declared that having his own record company would "allow me to help on projects, albums or recording sessions, even if I wasn't producing".

Banned by BBC Radio 1 after DJ Mike Read dubbed the record "obscene" – an action that doubtless assured its success – FGTH's debut single, 'Relax', hit the top of the chart and the one-million sales mark in November 1983, despite not being played on the hugely influential *Top Of The Pops* because of the futile ban.

FGTH went on to become the first group to top the British charts with their first three singles since Gerry & The Pacemakers over 20 years earlier. A second million-selling number one, 'Two Tribes', appeared in June 1984, followed a few months later by a third, 'The Power Of Love', while the Horn-produced debut album, *Welcome To The PleasureDome*, also entered the chart at the top spot. The success of FGTH completed a triumphant year for ZTT, which boasted a record in the UK top 75 singles chart in every week of 1984.

While both the band and Horn won BRIT Awards in 1985 – for Best Single and as Best Producer respectively – FGTH stayed together for only two more years, producing four further hit singles and the top five album *Liverpool*, which, with tracks produced by both Horn and Steve Lipson, cost a reported £800,000 to complete.

A temporary split in March 1987 turned into a permanent one, as the various members went their separate ways. Without Johnson and Rutherford, the other three members attempted to reform FGTH with a new singer, but a dispute over the use of the name ended any chance of a new record deal.

FGTH's contract with ZTT was for an initial period of six months; it could have been extended by the record company by two similar option periods and for up to five years with a minimum commitment of three singles and five albums if every option was exercised. ZTT was free to bring the contract to an end at any time and also had the right to reject recordings made by FGTH, which meant that the record company could in effect determine how long the contract lasted.

When singer Johnson signed a solo deal with MCA Records in July 1987, he was served with an injunction by ZTT and its sister music publishing company, Perfect Songs, within a month. ZTT claimed breach of contract and sought to prevent the singer from leaving the label.

Johnson's reaction was to fight the court order and also to claim royalties from earlier FGTH recordings released on ZTT, produced by Horn and published by Perfect Songs.

Before the case went to court, Johnson told *The Liverpool Echo*, "The court case is a drag. I think it is going to be an ordeal but I am willing to go through it because I believe I am completely in the right. It also means that plans for my solo career have to wait until we can sort things out."

Further details of FGTH's deal with ZTT – as disclosed by Johnson in his 1994 autobiography, *A Bone In My Flute* – included a £250 advance for all the members for the first single, and £5,000 for the publishing rights to songs written by the group.

Johnson also claimed that on *Welcome To The PleasureDome* he "took 60% of the composer's share on some of the singles and just 50% on other songs on the album", which, according to Johnson, was followed by a future deal that split the publishing royalties five ways while the band remained together. After that, earnings would revert to the respective writers of each song.

The singer, who claimed that the band received a UK royalty of 6% on the record-breaking single 'Relax', also stated that Perfect Songs took 35% of the publishing royalties, while Horn as producer received 4% of the retail price on each record. Horn also earned a return from the company's deal with Island and earnings from Sarm Studios, where the band recorded. Sarm was owned by Horn, his wife, Jill Sinclair, and their family.

Arguing that the recording contract he had signed with ZTT amounted to restraint of trade, Johnson and his solicitors marched head-long towards the High Court after attempts at an out-of-court settlement failed.

On January 18, 1988 in the London High Court, Johnson's action to remove the injunction banning him from pursuing a solo career opened before Mr. Justice Whitford, with Andrew Bateson QC representing ZTT and Perfect Songs.

The case was perhaps the first where the doctrine of restraint of trade was considered in a British court in relation to recording agreements, and many music industry observers were concerned about the legal precedent that might be set by a victory for the artist.

Bateson opened by telling the court that when Horn first heard the group, the producer – rated as one of the world's top three – believed they had potential. Following the success of 'Relax', Horn apparently dropped other work, at a cost of £50,000, to concentrate on the follow-up hit, 'Two Tribes'.

"On both those records there was no performance by the band", Bateson stated, adding that only the voice of Holly Johnson was heard alongside session musicians. The vocal had to be subjected to a considerable amount of work to "bring it into line musically."

Counsel added that in view of this work by Horn, whose expertise with high-technology recording equipment and session musicians had created the records' success, Johnson "has not done badly", earning royalties of nearly £500,000 between June 1984 and the end of 1986.

Bateson said that Johnson's contract obliged him to record as a solo artist "on the same terms" as when he was a member of FGTH. Documents supplied to the court by Johnson's counsel, Mark Cran QC, claimed that the part of his contract restraining members of the group who were leaving was "uncertain in meaning, application or effect".

Three days into the hearing, Mr. Justice Whitford transferred proceedings from the law courts to the Sarm Studios complex in London's plush Kensington district. Together with lawyers from both sides, the judge was given a demonstration of the latest in studio technology by ZTT's Stephen Lipson, and also heard two versions of 'Relax'. The first was a demo, recorded in just a few hours; the other was the finished, state-of-the-art version, which had taken three months to record. When that was played to the judge, he was reported to have said, "That's enough, we've just heard that."

Giving evidence a week into the trial, Lipson recounted his experience working with the band in Holland on *Liverpool*. With Johnson agreeing to work only in the afternoon while the rest of the band worked at night, the producer said, "It was like a constant pain. We were not pulling together."

In an attempt to accommodate the singer's wishes, Lipson said he only once asked Johnson to come to the studio in the evening. "He would not come. I called him at eight. He said, 'You know I do not work after six. I will come down tomorrow'." This behaviour upset the rest of the band according to Lipson, who told the court, "They got more upset towards the end of our stay. They spent more time looking for singers than working on the music."

Suggesting that Johnson's voice on *Liverpool* was "all right" but not "fiery", the producer of albums by Grace Jones and Annie Lennox added that the frontman was "not in sync", and his commitment to the album was "not particularly great".

While it was accepted that there had been no performance on the singles 'Relax' and 'Two Tribes' by the other members of FGTH, Horn gave them some credit for their contribution.

"All the music was by the band and the whole feeling came from the band," he said, while restating that there was no "actual playing" by FGTH. He admitted that the members of FGTH "hated the idea" of using session musicians, "but they went along with it".

As the case ran into February, Johnson was called to give evidence. He agreed with Lipson's testimony that he would only work in the day-time, explaining, "I think it is extremely unhealthy to work throughout the night", but he denied a suggestion that this attitude meant that records took longer to make and cost more.

Accepting that his determination to lead a normal life and "not get dragged into a rock 'n' roll lifestyle" alienated him from the rest of the group, Johnson stressed that he wanted to "do my own grocery shopping and other things at normal hours."

Johnson agreed that he'd made £980,000 from FGTH's records, but claimed he had not received all of the money. Asked by Judge Whitford why he wanted to leave the group and go solo, he replied, "I am just not happy working with them under the conditions of their contract. I do not really get on with them as people and I do not think they have respect for me."

Talking about his record company, Johnson stated, "All the other bands I know with ZTT are also unhappy. Quite a few of them have in fact split. It was not a happy, jovial atmosphere there."

During Cran's summing-up, as he went through a detailed analysis of the contract, Mr. Justice Whitford interrupted to comment, "Mr. Johnson could be 70 years old and still be bound to this contract; then I suspect even the Synclavier could not enhance his performance."

In the final days of the hearing, lawyers for both parties busied themselves with offers and counter-offers. In the end all were refused, and it was left to Judge Whitford to give his decision on February 10, 1988, after listening to 16 days of evidence. His ruling was that restraints in Johnson's contract were unfair and the singer should be free to pursue his career as a solo artist with another record label.

After dismissing the claims of both ZTT and Perfect Songs with the simple statement, "This was not a fair deal", the judge said, "Mr. Johnson, who I found entirely reasonable was, in my judgement, entitled to free himself from these onerous obligations. He is a singer. He wants to make a living singing."

The judge was also concerned with the Perfect Songs publishing agreement, which Johnson and other members of FGTH had signed without any choice since it had been offered as a package with the record deal. Judge Whitford considered the restrictions unreasonable and declared the agreement unenforceable, while stating that it was unfair that Perfect Songs should have control over the songs after they were delivered and that its 35% fee was too much.

After pointing out that ZTT directors Horn and Sinclair, a former maths teacher, had not been wilfully unreasonable but had acted through inexperience, Mr. Justice Whitford declared that as, in his view, Johnson was entitled to damages over the near £800,000 recording costs of *Liverpool*, an inquiry into the singer's entitlement should be held.

Johnson's reaction, following his victory, was to announce: "This is a great day for recording artists everywhere, and I believe this will help them in the future to get a better deal and contract."

Within weeks of the case ending, both Johnson and Sinclair traded verbal punches over the decision in the columns of the music press. The singer told *Melody Maker* (in an interview appearing in the February 27, 1988 issue) that in his view ZTT should have favourably amended FGTH's contract when 'Relax' was a hit, claiming that "any decent business person, any decent human being would have renegotiated the contract immediately and willingly.

"Their [ZTT] attitude is extremely difficult to deal with. With FGTH it was, 'They're the band, they're just puppets, we've created them.' They started to believe their own press. This is the first time ZTT has been shown publicly to be wrong."

Sinclair criticised both the judge and the defendant. "It was very sad that the judge only looked at the possibility of what could happen with the contract, how it could be interpreted, not how it had been... Holly is not an easy person to work with. I don't think any good artists are necessarily easy to work with, but that doesn't diminish their value to

(TERRY DISNEY/HULTON/GETTY IMAGES)

Liberace's victory was front page news – even in the *Daily Mirror*.

Flamboyant American piano star Liberace, out of sequins for once, arrives in style for his 1959 High Court appearance.

Press coverage of the 1967 lawsuit brought against The Move by Prime Minister Harold Wilson.

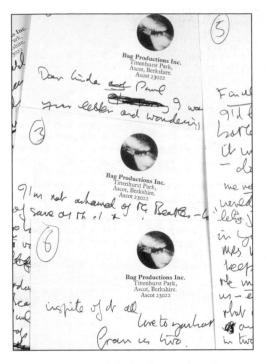

A hand-written draft of a six-page letter from
John Lennon to Paul McCartney, written around 1970
during the legal battle to break up The Beatles.
(REUTERS/CORBIS)

Paul & Linda McCartney stroll to court for the
hearing to end the Beatles partnership. (LFI)

George Harrison (right) and co-producer Phil Spector at work on George's *All Things Must Pass*
album which featured his copyright infringing song 'My Sweet Lord'. (BETTMANN/CORBIS)

'Exploited' Gilbert awarded a fortune

—Judge slams manager who cashed in on O'Sullivan's biggest hits

O'Sullivan's court victory was headline news in 1982.

Gilbert O'Sullivan, who sued Gordon Mills, the man who discovered, managed and produced him. (HULTON ARCHIVE/GETTY IMAGES)

Bernie Taupin (left) and Elton John, who jointly sued their music publishers over contracts and song copyrights. (MICHAEL OCHS ARCHIVE/GETTY IMAGES)

Judas Priest in court during their 1990 trial in Reno, Nevada, where they were accused of inciting two teenagers to shoot themselves. (DAVID PARKER)

Jason Donovan speaks to the media after his £200,000 "gay slur" victory in 1992.
(NEIL MUNNS/PA ARCHIVE/PA PHOTOS)

Morrissey lost the court case
and lost his appeal.
(PHOTO NEWS SERVICE/REX FEATURES)

Judge Weeks described Morrissey as "devious, truculent and unreliable"

Former members of The Smiths Andy Rourke (left) and Mike Joyce
(right), who went to court in 1996 to take on Morrissey and Johnny
Marr over their shares of royalties. (PHOTO NEWS SERVICE/REX FEATURES)

One of the judge's comments –
which Morrissey described as
"extreme and hateful".

Smiling on the steps of the High Court during their 1999 court hearing are former Spandau Ballet
members Steven Norman (left), Tony Hadley (centre) and John Keeble. (REX FEATURES)

Scary, Sporty, Posh and Baby Spice promoting the Spice Sonic scooters which featured in a high profile court case, brought by the cycle manufacturers after Ginger left the group. (REX FEATURES)

Emma 'Baby Spice' Bunton turns up prepared to give evidence at the Spice Girls court hearing. (HAYDN WEST/REX FEATURES)

Napster founder Shawn Fanning (left) watches his attorney David Boies in action in San Francisco in October, 2000, during the long running legal battle with the US record industry. (JERRY TALFER/SAN FRANCISCO CHRONICLE/CORBIS)

The Bluebells, who went to number with 'Young At Heart' in 1993 and ended up in court a decade later. (LFI)

Violinist and Clark Gable lookalike Bobby Valentino who successfully sued The Bluebells over his contribution to the hit song 'Young At Heart'. (STEVE MAISEY/REX FEATURES)

_eon Hendrix, brother of Jimi Hendrix, at the funeral f their father Al in 2002. Leon later sued the Hendrix Estate over Al's will. (JON FREEMAN/REX FEATURES)

Al Hendrix inherited his son Jimi's estate and caused a family dispute when he died. (GIGI CAMPANILE/REX FEATURES)

Former U2 stylist Lola Cashman fought the band over ownership of clothing and jewellery. (OSD PHOTO AGENCY/REX FEATURES)

Judge accepts Bono's word and gives him back his hat

U2 singer Bono went to court to fight for his "iconic" hat and a pair of trousers. (LFI)

Bono's victory was a big story.

Procol Harum's Gary Brooker, who described the 'Whiter Shade Of Pale' judgement as a "darker shade of black". (CARL DE SOUZA/AFP/GETTY IMAGES)

Ex-Procol Harum keyboard player Matthew Fisher claimed he was a co-composer of 'Whiter Shade Of Pale'. (CARL DE SOUZA/AFP/GETTY IMAGES) the record company. Holly was difficult to deal with and I'm flabbergasted by some of what he has to say."

Not surprisingly, given the bad feeling that so obviously existed between the claimants and the defendant, ZTT launched an appeal, which was judged by the Court of Appeal on July 26, 1989. Speaking for the three Appeal Court judges, Lord Justice Dillon outlined the three provisions in the arrangement between ZTT and Johnson and his fellow members of FGTH. The nature of these provisions persuaded the judges to reject ZTT's appeal against Judge Whitford's judgement.

They were concerned that the members of the group were bound collectively and individually for up to seven "option periods", that the agreements could have lasted up to nine years, and that the claimants (ZTT) were free to end the obligations at any time while the group were bound to record only for ZTT.

Next was the issue that ZTT had control of all matters, including approval of compositions and expenditure on recording costs, plus absolute discretion whether or not to release records by FGTH. Added to which was the fact that even if records were not released, copyright remained with ZTT.

Finally there was the issue that while the group and the individual members were bound exclusively to the companies ZTT and Perfect Songs, the arrangement was not reciprocal.

The Appeal Court found both the recording and publishing contracts to be "not a fair bargain" and in restraint of trade.

Meanwhile, the inquiry into the amount of damages to be awarded to Johnson continued. To this day there have been no public reports as to how much the singer received from his former employers.

The press reports of Johnson's Appeal Court victory declared that the judgement "set a legal precedent which rocked the music business", and claimed that ZTT had freed most of its artists from their contracts after the original case. By August 1989, the label was down to a roster of just two acts.

In the years after the break-up of FGTH, Johnson's ex-bandmates worked in a variety of line-ups, although Rutherford was the only one to achieve any chart success. At the same time, ZTT continued to release FGTH product, with remixed singles and a greatest hits package making the charts in the Nineties and 2000.

After a spell as an independent label, during which time it acquired Stiff Records, ZTT linked with the giant Warner Music Group and discovered the multi-million-selling singer Seal. He joined Horn's impressive list of production credits alongside ABC, Simple Minds, Pet Shop Boys, Tatu and the global charity hit 'Do They Know It's Christmas?', which Horn co-produced with Midge Ure.

In 1998, ZTT regained its status as an independent label. It now sits within the SPZ (Sarm Perfect ZTT) group, with interests including artists such as Lisa Stansfield and reissued Art of Noise and Propaganda releases alongside The Producers, a group consisting of Horn, Lipson and ex-10cc member Lol Creme.

In 2006, tragedy struck the Horn family when Sinclair was seriously injured in a shooting accident at the couple's Oxfordshire home. As of writing, she remains unconscious and in intensive care.

After the court case, the victorious Holly Johnson picked up where he had left off, notching up five hit singles between 1989 and 1990 and a number one solo album, *Blast,* before splitting with MCA Records after a dispute over the promotional budget set for his second, and less successful, solo album.

In a 1993 interview, Johnson revealed that he was HIV positive. He settled into a new life, painting and exhibiting his art, as well as writing and recording a third solo album in 1999, which featured a new version of 'The Power Of Love'.

In 2007, Johnson and the former members of FGTH faced each other in a court battle, this time over rights to the band's name. Johnson had applied for patents to use the name Frankie Goes To Hollywood on items such as beer mats, sunglasses, shoes and belts, and also for musical performances. Rutherford, Gill, Nash and O'Toole opposed the application on the grounds that the group was an equal collaboration between all five members.

While Johnson told the trademark adjudicator that the other band members had signed an agreement recognising that he had originated the name and that they had no rights to it when he left the group, drummer Gill claimed Johnson's bid was "in bad faith", that there had been an agreement between the members over the band's name and that profits had always been equally shared. Johnson's decision to register the group's name as a trademark came as the other four members announced their own plans to tour again as FGTH.

Eventually, the UK Intellectual Property Office ruled in favour of the quartet of Rutherford, Gill, Nash and O'Toole, and ordered the band's former singer to pay costs of £3,250 to his ex-bandmates.

Johnson's battle with ZTT was something that still rankled with him more than a dozen years after the original case. Speaking in 2001, he confirmed that he had left the label on very bad terms with Horn and Sinclair.

"They have never really forgiven me for winning my freedom in the law courts", the singer said, adding that the worst part of being in FGTH was "the contract we signed with ZTT".

Chapter 12

JUDAS PRIEST

Accused of hiding messages and causing suicides

Formed in Birmingham in 1971, heavy metal act Judas Priest, who took their name from Bob Dylan's song 'The Ballad Of Frankie Lee And Judas Priest', developed into one of Britain's leading rock bands, with flamboyant singer Rob Halford as their focal point.

In 1978, their fourth album, *Stained Class*, represented their second UK chart entry while also entering the US chart, albeit at number 173. By the mid-Eighties, they had notched up several US and UK Top 20 albums and built a solid following on the widespread "metal market". In 1985, they were invited to appear as part of the US Live Aid concert in Philadelphia. However, within a year Judas Priest were on the receiving end of a major lawsuit over the part their music allegedly played in leading two teenage fans to shoot themselves.

James Vance and Raymond Belknap, from Reno, Nevada, were teenage Judas Priest fans. Belknap's early present to his friend for Christmas 1985 was a copy of *Stained Class*.

On December 23, the pair of them ended up in a local church playground, where Belknap put a shotgun to his chin and shot himself, dying instantly. Vance followed suit, but his attempt at suicide failed even though he blew away most of the lower portion of his face.

A year later, Judas Priest, along with their label CBS, were named in a civil lawsuit brought by the families of Belknap and Vance. The suit charged that the band's music had caused the two to kill themselves. The official papers, filed in Nevada in early December 1986, alleged that the youths formed a suicide pact and shot themselves after six hours of listening to Judas Priest.

"The suggestive lyrics, combined with the continuous beat and rhythmic, non-changing intonation and the music combined to induce and encourage, aid, abet and otherwise mesmerise the plaintiffs into believing the answer to life was death."

It was claimed that listeners with emotional problems might interpret the band's lyrics as a plea to commit suicide as an act of social rebellion.

Washoe District Judge Jerry Whitehead turned down a motion to dismiss the suit and ordered a trial to be set. Before the case eventually made it to court – and nearly three years after the original shooting – Vance died from his terrible injuries.

Before the trial started, counsel for the families altered the focus of their case from the actual lyrics to the suggestion that subliminal messages planted on the album were responsible for the deaths. The argument centred on a track titled 'Better By You, Better Than Me', written by Gary Wright and originally recorded by Wright's band, Spooky Tooth, in 1969. According to the plaintiffs' lawyers, the song included the words "Do it, do it, do it", while other tracks contained hidden messages that supposedly said, "Try suicide" and "Let's be dead."

The use of subliminal messages was nothing new in advertising. Companies had used them in film and television adverts to subliminally batter consumers into submission, but governments around the world eventually introduced laws banning their use.

Rock acts – from The Beatles and Led Zeppelin to ELO and Queen – have all included backwards messages on their recordings with apparently little or no impact on their audience, although the lyrics of The Beatles' 1968 track, 'Helter Skelter', had arguably the most notorious effect when Californian mass murderer Charles Manson claimed that the song had told him to kill.

The Judas Priest trial finally took place in the Washoe County Courthouse in July 1990, and a nervous music industry waited with bated breath for a decision that could have serious and long-lasting implications for the future of their business. Artists too were concerned, with Frank Zappa warning, "If the lunatics prevail in this Judas Priest case, it opens up the possibility for medical malpractice insurance for musicians."

Judge Whitehead agreed with the argument that finding impartial jurors from the local community might be difficult, and elected to hear the case without a jury. Across the courtroom he faced Suellen Fulstone on behalf of both Judas Priest and CBS, plus Vivian Lynch, counsel for the Vance family, and Kenneth McKenna, representing the Belknap family.

Outside the court, Judas Priest fans waited for the arrival of the band, carrying copies of *Stained Class* for the group to autograph and holding up banners with slogans such as, "Honk If You Rock!"

Opening proceedings, Lynch told the court that the case was about mind control. "This was not suicide. This was an adventure, a journey to a better place. What they [Vance and Belknap] planned was good because Judas Priest said it was good."

She claimed that Judas Priest's records talked of violence, destruction and antisocial behaviour, but admitted that the band, "does not advocate this as a way of life. They are not soldiers in the army of Satan".

Lynch claimed that hidden messages in the music created excitement "as a way of making money", and accused the band of "irresponsible greed for embedding these messages" in their records. Adding that the band was "meddling in the mysteries of the human mind", she claimed that Vance and Belknap were part of the culture that believed the words of Judas Priest were "scriptures". "The hidden messages pushed them over the edge," she asserted.

McKenna added that the two youths were "compelled by a power they did not understand", and argued that both the band and CBS Records took "unreasonable risks with adolescent minds". He said their actions were "dangerous, irresponsible and negligent."

The prosecution's accusations were countered by Fulstone, who told the court that there were no hidden messages on the records. "There is a fascination with the possibility of mind control and manipulation," she said, "but this courtroom is no place for magic and experimentation".

Turning her attention to the deceased, defence counsel declared, "These two young men had many problems with drugs, alcohol, scrapes with law enforcement and loss of jobs." Fulstone went on to suggest that there was no suicide pact between the two youths, adding that just before he shot himself Belknap allegedly said, "Life sucks." After that, according to defence counsel, Vance "panicked and feared the police would charge him with homicide and then followed suit."

The defence concluded by stating, "Ray Belknap and James Vance had sad and miserable lives. They turned to drugs and alcohol, which only made their lives worse. In their anger and frustration they had fantasies of killing other people. On December 23rd Ray Belknap turned that anger onto himself."

Among the witnesses called to give evidence was Vance's mother, Phyllis, who was questioned by co-prosecution counsel Timothy Post, on behalf of the family's estate. Post morbidly chose to wear the suit that James Vance would have worn at the trial had he survived, explaining that, according to the family, he was the "closest thing they had left to a son".

Mrs. Vance confirmed that her son stopped going to church after discovering Judas Priest. "He couldn't do both at the same time. He was either true to the God of our church or he was true to the god Judas Priest," she said, before admitting under questioning that her son had assaulted her twice after the 1985 shooting, by which time he had stopped listening to the band's music.

One expert witness called to analyse the music of Judas Priest claimed that the message "do it" had been spread over 11 of the 24 recording tracks on 'Better By You, Better Than Me', while another, Victoria Evans, said that she had heard additional suicide messages on *Stained Class* and described the album as "a time bomb waiting to go off". However, she admitted that an innocent phrase such as "testing one" did sound like "no music" when played backwards.

Psychology professor Howard Shevrin gave evidence confirming that, in his view, subliminal messages subconsciously received could later surface consciously as the recipient's own thoughts.

The only member of Judas Priest to give evidence was Rob Halford, although guitarists Glenn Tipton and K.K. Downing and bassist Ian Hill were also present in court. Halford confirmed that on the track 'Love Bites', included on the band's 1984 *Defenders Of The Faith* album, he had deliberately recorded the words, "In the dead of the night, love bites" backwards, before playing it simultaneously with a forwards version.

Answering the judge's question as to why he did it, Halford explained, "When you are composing songs, you're always looking for new ideas, new sounds, just as an artist would add another piece of paint to a canvas."

Defence audio expert Anthony Pellicano told the court that in his opinion subliminal audio did not exist. To prove the point, Halford was invited to give a 10-second taped a cappella rendition of the line "Deliver us from all the fuss" from the song 'White Heat, Red Hot', a track on *Stained Class*.

Played backwards to the court, it showed that the words bore little resemblance to the message they were alleged to convey: "Fuck the lord, fuck all of you."

The former head of Reno's suicide crisis centre, clinical psychologist James Mikawa, testified that Belknap had decided to take his own life prior to the fatal shooting. "I concluded that Raymond Belknap was the one who was suicidal and James Vance was not," he said, adding that suicide "is not something that happens overnight".

The argument put forward by Judas Priest and CBS was that the "do it" sounds on the album were not any sort of hidden message, but simply an exhalation of breath by Halford plus a combination of drums, guitars and vocals.

In counsel's closing arguments at the end of the four-week trial, Lynch asked the judge to award the Vance family up to $5 million for pain and suffering and medical costs, while McKenna requested $1.2 million on behalf of the Belknap family.

On August 24, Judge Whitehead finally gave his ruling. He acknowledged that the plaintiffs had "submitted a forceful argument that the backmasked messages are present". He accepted that he had heard the words "do it" on the Judas Priest album and believed that both Belknap and Vance had heard them too.

The judge also acknowledged that the same words were subliminal, but concluded that they "are the result of a chance combination of sounds" and "were not intentionally formed". He agreed that the words were "a combination of the singer's exhalation of breath on one track and a Leslie guitar on another."

In his conclusion the judge ruled, "The plaintiffs have not lost this case because defendants proved that subliminal stimuli have no effect on human behaviour. Rather because they failed to prove that defendants intentionally placed subliminal messages on the album and that those messages were a cause of the suicide and attempted suicide involved in this case."

He ended with, "It is unknown what future information, research and technology will bring to this field."

While finding in favour of Judas Priest and CBS Records, the judge imposed a $40,000 sanction or fine against the record company for failing to comply with a court order to make the original 24-track recording of *Stained Class* available. While the company maintained that most of the master tapes of the album had either been lost or mislaid, Judge Whitehead was less than convinced. "Given their library, vault and security systems, it wasn't credible that those particular tapes all of a sudden couldn't be found."

CBS, which expressed surprise at the decision and claimed that it had complied fully, considered an appeal against the fine.

Relishing the victory, Halford said after the trial that Judas Priest had come out of the ordeal without blemish, but he had concerns about the judge's decision. "The judge's ruling has apparently left the door open for future lawsuits of this nature. He has in effect ruled that subliminals do exist as a form of manipulating the unconscious mind, and that has to be worrisome."

The singer believed that court testimony had shown that Vance and Belknap were "two walking sticks of dynamite that were going to go off whether they were listening to Judas Priest or not", and pointed out that the track 'Beyond The Realms' from *Stained Class* was in fact an anti-suicide song. "It talks about the way people withdraw from society and refuse to communicate when they can't stand things any more, but says they shouldn't kill themselves."

Downing said simply, "It will be another 10 years before I can even spell subliminal."

The reaction from the plaintiffs was that even though the judge had reached the wrong decision, he had not got it entirely wrong. Counsel Lynch, who announced that she was planning to file motion for a new trial, said, "I think the judge made all the right findings of facts but [he felt] the scientific evidence was not sufficiently developed to find cause. I disagree with him."

Soon after the trial, Lynch reportedly wrote a song called 'No More Deadly Music', with lyrics along the lines of, "I won't tell you death's the answer/Or sing of wicked Satan's creed." Her attempts to get Johnny Cash to record this dubious ditty proved unsuccessful.

A month after the trial ended, Judas Priest released a new album entitled *Painkiller*, which CBS chose to advertise with the rather insensitive slogan: "Awesome! Backwards Or Forwards."

For Halford this was the record company "playing on the lighter side of the issue", but he added, "Although it is a very serious venture for both Judas Priest and the record company, now we have to look at the ridiculous side of the allegations ... it's my personal belief that it sounds better forwards."

Lynch, on the other hand, was far from amused by the advertising message, which she described as "almost criminally irresponsible."

In November 1990, Judas Priest returned to Reno for a concert and donated the proceeds of the gig to the city's Community Runaway Youth Services Center. Within 12 months, Halford temporarily left the band to go solo, eventually suing Sony/CBS Records for restraint of trade. Even as Halford and the band parted company, the case of Belknap and Vance versus Judas Priest and CBS Records rumbled on into 1993, before the Nevada Supreme Court finally affirmed Judge Whitehead's ruling.

The judgement centred on the issue of whether subliminal messages were protected speech under the First Amendment, and for the second time in a decade a heavy metal act was cleared of being responsible for teenage suicides in America.

Chapter 13

THE STONE ROSES

Disputing a million pound record contract

W hen Manchester once again spawned a new wave of bands more than 20 years after its mid–Sixties heyday, The Stone Roses were one of the main acts leading the way. Fusing guitar rock with acid house beats, they helped to create the movement that became known as "Madchester".

Ian Brown, John Squire, Mani (Gary Mountfield) and Reni (Alan Wren) all hailed from the Greater Manchester area and by 1987 – after an earlier one-off record deal with local label FM Revolver – they had signed a deal with the emerging Silvertone label.

In just over two years – between 1989 and 1991 – The Stone Roses (a name created from a combination of the band's earlier identity as English Rose and The Rolling Stones) notched up half a dozen hit singles and one critically acclaimed eponymous Top 20 debut album.

As a band with attitude, the Roses rapidly became firm favourites with the alternative media and late-night radio. Alongside fellow Madchester trendsetters Happy Mondays, they made an unlikely debut on the mainstream *Top Of The Pops* in November 1989.

Loud and brash, the Roses took umbrage when their original label, FM Revolver, used an unauthorised video to promote a re-release of the band's 1987 single, 'Sally Cinnamon'. The band members forced their way in to the label's offices and spray-painted the interior, causing an estimated £23,000 worth of damage.

Hauled before the court, and in the midst of fan pandemonium, Brown, Squire, Mani and Reni were fined a total of £3,000 in March 1990. But further, much more serious, court action was just around the corner, as a dispute with their new record label looked set to turn into a major legal battle.

The deal with Silvertone required The Stone Roses to sign both recording and publishing contracts as a package, which gave the rights to the band's songs to the company for the life of copyrights although, after five years, The Stone Roses could ask for the rights in any songs not exploited.

As they were linked, both the record and publishing agreements could be extended indefinitely, and there were concerns over the level of advances and the lack of artistic or creative control enjoyed by the songwriters. Under the terms of the record deal, Silvertone had no obligation to release or distribute any records by The Stone Roses in the territories covered by the agreement – "the world and its solar system".

As one of the hottest bands around, The Stone Roses were now being pursued by others in the business, and Silvertone, part of the expanding Zomba Music Group, was keen to protect its investment. The label was granted an injunction in late 1990 to stop the group signing to a rival label.

Just months earlier, The Stone Roses had hit the UK Top 10 for the first time with 'One Love', but the wrangle with their record label looked set to keep them out of the charts and the recording studios for well over a year.

A date for the court case was set for November 1991 and, if it ran its full course, the Manchester four-piece faced being sidelined until well into 1992. With their lawyer, John Kennedy, saying, "We have permission to go back to the court if the injunction is interfering with the band's career," The Stone Roses and their manager, Gareth Evans, went to court in early 1991.

The High Court decided to bring forward the trial date to March, a move that even Silvertone managing director, Andrew Lauder, was happy with. "I am pleased that the court date has been brought forward so that this situation can be resolved."

The "situation" that needed resolving was Silvertone's allegation that the band and their manager were guilty of breaching the original contract they signed in 1988. In an effort to get a court ruling that The Stones Roses and Evans were still bound by the deal, Zomba sued for breach of the Silvertone recording contract and the publishing contract with sister company Zomba Music Publishing.

In the spring of 1991, the case opened at the High Court before Mr. Justice Humphries, with the band claiming that the contract they had signed with Silvertone and Zomba Music was unfair, oppressive and a restraint of trade.

Opening for Silvertone, Peter Prescott QC asked the judge to declare the contract enforceable and ban the group from recording for any other record company. Claiming that Silvertone had taken a major financial risk in signing the band before they were established, and had invested over £1 million before they returned a profit, Prescott added, "Unless you are an eccentric philanthropist, no record company is going to support a group in this way unless it has an exclusive right to their recording services.

"We say they can't now say, 'Boo-hoo, we want to get out'," Prescott said, going on to claim that as The Stone Roses' reputation grew while with Silvertone, they were poached by a rival record company, which he did not name. "It is particularly galling for my clients that the group said the contract is invalid and they are free to go off with another company."

However, Prescott did admit that one clause in the contract with Silvertone was "silly" and an error, but he suggested that it did not mean that the rest of the legal document should be scrapped.

According to the contract, the band was tied to the company until a record was released in the US. "If that's right you have a very strange state of affairs," said Prescott. "Until there was a release in the US you could never know when that period had expired." He urged the judge to ignore the implications of the clause and focus on the meaning of the contract as a whole, which meant that it ran for a year from the completion of the minimum commitment.

Under cross-examination by Barbara Dohmann QC, Silvertone's head of legal affairs, Mark Furman, said he was unaware that three members of the band were out of work when he met them to discuss signing.

Dealing with the terms of the contract, Furman told the court, "If there had been proposed amendments, there would have been points I would have been prepared to amend."

The court heard that since the original 1988 agreement, the band, their manager and Zomba had been negotiating to revise the terms of the contract, but a clause in the first deal stipulated that amendments to the contract could only be made with the band's full agreement.

The rift between The Stone Roses and their record company was not helped by their refusal to perform on Terry Wogan's prime-time TV chat show, the court heard. The appearance was set as part of the promotion for the single 'She Bangs The Drum', but, according to Mr. Ian Mills, counsel for the band's manager, *Wogan* was "the housewives' choice and people who appeared on the show reflected that fact", which, he said, was not in keeping with the band's cult image.

Steve Jenkins, managing director of Zomba Music Publishing, disagreed and told the court, "Obviously he's got to have topical musical guests. These will be from all areas."

At the start of the third week, music from The Stone Roses was at the heart of the hearing, as a track from the band's first album was played to the judge. 'I Wanna Be Adored' was used as an illustration of the type of music performed by the Manchester quartet. Bass player Mountfield (Mani) was questioned by Prescott about it.

The counsel for Silvertone suggested that it wasn't music that would be an instant hit and that it was a "cult" song, but Mounfield was not so sure. "I never thought of our music as being cult but something that should go straight into the mainstream charts," he said, before telling the court that he could not see the band being connected with Silvertone or Zomba in the future. "I don't trust them any more," he stated.

Explaining that from the time he joined the band in 1987 he had received no money other than "handouts" from their manager, Mountfield added that by 1989, as they became more successful, he was getting £60 a week, and by 1990 he was earning around £100 a week. He added that a solicitor representing the band had described the recording and publishing deal as "standard".

132

In closing the first week of the hearing, Kennedy told the court that the American company Geffen Records had made "a very good offer", but the US label was prevented from signing the band by the court order banning the Roses from recording while the legal wrangle was being resolved.

Arguing that the band's worldwide fame would fade quickly if they were not allowed to make new records, Kennedy said, "The Stone Roses can do live work at the moment but, without records, their value would tail off, very, very quickly indeed." The members would have to get a normal job or go on the dole "like anybody else".

With the hearing finishing earlier than expected, Judge Humphries adjourned proceedings and finally came back to court in mid-May to deliver his decision. He was in no doubt that The Stone Roses' exclusive recording and publishing contract with Silvertone and Zomba Music was "so entirely one-sided and unfair that no competently advised artists would ever have agreed to sign it".

Freeing the band from their 1988 contract, the judge said that the band had been badly advised before they signed the contract. "The Stone Roses themselves were not highly educated and had no legal experience and little or no business experience. They had little or no income... indeed, some were on social security."

Commenting on the role of a record company in the life of an artist, the judge added, "Clearly record companies take a considerable risk in spending money in supporting comparatively unknown artists who may never succeed. It must be very galling if they can't share in vast sums of money if the artists achieve success. But in my judgement those considerations did not, in the present case, justify taking such complete and exclusive control."

Judge Humphries said that Zomba was trying to make major changes in the contracts and tried to pass these alterations off as "tidying up", while also sending Gareth Evans a cheque in an effort to get the new agreements signed. "The plaintiffs knew full well what Evans was like. They knew full well that they had signed the cheque as a bait, hoping to hook him."

The judge confirmed that neither the band nor their manager had signed the revised contracts and, without any new agreement, the existing terms of the original contract amounted to "a contract in restrictive trade that allowed the plaintiffs to prevent The Stone Roses from making records". This would virtually "sterilise the band for seven years".

Dismissing the injunction granted against The Stone Roses, the judge also awarded costs to the band. Immediately the case was over, the members set about confirming their new recording deal with Geffen.

With Brown, Squire, Mani and Reni all in Rotterdam following Manchester United's UEFA Cup Winners Cup victory over Barcelona, manager Evans commented, "It's been a great week for United and the band. I'm very pleased with the result."

In the aftermath of the case, the band's lawyer, John Kennedy, admitted that the group had actually signed to Geffen before the court's ruling, but accepted that had they lost, the new deal would have been off.

Victory was going to bring new fame and fortune for The Stone Roses, according to Kennedy. "We're talking about a $4 million advance. Geffen are very excited about the deal and The Stone Roses could really have signed to almost any record company in the world. They met a lot of companies and Geffen were the ones who impressed them most. It wasn't down to money."

However, before the band could issue a record on their new label, manager Evans filed a suit alleging that he was owed £120,000 plus compensation. The dispute was subsequently settled out of court.

While Kennedy described his clients' original contract as "the worst I have ever seen", an unnamed chairman of a major record company admitted to UK trade magazine *Music Week* that he had been tempted to bankroll The Stone Roses through their case. "But then I thought about it and I couldn't do it. Effectively I would be helping someone to break a contract very similar to the ones I have with my own artists. I would be cutting my own throat."

EMI's business affairs director, Gareth Hopkins, said, "It does not add much, if anything, to what is already established. The factual background was such that I don't think this verdict will have any bearing on how my company does business."

Up in Manchester, music broadcaster and journalist Terry Christian used his *Manchester Evening News* column to voice his thoughts and opinions on the case. "Finally it's all over and, as in most of these cases of record companies versus artists over contracts, the artists have thankfully won.

"The judge in The Stone Roses case thought it was unreasonable that the band had to sign a contract which meant they were obliged to record songs on behalf of the record company, but the record company, in return, were under no obligation to release those records.

"The truth is that The Stone Roses deal was unfair but it wasn't unusual. Record companies are just like banks, except that at the end of the day it's easier to borrow money off a record company to put a record out than it is to borrow it from a bank."

Finally, five years on from their debut, the long-awaited second Stone Roses album – the wittily titled *Second Coming* – appeared in 1994, hitting the UK Top 10 in December. It was to be a short-lived romance with the Geffen label.

By 1996 – with Reni and Squire long gone and with Mani recently departed, singer Ian Brown announced that The Stone Roses were no more. However, the British public still had fond memories of the band and, in a 1998 poll to find the country's favourite album, the Manchester band's debut offering came second to *Sgt. Pepper's Lonely Hearts Club Band*.

In 2004, the story of the rise and fall of The Stone Roses was one of three rock'n'roll tales featured in BBC 3's television series *Blood On The Turntables*. Under the title 'War Of The Roses', the programme was branded by the BBC as a "tale of greed, naivety and deep-seated personal hatred".

Things had come a long way from Judge Humphries' closing remarks in the 1991 court·case when he observed, "There are many groups who would like to achieve national and international popularity – many are called but few are chosen."

Chapter 14

JASON DONOVAN

Outraged by a "doctored" photo of a T-shirt

Jason Donovan first became famous in his native Australia when he was only 11 years old. However, when he was just 18, he became something of a major celebrity thanks to the Australian television soap opera *Neighbours*.

Playing opposite Kylie Minogue – and amid rumours of their own off-screen romance, which included a photograph of him on holiday with his topless co-star – Donovan quickly became an idol for thousands of teenage girls both in the Antipodes and Britain, where the show attracted huge teatime audiences.

After an initial approach by an Australian record label, the Melbourne-born teenager travelled to London to meet with pop impresario Pete Waterman, who had already begun manoeuvring Minogue towards pop stardom.

What followed for Donovan was success on an unimaginable scale. After three chart-topping UK singles, including a duet with Minogue, he dropped out of *Neighbours* and soon recorded a number one album, *Ten Good Reasons*, which became Britain's biggest-selling record in 1989.

On the back of his huge record sales, Donovan set out on a series of sold-out concerts, with hordes of screaming teenage girls creating what the press dubbed as "Beatle-like scenes" as they "bayed for his body."

Despite being voted both Best Male Singer and Worst Male Singer in the 1990 *Smash Hits* Poll, and just five years after his *Neighbours* debut, in June 1991, Donovan was invited to play the title role in the Andrew Lloyd Webber/Tim Rice musical *Joseph And The Amazing Technicolor Dreamcoat* at the world-famous London Palladium.

The young Aussie was an instant success. Both critics and audiences were impressed by his performance and, as he set out to perform eight shows a week, he became the toast of London's West End, with both Princess Diana and the Duchess of York joining the sell-out crowds.

As a regular on the London club scene, Donovan was photographed with a string of women, variously described by the tabloid press as models, heiresses, actresses and singers, and the pop and stage star enjoyed his life in the capital to the full. Somewhere in the midst of it all he was described by his former co-star, Minogue, as, "Becoming more crazy. Nice crazy but sometimes he is a bit of a nutter".

Two months after his West End debut, Donovan went really crazy when he saw his photograph in one of the leading music and fashion magazines of the day.

Launched in 1980 as an up-to-the-minute, cutting-edge handbook for fashion-conscious young people, *The Face*, edited by respected former *New Musical Express* journalist Nick Logan, boasted a circulation of over 100,000 at its peak. Its writers included Tony Parsons and Julie Burchill, who had both been hired by Logan while at the *NME*.

Combining coverage of music, fashion, culture and politics with a modern attitude, *The Face* was aimed at "culture-hungry non-conformists" according to *The Independent* newspaper, which listed it among its top 10 post-war magazines. But even the "Eighties fashion bible" made enemies, and the magazine was withdrawn from sale in Singapore when it featured a photograph of a topless woman.

In August 1991, the magazine ran an article by Ben Summerskill, associate editor of what was then Britain's only newspaper for homosexuals, *The Pink Paper*. Summerskill wrote: "In the case of Jason Donovan speculation has surfaced time and again about the preferences of the boy with bleached hair. No proof has ever been offered. No newspaper has ever been brave enough to back it up with a direct suggestion. Peter Waterman explained to tabloid hacks that Jason couldn't be gay 'because he drinks three pints of beer and goes surfing'. Some of the prettier boys on Bondi Beach might not follow the logic."

The article also carried quotes from another magazine in which Donovan was quoted as saying, "There's absolutely nothing wrong with homosexuality. I am not gay. Some of my best friends are gay but it is not the way I choose to live my life."

A huge "outing" campaign in the UK was launched in 1991 by the homosexual group Gay Pride, on the back of an American initiative. A list of 200 British "gay" celebrities was apparently drawn up before the organisers eventually announced that the whole campaign had been one big, elaborate hoax.

Accompanying Summerskill's article was a "doctored" photograph of Donovan wearing a T-shirt with the words "Queer As Fuck" superimposed, his name in bold letters above the picture and the word "OUT" included below the image.

Donovan instructed his lawyers to issue a writ against *The Face*. Named in it were Logan, Summerskill and the magazine's parent company, Wagadon. In an article printed a month before the libel trial opened, the music industry's major trade magazine, *Music Week*, carried a story that said that if Donovan won the case and was awarded the punitive damages he was believed to be seeking, "then *The Face* faces closure".

Before a jury of seven women and five men, and with Mr. Justice Michael Drake presiding, Donovan's counsel, Mr. Charles Gray QC opened proceedings in London's High Court on March 30, 1992. He took the opportunity to confirm to the court that Donovan's preference was and had always been for the opposite sex, describing what *The Face* printed as an "injurious and insidious slur on this young man".

Describing the photograph as "crude and deeply offensive", Gray told the court that the publication of the picture and the words on the T-shirt could "only intimate to readers that Jason Donovan is gay, is queer, is homosexual", and he added that it also suggested that his client's protests that he was heterosexual were "a dishonest and deceitful pretence".

THE WORD IS HOMO.

While the magazine argued that it was obviously a composite photo-graph with the words superimposed, Gray – echoing words that had been used in Liberace's infamous libel case in London some 33 years ear-lier – posed the question to his client, "Are you or have you ever been a homosexual?" The Australian singer-turned-actor answered, "No."

Giving evidence in the witness box on the first day of the case, Donovan said he had been disgusted by the article, and recalled that the photograph in question was taken in 1986 when he was in *Neighbours* and he was wearing a plain white T-shirt.

"Suddenly I pick up a magazine that I read and which influences my friends and people in the entertainment industry, and now I am stand-ing with the words "Queer As Fuck" on the front of the T-shirt."

Acknowledging that people did look up to him and that he saw him-self as a role model and as someone who had set up an image, Donovan said: "I don't try to tamper with that too much. I don't wear outrageous clothes. I am me, I am what you see."

Donovan referred to Summerskill's article as "nod and wink" report-ing, which was totally unethical. "It insinuates that I have got something to hide, that I am lying about my sexuality when I am not. It's some-one's point of view. I'm saying I'm not gay and yet these people are say-ing, 'We think he is'."

The entertainer finished by stating that he was not in any way anti-gay, that his private life was something he attempted to keep private and, "As to the boy with bleached hair, I don't have bleached hair."

Day two began with more references to Donovan's hair colour. He again denied using bleach but admitted dousing his locks in lemon juice – a practice that, he said, was quite common in Australia.

Defence counsel for *The Face*, Mr. Jonathan Crystal, brought up the subject of a feature in *Elle* magazine and read to the court a quote from the article in which Donovan said, "People would brand me a male tart if they really knew what I do."

Perhaps unfamiliar with the phrase "male tart", Judge Drake asked Donovan what he meant by using that description. "The purpose of saying these words was to work against the idea of what *The Face* had set up. I am a normal heterosexual. I do go in for relationships at the age of 23 like most people do."

Seeking further clarification, the judge then asked if Donovan was referring to relationships with men or women. Apparently with a blush, Donovan replied, "I was saying I had relationships with women."

While admitting that he had posed in a photograph for *Elle*, lying half-naked on a bed, Donovan said the magazine had suggested that it was in the public interest to know who Jason Donovan "is shagging". He disagreed, telling the jury, "It is not necessarily in the public interest to know who I am going to bed with – no, it is not."

While he attempted to keep his private life private, Donovan acknowledged that rumours about him being gay had been circulating in London for the previous 18 months, and it made it difficult for him to go out with male friends.

"I hear rumours all the time," he told the judge and jury. "If I go out with a friend of mine that's male, suddenly it becomes a boyfriend or a partner – no longer a friend, a mate from Australia."

The West End star claimed that *The Face* photograph and article suggested he was gay and that he was dishonest when he maintained he was heterosexual, and he dismissed the magazine's argument that it was criticising the way Donovan had been made a victim of posters put up by militant gays. "That picture and the text that follows says these are not rumours. If people were to read this they'd turn round and say, 'The guy's gay'."

Answering Crystal's point that nowhere in the article did it say that Jason Donovan was a homosexual, the teen idol reiterated, "It's the ambiguity of the article. It's the suggestion of the article that I am being hypocritical. There is no direct thing that says Jason Donovan is gay."

Crystal told the court on behalf of his clients that *The Face* was not suggesting Donovan was gay, and he wanted to make it absolutely clear they "unreservedly accepted that Jason was heterosexual."

A smiling Donovan told the defence counsel: "Thank you. I am as eager as you are to make that publicly clear."

Before the end of the day's proceedings, Donovan said that he would have been happy with a prominent apology in the magazine's next issue but one had not been printed. Explaining why he had not sued the *Daily Mirror* over an article that reported that he was the victim of a gay campaign, he said that the paper did not use the F-word and "obviously has a certain amount of respect for its readers".

Summerskill told the court that he had heard 4,000 people singing an alternative version of Donovan's hit song 'Any Dream Will Do' from the *Joseph* musical at a gay parade. It had been adapted to become 'Any Queen Will Do', but *Face* editor, Sheryl Garratt, said that she had deliberately removed all references to the song from Summerskill's original copy.

"It was irrelevant to the story and was spiteful," she said, while explaining that she ran the picture of Donovan only after spotting it on posters around London.

After explaining that she chose Summerskill to write the article because he had contacts with the homosexual community, Garratt told the court she thought "outing" was nasty, and that she wanted to reflect this in the article. "It wasn't an article about exposing gays because I didn't think Jason was gay," she stated.

Close to tears, Garratt admitted that she was upset at seeing Donovan giving evidence in court ("I didn't want to watch that man go through this. It was not pleasant"), and admitted having feelings of guilt that she was not named in the writ.

"This was my idea. I did the best I could and didn't set out to insult anybody. Because of what I have done, people might lose their jobs and my boss might lose his home."

With the evidence in and the arguments made, Mr. Justice Drake addressed the jury on the issue of damages if they found in Donovan's favour. Warning them not to "go over the top", he declared, "Don't think you have to fix sums with lots of noughts on the end because it's fashionable."

Reminding them Donovan's hurt had lasted less than a year and would be all over at the end of the case, he added that there were people "out there" with injuries that could never be put right. "What does a miner who has irreparable damage to his lungs and lives a miserable life say when he reads of huge awards of damages in libel action?"

Despite the judge's warning, after three hours' deliberation, the seven women and five men decided on a massive award to Donovan of £200,000, with costs against *The Face* estimated to be a further

£200,000. Donovan's huge payout put him at ninth place in the list of all-time awards in the British courts, a long way behind the £1.5 million paid to Lord Aldington but ahead of Teresa Gorman's £150,000 and Sara Keays' £105,000.

All these sizeable awards had been handed down between 1987 and 1992. In at least six of the top cases the unsuccessful defendants were newspapers and magazines, which prompted former Master of the Rolls Lord Denning, who observed "these awards are crippling magazines and newspapers", to seek a change in the law.

While Donovan celebrated his victory, a shouting match developed outside the court between teenage girl fans and outraged gays, who paraded placards saying "Queer Is Not Libel" and "Queers Surf Too".

A lot richer than when he went to court, Donovan delayed his departure long enough to read out a prepared statement. "This has not been a case about homosexuality and I resent the suggestion that it was. Everybody should be free to live their lives as they wish. I am heterosexual."

Although he confirmed to the waiting scrum of media and fans that "damages have never been uppermost in my mind", Donovan's opponents accepted the fact that they faced potential financial ruin. With a massive bill of £400,000, the monthly magazine and its sister publication *Arena* were in danger of folding, and the jobs of 14 employees were at risk. As they prepared the May issue of *The Face*, the hope was that it would not be the last edition.

Following the court's decision, the magazine's lawyer reacted angrily to the outcome. "Jason Donovan has known for a long time that the defendants are not rich. He knows that *The Face* has repeatedly offered to apologise unreservedly, but the offers have been turned down time and again."

The only light at the end of a very dark tunnel for Logan and Wagadon came from an unexpected source, when Donovan indicated that he was keen to save *The Face* from closure. Within hours of the court victory on April 3, 1992, Donovan's manager, Richard East, announced, "He still very much likes the magazine despite what they did to him and he is prepared to give up as much of his damages as necessary to save the magazine."

With the judge granting a 28-day stay on payment of the damages pending an appeal, lawyers representing both parties began negotiations over a rescue plan for the 12-year-old magazine. According to *Music Week*, Donovan cut the damages and costs by 70%, thereby lifting the immediate threat of closure, but it seemed that Wagadon still faced a bill of over £100,000 and possible closure.

The fight to save *The Face* attracted support from the music industry, with offers of benefit singles, club nights, live shows and even a Lemon Aid Fund (making light of Donovan's comments about using lemon juice on his locks) to help raise the cash to keep the magazine afloat.

The Face did carry on under Logan's guidance until 1999, when the magazine and Wagadon were sold to the mighty EMAP publishing group. However, five years later they decided that *The Face* had run its course and, as news of the magazine's closure emerged, there were reports that Donovan was again riding to its rescue.

Whether or not he actually made a bid to buy the title from EMAP is unclear. Either way, nothing seemingly came of his rumoured interest as *The Face* did finally cease publication in May 2004, just over 12 years after Donovan so nearly brought it to its knees.

Despite his best efforts to save the magazine that libelled him, Donovan reportedly endured something of a backlash from some fans, who thought his legal action was too severe. In the late Nineties he suffered from a well-publicised drug problem but, as the father of two young children, he eventually settled into both serious acting and more musicals, including *The Rocky Horror Show*, *Chitty, Chitty, Bang, Bang* and *Sweeney Todd*.

Writing in his 2007 autobiography, *Between The Lines*, Donovan looked back on his decision to sue and commented, "I have no regrets in my life … but if there is one moment I'm not particularly proud of it is taking *The Face* to court. I still stand by the view that I was right and they were wrong but with hindsight I would have done things differently."

While he revealed that he agreed to stagger payment of his £100,000 costs over 18 months, Donovan remained convinced that the publication did not face closure as a result of his actions, suggesting that it had the financial backing of a major publishing company, "… but no one else seemed to know that."

Chapter 15

GEORGE MICHAEL

Objected when his record company turned Japanese

While Sony Music only came into being in 1988, the origins of the world-famous Columbia label go back to 1887. Indeed, CBS was still part of the Columbia Broadcasting System when two young London hopefuls named George Michael and Andrew Ridgeley linked with a small independent label funded by CBS's UK division.

The duo, known as Wham!, signed to Innervision in March 1982, staying there until the conclusion of a series of legal moves that could – and should – have served as a warning of things to come. With four Top 10 singles and a number one album, *Fantastic*, under their belts, Michael and Ridgeley were a hot property, and Innervision were not about to let go of their biggest act without a fight. They opposed an action brought by Wham!'s lawyer, Tony Russell, in October 1983 in which he said the duo were seeking to break their contract and retain all their master recordings because they claimed the contract was unfair.

In November, the case of Wham! vs Innervision went to the High Court. Mark Dean's small dance label won the first round when Mr. Justice Harman granted Innervision a temporary injunction preventing the two singers from signing to any other label. The judge observed that just because Wham! saw "fresh fields and pastures new and longed to get in them", it did not, in his view, amount to a breakdown in confidence between the act and their label.

As a major legal battle loomed on the horizon, the two parties chose to settle out of court. In March 1984, Wham! were released from their Innervision deal and set free to sign with CBS's Epic label, originally founded in America in 1953 for classical and jazz recordings. In 1986, however, after selling over five million singles in the UK alone and top-ping the UK and US charts on three occasions, Michael and Ridgeley parted company.

Although Wham! were no more, CBS wisely saw where the talent lay, and within months exercised their option for five more George Michael solo albums. By re-signing to Epic, Michael would join a long list of successful solo artists ranging from Bobby Vinton, and Johnny Nash to Michael Jackson, whose *Thriller* album totalled 50 million sales around the world.

In 1988, Michael signed a new solo deal with Epic, which was then swallowed up by the mighty Japanese electronics corporation Sony as part of its $2 billion deal to acquire CBS Records. As the established CBS film and television corporation insisted on retaining the distinctive name, Sony Music decided to acquire the rights to the name Columbia for the world. For over 50 years this name had belonged to EMI in many international territories, including the UK, now Sony wanted it – to put up there alongside its successful Epic imprint.

Within 12 months of signing – and in an echo of the Innervision sce-nario – the first contractual issue between George Michael and his label reared its ugly head as the financial terms of the deal were amended in the artist's favour. Following three number one singles and four more Top 10 hits, plus the multi-million-selling album *Faith*, the terms of Michael's deal were once again revisited, just in time for his 1990 album, *Listen Without Prejudice Volume 1*.

Issues that had been simmering for close to five years boiled over and, in October 1992, Michael's solicitor, Tony Russell, informed the pow-erful Sony Entertainment parent company that Michael was no longer bound by his contract and that the master recordings belonged to him. Having gained no satisfaction, Russell then took things a step further.

Before the month had ended, he filed a writ against Sony, which, unsurprisingly, disputed all the claims.

At the heart of the writ were Michael's concerns over his deal with Sony. Under the terms of the deal, it was claimed:

• Sony owns George Michael's recordings, released and unreleased, although the singer has paid the cost of recording.
• Sony has no obligation to release any album anywhere in the world except, under certain circumstances, in the UK and some other territories.
• Sony has the right to reject Michael's material.
• Michael has no right of audit over Sony.
• Michael is prevented from appearing in any film produced by a third party.

In addition, the writ claimed that proceeds from sales of *Faith* and *Listen Without Prejudice Volume 1* were shared "inequitably", with Sony earning £1.83 per unit and the singer 57p. Apparently, at the time, Sony was paying only 75% of the royalty on CD sales of *Faith* and 80% on copies of *Listen Without Prejudice*. Also, as detailed in the writ, 9% of album sales earned no royalties at all for the singer because of the high level of "free" units given to retailers and wholesalers.

In an effort to explain his actions, Michael issued a statement in which he made clear his animosity towards the Japanese corporation:

"Though I have been advised that my contract with Sony is unfair financially, my personal reasons for taking this action are entirely different. Since the Sony corporation bought my contract along with everything and everyone else at CBS, I have seen the great American company that I proudly signed to as a teenager become a small part of the production line for a giant electronics company which, quite frankly, has no understanding of the creative process.

"Sony appears to see artists as little more than software. Musicians do not come in regimented shapes and sizes but are individuals who change and evolve together with their audiences. Sony obviously views this as a great inconvenience.

"I have reached the conclusion that divorce is the only solution. In my opinion, my relationship with CBS Records was a successful affair, whereas this arranged marriage to Sony simply does not work. We do not speak the same language."

Sony's more restrained and corporate response to Michael's statement read as follows: "We are saddened and surprised by the actions George has taken. There is a serious moral as well as legal commitment to any contract and we will not only honour it but vigorously defend it."

A court case now seemed to be the only way of settling the dispute, but this was not going to happen any time soon. Michael's lawyers argued that a long wait would mean that their client would face the "unpalatable choice" of releasing his next album either early in 1994, a bad time for sales, or waiting for the Christmas market.

Their request for a hearing in June 1993 was rejected by Mr. Justice Knox, although he did agree to grant a speedy hearing and set the case for the autumn of 1993. By the time the case came to court, *Listen Without Prejudice* was established as a global best-seller, followed by Michael's number one duet with Elton John on 'Don't Let The Sun Go Down On Me'. There was also a final release under his Epic contract, the top five hit, 'Too Funky', released in June 1992.

On October 18, 1993, the plaintiff, George Michael, and the defendants, Sony Music, came face to face in the London High Court under the watchful eye of 56-year-old judge Mr. Justice Jonathan Parker, who listed his hobbies as painting and gardening. Representing the singer was Mark Cran QC, while the Japanese company retained Gordon Pollock QC. The trial was predicted to run for at least two months.

While both Michael's fans and the media were fascinated by the impending trial, which would expose to public gaze the inner workings and financial details of a major artist's recording contract, music industry executives were just as interested – but for entirely different reasons.

Leading music industry lawyer John Kennedy, who represented The Stone Roses in their 1991 court case, said that the case could run for up to five years, and that it was unlikely Michael would record again until it was all over. "It's probably the case the industry has been waiting for to resolve the ambiguities that remain."

The manager of Dire Straits, Ed Bicknell, warned that if Michael won the case it would have an "unbelievable" impact on the UK music industry, rendering most recording contracts potentially "unenforceable".

In front of a packed public gallery, the court heard on the opening day that it was Michael's conscious decision to abandon his previous sex-symbol image to focus on more serious music that had created the conflict with Sony, and not the financial imbalance of their arrangement.

Opening the case for the singer, who appeared under his real name of Georgios Kyriacos Panayiotou, Cran told the judge that the Sony contract prevented the artist from recording with another company. "Without recording, his career and his livelihood are stultified." He explained that under the contract, Michael could write songs but not record them for another company, could tour but not produce recordings, and could appear on film or video but not sing.

Focusing on the financial side, Cran detailed the imbalance of the contract, which gave the singer just 37p per CD and 34p for each cassette sold in the UK, with the plaintiff paying for production and packaging costs. He calculated that, after payment of manufacturing and distribution costs, Sony pocketed £2.45 for a CD and £1.49 per cassette.

Michael's total worldwide royalties in the five years up to December 1992 had been, according to Cran, £16.89 million – with profits of £7.35 million – while his record company's share was £95.5 million with profits of £52.45 million. Acknowledging that his client had received a £1 million signing-on fee from Sony, Cran added that fellow Epic act Michael Jackson had been given a 50/50 profit share agreement by the company.

In an effort to back up his argument, Cran brought details of a case heard in Ireland in 1919 to the judge's attention. The Ballymacelligott dairy co-operative apparently fixed milk prices and paid its members the equivalent of advances in the form of seeds and manure. This was ruled to be illegal, and Cran argued that the same principles applied over 60 years later in the case of a recording contract.

However, counsel explained that money was not the issue at stake. "It's not about the wish of somebody to benefit from being free of a contract which he has freely entered into. It's about restraint of trade. It's about an agreement which binds George Michael for the whole of his professional career in terms which are capable of being worked to his substantial disadvantage."

While Cran claimed that Sony had "almost no obligation" to promote Michael's records, yet retained the copyright on any material he provided under the terms of the deal for the next 50 years, the Japanese company pointed out that Michael's contract was no better or worse than those of other high-profile Sony artists such as Bruce Springsteen or Billy Joel.

Cran also revealed a series of personality clashes between his client and the executives of Sony Music's American operation. He revealed that the singer's relationship with Don Ienner, the head of Columbia, the label on which Michael's recordings were released in the US, became so bad that the singer attempted to switch to the sister Epic label. After initial agreement, the move was blocked by Sony US chief, Tommy Mottola, who, it was claimed, did not feel "particularly sympathetic" to the British singer's position.

Counsel also claimed that when Michael sought to renegotiate his 1987 contract, the then head of CBS, Walter Yetnikoff, had only allowed him to do so if he chose lawyers Allen Grubman or John Branca, both friends of Yetnikoff, to represent him.

The final part of Cran's opening argument focused on advances in technology, which, he claimed, could cost his client millions of pounds. He pointed out that under his Sony contract, Michael would receive the same royalty for sales via new technology – such as music videos on compact disc – as he would for vinyl sales.

"He is getting the same rate for CDVs as he would be for vinyl. It may be that the vinyl rate is appropriately low," said Cran, who concluded by claiming that the contract between Michael and his record company was to the "detriment of the artist and the benefit of Sony".

Giving evidence from the witness box during the second week of the trial, Michael accepted that he was motivated by royalties because, he claimed, record companies would work harder to exploit an artist's work if their share of the profits was reduced. The singer also agreed with Sony's counsel, Pollock, that he had "effectively blackmailed" his first record company, Innervision, in 1983 by refusing to deliver the first Wham! album unless the duo's contract was renegotiated.

"This was the first example of you breaking your promise to get what you want?" asked Pollock, to which Michael replied, "Yes."

Confirming that his lawyer had proposed to CBS UK a royalty of 22% in the UK and US and 19% for the rest of the world during the 1987 renegotiations, Michael accepted Pollock's assertion that he was "asking for the world".

"Absolutely," agreed the singer. "I would presume we were doing what was commonplace. You ask for too much and you'll get something lower, but better than what you had."

Asked by Pollock to give the court an estimate of his worth, Michael said that press estimates were alarming. Before writing a figure on a piece of paper, however, he let slip, "I have more money than I know what to do with."

Returning to the subject of his relationship with Sony Music US executives Michael Schulhof, Mottola and Ienner, Michael accepted that there was a difference between how Sony Music UK and its American counterpart treated their artists.

"[In the US] I was given the impression that I was a difficult British artist who took himself too seriously and needed to be brought into line."

Suggesting that Ienner was responsible for killing off *Listen Without Prejudice* "to teach me a lesson", Michael added that the company's decision to release only four singles, as opposed to the six issued in the UK, was "their way of saying they didn't want to be bothered with this project any more".

Concerned that Sony did not "prioritise" the album, Michael was also anxious about the singles issued in the US stopping or slowing down after their initial high chart entry. "They were not making that last effort or putting money into what creates a top five single," he claimed.

Answering Pollock's suggestion that the singer was claiming that the company had deliberately decided to stultify sales in America in order to teach him a lesson "despite the loss of money it would involve to themselves", Michael replied that the failure of his album in America would "hardly make a dent in their profits".

The singer also told the court that he was offended that Ienner and Mottola left one of his concerts halfway through. In addition, Ienner had suggested a remix be done of the track 'Too Funky'. "It was the first time an executive tried to make a creative decision for me."

The rise of Schulhof to run the former CBS music operation after its takeover by Sony was also seen by Michael as a key contribution to the breakdown in his relationship with the corporation.

"There's a big difference between a company which is run by a record man and a company which is not. The reason we are here now is probably directly attributable to the fact that there was no one over-seeing the relationships between artists and Sony at the head of the music division."

Sony's decision to work with American disc jockeys to plug Michael's anti-war song, 'Mother's Pride', during the Gulf War was also addressed. The singer told the court that his song had been interspersed with messages between mothers and their sons in the Gulf.

"I found it extremely distasteful and totally at odds with the lyrics of the song. I think it was unreasonable, once they knew of my objections, to go on in this way. Most artists would take objection to this and their objections would be listened to."

Accused by Pollock that he was "too grand" to help Sony with the marketing strategy for *Listen Without Prejudice*, Michael denied the sug-gestion. "I'm not too grand to sit round a table with the marketing people, but I pay a manager to do that. You don't get respect that way."

As the trial moved into November, the 30-year-old writer and per-former was forced to deny claims that the Walt Disney company had approached him with a £2 million film deal in the months leading up to his contractual dispute with Sony, and that he had opened negotia-tions with another record label. Michael told Mr. Justice Parker and a crowded courtroom that he had received "no serious offers" from any-one, adding that he might have a new album finished by the summer of 1994. "I have no intention of negotiating with any record company until my next album is completed, which could be six to eight months," he confirmed.

Referring to his 1992 charity album, *Red Hot + Dance*, which, it was claimed by Cran, Ienner "hated", Michael admitted that he had decided to leave Sony soon after its release but had held off telling the company. "I wouldn't have wanted to have started those type of discussions until the charity album had run its course."

In his evidence, the singer's manager, Rob Kahane, stunned the courtroom with an allegation that Sony boss Mottola had links with the Mafia, and had tried to bribe him into persuading Michael to sign with CBS in America. Kahane claimed that the American record chief also offered him a consultancy and an annual retainer if he came under Sony's "wing". Kahane explained that he did not tell Tony Russell of his conversation with Mottola because of the latter's reputation.

Kahane accepted Sony counsel's claim that he did not always tell clients of his dealings on their behalf because "they are artists and not businessmen". Kahane also admitted that he rarely kept notes of his conversations because "he trusted record companies to do what they said they would do". He did, however, allege that Sony deliberately failed to fully support Michael's second solo album because they were angry at the singer's decision not to make a video or give interviews in support of *Listen Without Prejudice*.

Dick Leahy, a partner in the company Morrison Leahy Music and the man responsible for publishing Michael's songs since 1982, was alleged in court to have been approached by Russell in 1991 to become the artist's manager throughout Europe. This was in return for a 6% commission on sales of the next album release.

Under questioning from Sony counsel, Leahy, regarded as one of the plaintiff's closest advisors, admitted he had considered an offer but denied that any financial details were ever discussed. Pollock also accused Leahy of advising Michael not to tell Sony of his change in artistic direction until after the 1990 renegotiations were complete.

Tony Morris, the former managing director of both Polydor and Phonogram Records, was called to the stand as an expert witness on behalf of Sony. He denied that the record company had failed to give proper marketing and promotional support in America to *Listen Without Prejudice*. Explaining that the single 'Praying For Time' got to number one and 'Freedom' had reached the Top 10, Morris added, "Both were better placed than in the home market and, unlike *Faith*, did not receive the co-operation of the artist."

Morris claimed that Michael refused to allow his name to be used on promotional items, and failed to appear at a party held in his honour at the annual convention of the influential US radio tipsheet, *The Gavin Report*.

Accepting that sales of the singer's second album were only a quarter of those of *Faith*, Morris explained, "The US is vastly different to any other territory because of its complexities. In smaller territories you can reach the market much more easily than in the US."

Answering questions from Pollock, Morris detailed areas where the million-selling singer was allowed "considerable scope" by Sony. The stipulation that Sony could not release the artist's masters without his consent he described as "exceptionally unusual, maybe unique", while Michael's control over artwork, remixes and videos" Morris considered "not common by any means".

The veteran record company executive denied that major labels issued standard contracts to their artists. "I have never seen one contract which resembled another," Morris told the court.

Following the UK record company boss into the witness box were Sony US executives, who were questioned by Cran about the company's attitude towards the singer and *Listen Without Prejudice*. Claiming that Sony decided to "pull the plug" on the album in November 1990 because it had only sold 1.8 million units, Cran questioned Fred Ehrlich, Columbia US vice-president and general manager.

Ehrlich denied there had been a move to scale down the marketing and rejected Cran's description of the $188,000 promotional spend to launch the album as "derisory". He added, "Columbia has a marketing strategy for the life of an album, not just for the first week."

Columbia's East Coast promotions vice president, Burt Baumgartner, defended the two million sales of *Listen Without Prejudice* compared to *Faith*'s "extraordinary" eight million. "It was in the top one per cent selling albums that year, but did not do as well because Michael tried to appeal to a different audience. But it was not clear why he did it. There was no explanation as to why he was no longer releasing upbeat, fun records and everybody – particularly in US radio – was confused." Baumgartner also denied that the second single, 'Freedom', was deliberately released early because Columbia was unhappy with the first, 'Praying For Time', which had reached number one.

Answering Cran's suggestion that he provided "a very incomplete picture" to back up his claim that all the stops had been pulled out to push the singles on US radio, Baumgartner said that US radio programmers became "extremely disenchanted" with Michael after he cancelled interviews and promotional appearances in the US in both 1990 and 1991.

Six weeks after the start of the trial, Michael and Kahane were among those recalled to give evidence on documents supplied to the court after the proceedings had begun. The singer's manager confirmed that he had considered asking Sony for a $400,000 loan in late 1991 in order to save his company from financial difficulty. He had previously received a sizeable loan from the record company, guaranteed against his income from Michael's future royalties, but on this occasion the singer had made a direct loan to his manager of $360,000.

Kahane subsequently agreed that this money was included in sums totalling $458,000 that the plaintiff had later written off. While Kahane denied that there had been a plan to deliver one more album to Sony and then break the contract, he told the court that he planned at one stage to press for a $20-million advance for the remaining four albums on Michael's contract to ensure that the record company would work hard to recoup the money.

Michael claimed that he did not remember his manager's negotiations with Sony for a $4 million advance for his third solo album, adding that Kahane was "always pressing about money".

The singer did receive one advantage during the hearing, when Mr. Justice Parker agreed to allow Sony contracts with other top artists such as Michael Jackson, Barbra Streisand, Billy Joel and Bruce Springsteen to be considered by the court. However, ruling that full disclosure of the contracts could cause Sony "serious financial damage", and accepting that the artists may not consent to disclosure, the judge ruled that all evidence regarding the contracts had to be heard in camera.

In December 1993, the seventh week of the hearing brought former Sony Music UK chairman, Paul Russell, to the stand to give evidence on behalf of the defendants in his role as Sony's European president. He began by describing his shock when Michael returned a $1 million advance cheque in September 1992. "It was an industry first for an artist to return that amount of money to a record company. It posed a practical problem because our year end is March 31, and we paid the money out in one year, only to get it back in the next."

Russell said he had been assured by Michael's solicitor, Tony Russell (no relation), that there was no "hidden agenda" behind the return of the money. It was a precursor to the singer's restraint of trade case against the record company that began with the writ issued in November 1992.

Paul Russell explained Sony's apathetic attitude towards the *Red Hot + Dance* album by saying it had "lost its sizzle" after Prince and Michael Jackson dropped out, and that poor artwork and having only 13 tracks were other factors.

Cran questioned Paul Russell about the eight-album deal his client signed with Sony, and suggested that the vast majority of successful Sony acts since 1980 achieved success with their first albums. "Why is an eight album deal necessary? Since 1980, either a Sony artist has achieved success in the first three albums or they have been dropped."

Citing acts such as The The, Prefab Sprout and The Psychedelic Furs as acts that Sony continued to back even after weak sales on their first three albums, Russell responded by stating, "A six-album deal is appropriate for signing a new artist. Record companies take a considerable risk and put up a lot of money, so they must have a return on their investment."

Russell admitted that Sony only invested large amounts of money at the beginning of an artist's career because it knew it could recoup the money over eight albums, and that even a five-album deal would affect the amount invested in new acts. Talking about the 1987 renegotiations after the release of *Faith*, Russell said he favoured the discussions being held in London rather than America, and accepted that the appointment of Allen Grubman as Michael's US lawyer "sidelined" the artist's UK solicitor, Tony Russell.

Russell confirmed that prior to the 1987 renegotiations, he met with Walter Yetnikoff and agreed that Michael would be awarded superstar status if sales of *Faith* topped the 10 million mark.

Cran suggested that the album had passed that mark by December 1988 but the US royalties were not forthcoming, while Paul Russell said that extra advances were agreed. When Russell denied that Michael's royalty rates for *Faith* – 14.5% in the UK, 13% for major territories and 12% for the rest of the world – and for his next three albums 15%, 14% and 13% respectively – were lower than for similar artists,

Cran produced rates for a number of unnamed Sony acts to support his case.

At this point, Russell acknowledged that most were better off than Michael, but claimed that many had sold more units at that time. While the six Sony acts were supposed to be kept anonymous, and were identified by the letters A to F, singer Paul Young was inadvertently identified in court as act A. His royalty rates were disclosed as being 15% in the UK on his first album, released in 1983, rising to 16% by 1988.

Commenting on the idea of Michael moving from Columbia to Epic in America, Russell said he was never in favour of the move but had discussed it with Kahane. The Sony man said he was worried about the impact on Columbia morale. "If we let an artist switch labels every time they are unhappy or their management is unhappy, you would have artists switching over and it would be like Charing Cross station."

Russell, who spent more than 20 hours in the witness box, was followed by fellow Sony executive Richard Rowe, who led the business affairs team in 1987. He pointed out that Paul Young's higher royalty rate, agreed in 1988, included his music publishing.

"You can't isolate royalty rates but include them as part of the overall contract," Rowe stated, adding that when he referred to Michael being offered "very high" royalty rates, he was talking about the singer's deal as a whole, including multi-million pound advances for his "tax out" year in 1988.

"We try hard to balance royalties and advances," he continued. "It may not be in the artist's interest to give him all the money at once. This can be a terrible warning for people spending too much money too quickly."

At the same time, Tommy Mottola flew into the UK to give four hours of evidence, which included brief sessions held in camera. He told the judge that he and his family were "outraged, shocked and offended" by Kahane's claims that he had Mafia links. He denied that he had any connection with "unsavoury criminal elements", or had put Kahane in fear of his life or offered him a bribe and a consultancy. Mottola admitted that his relationship with Kahane was "always tough and strained", and that he felt the manager did not always act in Michael's best interests.

Another Sony executive who gave damaging evidence against Kahane was director of corporate business affairs, Sylvia Coleman, who told the court how Michael's manager behaved when he was seeking a loan from the company. "He telephoned me once and, without saying hello or any formal introduction, he asked, 'Where's my fucking money?' which I thought was bad form."

Before the court rose for Christmas 1993, Sony Music International executive, Tom Tyrell, said that the proposals put forward in 1987 by Tony Russell on Michael's behalf were "crazy – he was asking for $20 million and royalty rates far higher than we pay anyone else". Tyrell, who at that time was CBS Records' senior vice-president administration, agreed with Michael's counsel that the phrase "brain damaged" in his notes from the meetings was a reference to Tony Russell, although it was later crossed out. He added that Russell had "exploded" during a meeting in which CBS refused to set Michael's CD royalty rates at 100%.

The Yuletide break over, court proceedings recommenced in late January 1994. They began with Pollock succeeding in getting parts of the witness statement from Michael's accountancy expert, David Ravden, (from the company Martin, Greene, Ravden) struck out. Mr. Justice Parker agreed to rule out a number of passages on the basis that they were hearsay, including Ravden's references to the "lavish offices and lifestyles" of the major record companies.

In court, Ravden rejected Pollock's suggestion that Sony's 1988 $14 million advance represented "a high risk" for the record company. "*Faith* had already sold very well and the company was set to make profits covering any risk on the advance."

After the court had heard that Sony Music had earlier faced the possibility of a restraint of trade action from singer Terence Trent D'Arby, who was also represented by Tony Russell, the company's UK legal affairs head, Jonathan Sternberg, accused Russell of using "bullying and blackmail" tactics in his 1990 renegotiations of Michael's contract.

Sternberg claimed that Russell had warned that failure to agree new terms would delay delivery of *Listen Without Prejudice*, and that Sony agreed that "we should not allow ourselves to be blackmailed or bullied". When he was recalled to the stand, Tony Russell denied the accusations and also rejected Cran's claim that he had raised the subject of Holly Johnson's restraint of trade action against ZTT Records.

The opposing counsel set about presenting their closing arguments when the court resumed in February after 51 days of legal wrangling.

Pollock began his final address by asking, "Is this really a case where public interest requires that the contract should be set aside? This is a case of a young man who, in order to achieve fame, success and fortune, signs a contract with CBS and, 10 years later, after two renegotiations, he has achieved everything he set out for – fame and riches beyond the dreams of everyone apart from pop stars."

Counsel estimated that a successful artist's earnings from the contract would range from $40 million, if they became a superstar, to between $10 million and $20 million if they were only moderately successful. "If [Michael] was unsuccessful, he would not suffer because the record company would cover his expenses. Then he would most likely be free of his contract because [Sony] would not exercise its options on future albums.

"The irony of the situation is that Michael is being paid a lot of money and would only find himself 'restrained' by the duration of the contract. We argue that in return for Michael being with Sony for a long time he is paid a lot of money."

Pollock told the judge that he would have to decide whether the contract "merely regulates a normal commercial relationship" or was a restraint of trade, and concluded that while Michael was prompted by financial motives, he was supplied with "not always accurate" information by his advisors, which made him unhappy with his Sony contract.

Michael's action alleged that his Sony deal contravened Article 85 of the Treaty of Rome, the European Union law covering prevention, restriction or distortion of competition. Pollock argued, "If competition is altered it does not necessarily give rise to an effect on community trade. You can alter competition, but still have trade flowing." He also said that Michael's call for single album deals would be "a disincentive to the exploitation of back catalogue", before adding, "If one purchases rights, one is entitled to decide what to do with them."

In response, Cran described his client's deal as an "exclusive supply agreement" weighted in favour of the record company on the following counts: Michael cannot re-record his songs until five years after the end of the contract; Michael cannot terminate the contract yet Sony can, by exercising its options after the release of three albums; Sony is not bound to release Michael's works in major territories outside the UK and US; and Sony is not obliged to release material produced outside the delivery agreement of eight albums.

Responding to Pollock's suggestion that Sony had "bought" rights to the artist's material by payments such as the $14 million advances in 1988, barrister Jeremy Lever QC, a European law expert called by Michael, said, "You can't justify a restriction on the basis that you pay a lot of money for it."

Lever suggested that assigning copyright in Michael's recordings to Sony for 50 years was an interference with market forces. "One has to satisfy the [European] Commission that tying George Michael up for 50 years is reasonable," he said, and claimed that the length of the contract – 15 years – further restricted the singer's freedom.

Describing Michael's recordings as raw material to be used by Sony as a manufacturer, Lever added, "George Michael was restricted from selling his raw material to another manufacturer. The contract takes him out of the market, thus restricting competition between record companies."

As the case finally swung towards a conclusion – some time after the judge's March 30 estimate – there was a significant move away from Michael when Mr. Justice Parker queried the singer's decision to challenge his 1988 Sony contract rather than the 1984 agreement he had signed as a member of Wham!

Cran claimed throughout the hearing that the 1984 deal was unenforceable, but it was an assertion that was not included in the lawsuit. As a result the judge was forced to ask, "How can the effect of the 1988 agreement have been to take [Michael] off the market if – and it's a big if – he was already taken off by the 1984 agreement?"

Pollock claimed the issue had to be cleared up or the case could collapse, so the judge adjourned the hearing to give Michael's counsel the chance to amend his case. However, Cran rejected the offer, stating that the 1988 contract was the only standing agreement, while Sony argued that the 1984 deal was relevant on the grounds that it had settled the litigation between Wham! and Innervision. Sony also claimed that if it was not contested then it must have been valid, even though Michael's lawyers based their restraint of trade claim on the 1988 deal.

Bringing the legal arguments to a conclusion in mid-April, Pollock argued that Michael's contract was not the result of one-sided negotiations. "At all times during negotiations, he knew what he was doing, received full advice and actually had a choice – he could walk away from the deal if he didn't like it."

Answering the question of Sony's alleged under-promotion of *Listen Without Prejudice*, Pollock claimed that no record company ever deliberately under-promoted an album because it was not in their interest to do so.

"No one could provide evidence of a release lacking any form of exploitation or promotion for contractual reasons. It is inconceivable that the record company would seek to operate against the business relationship."

Finally, on June 21, eight months after proceedings had begun, Mr. Justice Parker delivered his judgement in a lengthy 273-page ruling that found in favour of Sony and brought a crushing defeat for Michael.

Describing the terms of the Sony deal as "reasonable and fair", the judge threw out the claims that the contract was in restraint of trade and that European competition laws applied to UK recording contracts. Commenting on the fact that *Listen Without Prejudice* sold only half as well as the earlier *Faith*, Justice Parker said, "Mr. Michael expected that the consequences of his change of direction would be a loss of sales. He cannot blame Sony for the fact that he was right."

The judge added that there was "no oppression or misuse of bargaining power on the part of Sony Music, not was there any compulsion on Mr. Michael" to sign contracts firstly with CBS in 1984 and then with Sony in 1988. Explaining that Michael, whom he considered to be fair and honest, had twice renegotiated the contracts, so reaffirming the agreements, the judge added that the singer knew the kind of contract a major record company would offer, "which, if he proved to be a success, would be likely to last for the greater part, if not the whole, of his working life and in the process make him very rich". He concluded that he was satisfied that "there is no substance to George Michael's claim of unfair conduct by Sony".

While pointing out that Michael was also intelligent, articulate and had access to the best legal advice before signing, the judge was scathing about Kahane, whom he described as "a thoroughly untrustworthy witness". Mr. Justice Parker made it clear that he believed that Kahane had misled his client about Sony's actions, lied to both the singer and his UK lawyer, Tony Russell, and demanded advances so he could earn commission. Kahane was constantly complaining and adopting a "thoroughly hostile attitude towards Sony". At the same time he was "sowing in Mr. Michael's mind the notion that Sony was acting in bad faith and spitefully towards him by feeding him with exaggerated and misleading reports concerning Sony's competence".

Before the end of his ruling, the judge added, "I cannot help feeling that, had Sony US seen rather more of Mr. Michael and rather less of Mr. Kahane from 1990 onwards, events might have turned out differently."

At the end of the 75-day hearing, Mr. Justice Parker rejected every argument put forward by Michael's lawyers and made it clear that he was more inclined to believe the evidence given by Sony executives such as Mottola, Coleman and Paul Russell rather than Michael's team of advisers. He also ordered that the singer pay the costs of the case, which estimates put at close to $7 million.

While the UK record industry breathed a huge sigh of relief at the outcome of the lengthy case, the defeated singer was rather less pleased. Vowing to continue the fight with an appeal and threatening never to make another album for Sony, Michael commented, "I am confident that the English legal system will not support Mr. Justice Parker's decision or uphold what is effectively professional slavery. There is no such thing as resignation for an artist in the music industry. Effectively you sign a piece of paper at the beginning of your career and you are expected to live with that decision, for good or bad, for the rest of your professional life."

Less sympathetic to the singer's cause was successful record producer Pete Waterman, who commented, "Anyone who is worth £70 million and claims he is being hard done by should look at the rail strike," while Sony diplomatically stated, "We have great respect for George Michael and his artistry and look forward to continuing our relationship with him."

At the same time, Dick Leahy denied reports that, in the aftermath of the court ruling, he had been appointed as the singer's European manager. At the same time, he gave the much-criticised Kahane a vote of support. "Rob Kahane is still his manager and will continue to be. George has been involved with Rob in some capacity for nine of his 12 years in the business."

In its influential leader column, *The Times* announced: "Mr. Justice Parker has rightly ruled against George Michael," stating the "carefully crafted" judgement should "dispel the sentimental notion, which will arise inevitably in certain quarters, that Sony has succeeded in biting the hand that feeds it… Had the decision in the High Court gone in Mr. Michael's favour, it would have sent shock waves through the music industry, which is one of Britain's most successful exporters."

Speaking a month after the case closed, Michael told television interviewer Sir David Frost, "I didn't want to pick a fight. I just wanted to work with people who wanted to work with me and who would have some respect for the fact that I was growing up."

At the same time, a senior legal aide to the singer rejected reports that Michael was likely to reach an out-of-court settlement with Sony, explaining, "We're building our grounds for appeal. As George says, we believe we have a strong case for overturning the judgement."

In May 1995, Leahy went public to further play down reports that the singer and Sony were on the verge of reaching a settlement. Denying that Michael was about to sign new territorial deals, Leahy confirmed, "Nothing at all has happened to change George's case and we still intend to take it to the Court of Appeal."

However, within two months there was public confirmation of the deal, which the music business had been talking about for months. In July, Michael and Sony announced that they had settled their differences and reached an agreement. Under the terms of the settlement – described by the media as an "honours even deal" – Michael agreed to record two new tracks for Sony that would feature on a greatest hits package set for release by the company in 1997. The artist was given the right to control the timing of the compilation, which he would also personally assemble.

In return for agreeing to release the singer from his Sony contract, the company also reportedly received a $40 million one-off payment, in addition to 3% of retail sales on the artist's next two solo albums. It was also agreed that both parties would share the $7 million legal costs emanating from the court case.

At the same time, Michael signed new deals with Virgin Records for international territories and DreamWorks for the US, and received a $10 million advance for two albums. Announcing Virgin's part in the deal, which reportedly gave Michael ownership of his recordings alongside a near 20% royalty rate, Virgin Music chairman, Ken Berry, confirmed that the deal was concluded in "an extraordinary set of circumstances, unique in the history of the industry".

The next thing on the horizon for Michael was to find a new manager to replace Kahane, who resigned in late 1994. In July 1995, the singer appointed former Sony executive Andy Stephens for the world outside North America. Stephens had worked closely with Michael both as a member of Wham! and as a solo artist, and was described by the singer as "a friend and professional ally of mine in his position at CBS/Sony since day one of my career in music".

Under new management, free from his Sony contract and linked to two new record companies, Michael re-emerged as a major-selling top five artist around the world thanks to singles such as 'Jesus To A Child', 'Fastlove' and 'Spinning The Wheel' from his third solo album, *Older*, which was released in 1996, selling over 12 million copies. The greatest hits collection that formed part of the settlement was issued in November 1998. *Ladies And Gentlemen – The Best Of George Michael* became an international best-seller, and was issued in both the UK and the US on Sony's Epic label.

At the end of 1999, Michael's fourth solo album, *Songs From The Last Century*, hit the charts, but his relationship with Virgin and DreamWorks was soon to come to end as he signed an unprecedented deal for just two singles with Universal in 2001.

Ironically, in 2003, Michael returned to the company that had been involved in his long-running and bitter legal dispute ten years earlier. The following year, his first new Sony releases were issued, bearing his own personal Aegean imprint. His fifth solo album, *Patience*, gave the corporation its fourth number one album from George Michael – the artist who once vowed never to record for them ever again.

Soon after the return of its prodigal son, Sony entered into negotiations with the German media company Bertelsmann, and the result was the creation of Sony BMG Music Entertainment, in August 2004. Owned equally by the Sony Corporation of America and Bertelsmann AG, the new music operation oversaw the release in 2006 of Michael's hits collection, *Twenty Five*, which actually appeared on the neutral RCA label while the two corporations awaited a final ruling from the European Union on the proposed new company.

The clearance given by the European Commission was annulled by the Union in July 2006, and a re-examination of the merger between BMG and Sony was ordered. However, the merger was given final approval by the EC in October 2007 – and George Michael featured on the roster as one of the new company's major assets.

Chapter 16

THE SMITHS

Seeking satisfaction over a fair share of the profits

The Smiths – once tagged as having the most forgettable name of any new band – quickly became the darlings of the early Eighties independent scene. By signing to influential indie label Rough Trade and turning down more lucrative offers from the majors, the Mancunian band signalled their decidedly un-hip attitude towards the music business. Their hardcore fans wallowed in the despair, pain and boredom represented and celebrated in The Smiths' music.

Voted the *NME*'s Best New Group in 1984, The Smiths (singer Morrissey, guitarist Johnny Marr, bassist Andy Rourke and drummer Mike Joyce) grew to a level where they were considered by some to be the most perfect four-piece group since The Beatles. Despite these accolades, the band's chart record was bizarrely uneven: out of 16 UK hit singles only two reached the Top 10; while, of their seven chart albums, four stalled at number two while just one reached the top spot.

America predictably failed to take to the quintessential Englishness of The Smiths and in particular the group's pale, thin, hearing-aid wearing, gladioli-carrying frontman. But Morrissey's talent as a lyricist was

matched by Marr's ability as a tunesmith, and they established themselves as a songwriting team that some critics compared with Lennon &
McCartney or Jagger & Richards.

"Groundbreaking" and "inspired" were just two of the words regularly used to describe the band, whose 1986 album, *The Queen Is Dead*,
was voted Best Album of All Time in a 1988 *NME* Reader's Poll.

A year earlier, the band had announced their signing to EMI at the
completion of their Rough Trade deal. The indie responded to the
news by saying that the band had to deliver two more albums before
they would be free and the major "could have quite a long wait before
they can release any records". In fact, EMI never released a Smiths
record, although they did eventually claim Morrissey as their own as he
sought greater international success.

The first telltale signs of unrest in the band came in the form of newspaper reports of a serious clash of personalities between Morrissey and
Marr. The singer was apparently upset at the guitarist's involvement
with other acts such as Billy Bragg, Bryan Ferry and Talking Heads. For
his part, Marr was telling friends that he'd had enough of Morrissey acting "the self-centred star".

In December 1988, Morrissey, Rourke and Joyce, without Marr but
with ex-member Craig Gannon, played an official farewell Smiths gig at
Wolverhampton Civic Hall. After six years, it was now all over, except
for the small matter of a lawsuit brought against Morrissey and Marr by
Joyce, claiming a share of past profits and a stake in all future royalties
from the band's sales. Joyce and Rourke – the non-writing members of
The Smiths – were paid 10% of the band's royalties from everything
except songwriting, which, as composers, Morrissey and Marr shared. It
was an unwritten arrangement that had been in operation since the very
earliest days of the band, but, according to Joyce, he had been unaware
of his share until the band's break-up in 1987.

Believing he was earning a 25% share of royalties, Joyce had
accepted the situation, despite once questioning the group's financial
arrangements and apparently offending Morrissey in the process. When
Joyce and Rourke discovered that Morrissey and Marr were sharing
80% of the band's royalties, they initially planned a joint action against
their two former bandmates. In 1989, however, Rourke settled out of

court and accepted an offer of a 10% share of future royalties plus £80,000.

While this left Joyce to fight on his own, he understood why the bass player had backed down. "Andy said he had to accept. It seemed that the last couple of years had been futile. But then again, Andy didn't realise how difficult it was going to be. I don't think people do when they enter litigation."

Difficult or not, Joyce stuck to his guns, turned down the offer made to him by Morrissey and Marr and continued with his legal action, which finally came to the High Court in December 1996 – nearly 10 years on from the break-up of The Smiths.

Despite the fact that they had barely spoken since the band split, Morrissey and Marr found themselves on the same side when the hearing opened on December 2 before Mr. Justice John Weeks. While they were both listed as defendants, the two musicians opted for separate legal representation, with Ian Mill QC acting for Morrissey and Marr retaining Robert Englehart QC.

Counsel for Joyce, Nigel Davis QC, confirmed to the court: "It may be that some will say this claim is a cynical piece of opportunism prompted by the dissolution of the group. We submit that's not fair. Mr. Joyce's case is that it was only when the group dissolved [that] he went to see his accountant and was told that he's been getting only 10%."

Describing The Smiths' success as "very considerable", Davis added that the band "released a number of highly successful albums and highly successful singles". As Morrissey wrote the lyrics while Marr wrote the music, they were "clearly entitled" to the royalties from the group's songs.

However, Davis explained that royalties from recordings and profits from concerts were paid to a company called Smithdom Limited, and that Joyce claimed that as a partner he was entitled to a quarter-share. "Now that it is admitted there was a partnership agreement between the four members of the band, the presumption is one of equality." Davis also informed the court how the two defendants "place emphasis on how much more important they were for the group".

Suggesting that Morrissey – who appeared under his real name, Stephen Morrissey – treated the rhythm section as "mere session musicians as readily replaceable as the parts of a lawnmower", Davis summed up the position, as he saw it, according to the group's singer and lead guitarist: "They had the highest profile so far as the public were concerned, but it would seem they'd go further and claim they are much more talented. They seek to play down the importance of Joyce and Rourke."

Suggesting that it was "wrong to rubbish" the contribution of Joyce and Rourke, Davis acknowledged that after the plaintiff raised the matter of the pair's role in the band and their earnings, they subsequently received £270,000. Summing up his client's view of how things worked in The Smiths, Davis said, "It was Mr. Joyce's perception throughout that all the real decisions were made by Morrissey and Marr. In particular, the financial decisions were made by Morrissey. Mr. Joyce was happy to do so because he trusted them. Morrissey now seeks to disparage Mr. Joyce and Mr. Rourke."

On day two of the hearing, Morrissey took the stand to give evidence and to dispute Joyce's claim that he and Marr had denied the drummer royalty payments. The Stretford-born singer was questioned by Davis about the alleged "hierarchy" within the group. Referring to a copy of *The Severed Alliance: The Definitive Biography Of The Smiths* by Johnny Rogan, Morrissey stated: "There are only two names on the cover – Morrissey and Johnny Marr. Did you notice that? Two names only, not Michael Joyce or Andy Rourke."

Davis responded by telling the singer, "I'll ask the questions", and then asked about an alleged secret plan to replace Joyce as The Smiths' drummer. "Johnny wouldn't have wanted Mike to go, nor would I, but we could live with it," Morrissey replied.

The verbal sparring between Morrissey and Davis continued, with the counsel for Joyce at one point being forced to ask, "Could I please finish my question?" to which the singer replied, "It's much too time-consuming." Davis retaliated by suggesting, "It's more time-consuming if you don't allow me to finish the sentence," to which Morrissey shot back, "I don't agree."

The singer also denied claims that he ran the band's finances, saying that he had no grasp of money matters and adding, "I didn't ever agree to deal with [Joyce's] affairs. Why should I?" Asked why Joyce hadn't accepted the settlement figure agreed with Rourke in 1989, Morrissey said, "He didn't want it. He wanted more. The fact he was trying to sue me was extremely unfair."

Davis told the court that Morrissey and Marr had "reluctantly" consulted a firm of accountants, which sent them a letter confirming that they both felt the pair were each entitled to a 40% share of the group's profits. Quoting from the letter, Davis read out a section that said, "Unfortunately this has never been formally agreed. We should take steps to draw up some form of agreement with Mike Joyce and Andy Rourke."

Nine years after Morrissey had publicly vowed that he had no intention of ever having any more contact with his former songwriting partner, Johnny Marr was called to give evidence in support of his former collaborator. The guitarist told the court that, "The Smiths was me and Morrissey", and that was the reason only the two of them signed the contract, while a verbal agreement was made with Joyce and Rourke.

In an attempt to justify the difference in payments, Marr said the band's rhythm section had "less pressured lives". While the two defendants had to "deal with shit from managers or record companies, Mike and Andy could skedaddle when their work was done."

In his closing speech to the court, Marr's counsel acknowledged that his client and co-defendant never thought they would share the sizeable earnings from The Smiths with the other two members of the band.

"Some 13 years on, it is extremely difficult to pinpoint when the 40/40:10/10 profit split came into being," said Englehart. "But Morrissey and Marr acted throughout on the basis that they would be getting 40% each of the net profits from The Smiths' earnings."

Claiming that Marr came over in evidence "as a very decent, honest person, scrupulously fair – who was not going to cheat his friends", Englehart added, "But the court has heard that both Michael Joyce and Andy Rourke accepted from an early stage that both Morrissey and Marr would get more than them."

As the case came to a close, Mr. Justice Weeks raised the issue of The Smiths' debut appearance on *Top Of The Pops*, saying that he was astonished that the singer could not remember the night. "The Smiths' first time on *Top Of The Pops* and your client cannot remember that evening?"

It was claimed that the date in January 1984 – when the band performed their first Top 20 hit, 'What Difference Does It Make?' – was also significant because it was the day on which Marr phoned Morrissey to tell him that Joyce would not accept a suggested 10% share of the band's earnings.

Admitting that the attitude of Morrissey had on occasion "betrayed a degree of arrogance", Mill told the judge that the reason his client could not recall the *Top Of The Pops* appearance was because, "To Morrissey the success of The Smiths was inevitable. He had an inherent belief that his partnership with Johnny Marr would succeed and that an appearance on *Top Of The Pops* was an inevitable and automatic step along the way."

On December 11, after a week-long legal battle, Mr. Justice Weeks gave judgement against Morrisey and Marr and in favour of Joyce. The judge ruled that the band's royalties had been unfairly split, and that Joyce was entitled to an equal slice of the income. A private hearing was set to decide the exact amount owing, but reports suggested that a 25% share, backdated to 1983, could earn the successful plaintiff around £1 million.

Morrissey (who was in court to hear the decision) and Marr were also ordered to pay the costs of the hearing, which were estimated at around £250,000. Giving his decision, Judge Weeks said that when Joyce had applied for a mortgage, his accountant wrote to the building society stating that his share of the annual income from the band was in excess of £20,000, which, accounts showed, was a 25% share of the profits from 1984 and 1985. When he was sent a copy of the group's accounts in 1986, Joyce put it in a drawer without studying it, said the judge, who was satisfied that even if the plaintiff had looked at the figures, he would not have realised the implications and that he was receiving only 10%.

Acknowledging that none of The Smiths had any business experience, the judge said that Morrissey took all the decisions. Although he controlled the band's finances, however, he "lacked the will" to tell Rourke and Joyce of his decision over profit sharing.

"He left it to Mr. Marr to give the unpalatable news to the other two," said Mr. Justice Weeks, who said there was no evidence of a

40/40:10/10 agreement and there was never an assumption by Joyce and Rourke that that was what they would receive. Shortly after the pair joined the band, in 1982, Morrissey and Marr had signed a "curious document" that claimed they had contractual rights over the other members of the band, who had never been shown this paperwork.

Joyce and Rourke impressed the judge as "straightforward and honest", although they were "not intellectuals and certainly not financially sophisticated or aware." While Marr was the most intelligent of the four with "a more engaging personality" and "a more reasonable character", he "seemed to me to be willing to embroider his evidence to a point where he became less credible".

However, the judge's criticism of the guitarist was nothing compared to his opinion of the founder and leader of The Smiths. "Morrissey was more complicated and didn't find giving evidence easy or a happy experience. He was devious, truculent and unreliable when his own interests were at stake."

Unsurprisingly, Morrissey was less than impressed at the outcome and in a statement issued through his solicitors, he said, "I am disappointed and surprised at the judge's decision, particularly given the weight of evidence against Mike Joyce's claim. I will be considering the terms of the judgement with my solicitors to assess possible grounds for an appeal."

Marr left the court without uttering a word or issuing any sort of statement. Joyce, on the other hand, was delighted at the result. "I still have the highest regard for Morrissey," he said before adding, "But I always knew 10 years ago when I started this action that I would win. This was never about money. It will not change my lifestyle but it will secure the future for my wife and children."

For Rourke, the only satisfaction was that after fighting a battle with heroin addiction and being "desperately short of money", he had in his 1989 settlement attained some sort of financial security for himself.

With the case over, Marr apparently did the decent thing and paid his part of the settlement soon after the final figure had been agreed. Morrissey, however, was seemingly less inclined to hand over the money or let things lie. He suggested that the court had sided with Joyce only because the judge had been "primed" as to Morrissey's character through his public attacks on the Queen and Margaret Thatcher.

"It's likely that Thatcher had appointed the judge, so I was not a very sympathetic character, whereas Joyce was playing the part of the wounded soldier," he claimed.

Morrissey also launched a blistering personal attack on the drummer, alleging that Joyce had begun turning up at the singer's solo concerts to ask for his money. Morrissey's appeal was decided in November 1998, when three Appeal Court judges decided against the singer's claim that Judge Weeks' "unjust and gratuitous attack" on his character had led him to rule in favour of Joyce.

Lord Justice Thorpe ruled, "It is unfair to suggest that the adverse view that he [Judge Weeks] formed of Mr. Morrissey in the witness box dictated his findings on the individual matters."

Despite the legal setbacks, Morrissey's solo career went from strength to strength, demonstrated by the singer receiving the 2004 Nordoff-Robbins Silver Clef award for "his amazing contribution to music".

Marr teamed up with The The, formed Electronic with ex-New Order member Bernard Sumner and, in 2007, began work with Seattle band Modest Mouse, in addition to achieving a Q Lifetime Achievement award.

For Joyce and Rourke, life after The Smiths made fewer headlines, with both appearing briefly in The Adult Net. Rourke later linked up with Delicious, Killing Joke and Foreign Bodies. In January 2006, he teamed up with Marr for the first time in 19 years for a cancer-charity show at Manchester's MEN Arena. Having briefly played in a reformed Buzzcocks, by the time the court case came around, Joyce was in Wah Now before moving on to play with Vinny Peculiar (Andy Rourke also played with Vinny Peculiar).

Morrissey, who relocated to Los Angeles soon after the 1996 hearing, was subsequently refused leave to appeal to the House of Lords in early 1999. In 2004 there were reports that Joyce was still waiting to receive his half of the settlement from the singer, who continued to contest the decision.

Speaking to *The Guardian* in 2004, he continued his rant against Judge Weeks. "How a judge can offer a judgement with 50 mistakes is absolutely unbelievable. Of course, judges speak with such extreme authority and their own error is completely unthinkable. You can see that if they still had the power to hang you, they'd do it with a smile on their face. They're enraged they can't actually hang you."

Any chance of Morrissey remembering The Smiths with any fondness was immediately dismissed. "It's destroyed. Because Joyce, Rourke and Marr could have stepped in and said something in my defence but they didn't. They let the judge say the most extreme and hateful things about me, which they knew weren't true."

With that the man who founded one of the UK's most innovative and creative bands seemingly put paid to any chance of a Smiths reunion.

Chapter 17

SPANDAU BALLET

Friends' falling-out over the publishing payout

One of the pioneer groups of the 'New Romantic' style, Spandau Ballet – a move on from earlier names such as The Makers and The Roots – created their own Reformation label and signed a licensing deal with Chrysalis Records in the spring of 1980.

Named after the prison in Berlin where Nazi war criminals were held, all five band members were born in Islington, north London. With former girl's magazine model Tony Hadley on vocals, child actor brothers Gary and Martin Kemp on guitar and bass respectively, John Keeble on drums and Steve Norman offering rhythm, guitar, saxophone and percussion, Spandau Ballet began to make an impression around London's club scene in 1980.

Resplendent in kilts, frilled shirts and lavish hairstyles, and managed by Islington schoolmate Steve Dagger, the band debuted in the charts with 'To Cut A Long Story Short'. Over the next decade, Spandau Ballet made the UK charts with 20 hit singles and six albums, including the double number one, *True*. During that time they also sued Chrysalis Records to release them from their contract, alleging the label's poor promotion was the reason for their lack of success in the US, where only the single 'True' went top five.

Freed from the deal in 1986, the group took their Reformation label to CBS. They continued to chart for three more years, until a dispute over the release in America of what would be their last album ended their contract with CBS.

The Kemp brothers, who starred in the 1988 film *The Krays*, and the other band members drifted apart, with Hadley signing a solo contract with EMI as Spandau Ballet finally ground to a halt.

However, the end of the band was only the beginning of a lengthy dispute between Hadley, Keeble and Norman on one side and Gary Kemp on the other, over publishing royalties paid to them through the band's company, Marbelow. The arrangement regarding publishing royalties for songs written by Gary Kemp – the band's chief songwriter – and recorded by Spandau Ballet was that Kemp would receive 50% while the other half would be shared between the other members.

Writing in his autobiography, *To Cut A Long Story Short*, Hadley claimed that in 1993, when he noticed there was little money coming through from the company, he rang the office. "That's when I believe I found out that I was no longer receiving an income from publishing royalties," he said. "It was a huge shock and made no sense. There had never been a disagreement over these payments from Gary in the past. The split had suited everyone for years. I couldn't understand why the payments had stopped."

The issue revolved around whether the royalties Kemp paid to the other members constituted an act of generosity on his part, or whether there was an agreement dating back to the band's formation giving a portion of his song royalties to the others. The other three band members – Martin Kemp was not involved in the dispute – were forced to consider whether to take legal action in pursuit of their claim that they had not been paid by Gary Kemp since 1988.

Deciding they had no option, Hadley wrote that he, Keeble and Norman believed they had been wronged. "We were as entitled to receive an income from publishing royalties as we had been in the past. I thought it a way of acknowledging our contribution to Spandau Ballet songs. There was more than a principle at stake; we were counting on the income as a kind of pension. We had to fight."

The fight began in London's High Court on January 27, 1999, when the three plaintiffs sued Gary Kemp over the alleged unpaid royalties. Even before the proceedings began, Kemp took the opportunity to issue a statement outside the court in which he said, "It has besmirched the history of the band I was proud of. These songs were written by me as long as 20 years ago, and only in the last 18 months has this claim been made."

In court, before Mr. Justice Park, Andrew Sutcliffe, counsel for the three plaintiffs, claimed they had contributed to the songs but that Spandau Ballet was more than just music. "The band's look was crucial to selling the band's songs."

Referring to the original contract with Chrysalis Records – which earned Spandau Ballet a £40,000 advance plus a further £15,000 on delivery of their first album – Sutcliffe told the judge, "It is the plaintiffs' case that although they were taken through the contracts, they didn't have any idea how the arrangement was going to operate."

Explaining that the band had discussed how royalties would be split before they signed with Chrysalis, Sutcliffe added, "They all say that Gary Kemp agreed from the early stages of the discussions that it was fair that all members of the band should have some share of the publishing royalties, despite the fact that he wrote the lyrics, music and basic chord structure of all the songs."

Sutcliffe claimed that his three clients were told by Kemp and Dagger that Kemp would take half the royalties and the rest of the band (including Kemp and Dagger) would keep the other half, which meant that Kemp would receive a total of seven-twelfths of the earnings.

"They all considered that split to be fair because of the way they worked together," said Sutcliffe, who warned that Kemp and Dagger's version of affairs "was very different". He said they both denied there was any discussion about sharing publishing royalties, and things had started to go wrong in early 1988 when Kemp "resolved that he was stopping paying publishing royalties to the other band members and wished to keep all the publishing monies for himself".

The court heard that while the Kemp brothers forged new careers for themselves – Martin starring in the popular TV soap *EastEnders* – the other three struggled with their careers after the band broke up. Judge

Park was also told that Gary Kemp's claim was that he only gave up a portion of his publishing royalties to fund the band's expenses.

When the court resumed on February 1, the judge reflected that there was a "stark contrast" in the two sides' arguments. A selection of the band's music was also played in court and Mr. Justice Park admitted, "I spent a large part of the weekend listening to this. It's very good."

Giving evidence, Hadley said he had suffered financially after his solo career failed. When the band were at the height of their success in the early Eighties, Hadley earned £120,000 a year, but the failure of his solo recordings meant he had to sell his home to clear a £50,000 overdraft. "Maths has never been my forte. I would just go, 'Wow, lots of figures', and sign forms. I was in a desperate financial situation," said Hadley, admitting that he was dependent on his share of the publishing royalties from Kemp's songs.

Keeble repeated his counsel's statement that the band shared everything, and told the court that Kemp could be extremely pedantic about matters relating to the group and their music.

The week ended with Gary Kemp giving evidence in his defence. He told the court that Spandau Ballet was not a democracy but a hierarchy. "My brother Martin dominated the way we looked. There were many, many arguments, particularly towards Tony [Hadley], feeling that he wasn't looking right or pulling his weight on that side of things."

The band's guitarist and main songwriter conceded that other band members did contribute ideas towards his songs. "People made some suggestions for free-form solos, particularly Steve, who was the most instinctive musician among us. But I would come up with a full song," he asserted. "The songs, the melody, the lyrics all came from me. I would always come to rehearsal with a song, with a title, with the vast majority of the lyrics finished, if not all of them."

Kemp admitted that it was "intimidating" playing his new songs to the other band members. "It was a nerve-racking thing playing to people who hope your song is good enough to be a hit record. None of us were great musicians. We were simple musicians and it was important for us to sound tight as a unit. There is more responsibility being Tony Hadley than being Gary Kemp. I would find it frightening."

Describing his own musical ability as "simple", Kemp admitted that he gained a lot of attention. "I tried to be humble with my name all over the record sleeve as the songwriter... it is not in my instinct as a person to sing my own praises of my abilities."

Continuing his claim that there was no formal agreement between the band members over publishing royalties, Kemp explained that he gave Marbelow half his royalties to help ease the "disparity" between himself and his colleagues. "It was a voluntary action and I didn't need to do it. I certainly would not have led them to believe the money would be coming to them for the rest of their lives."

After an adjournment lasting nearly three months, Mr. Justice Park returned to the High Court on April 30 to give his decision in a 68-page judgement, finding in favour of Gary Kemp and his Reformation Publishing Company.

Describing the case as "important and difficult", the judge declared that the case brought by Hadley, Keeble and Norman "fails in its entirety", although he felt sympathy for the plaintiffs and accepted that his ruling would be a "heavy blow" to them. However, Judge Park said he found it "unconscionable" for the three former band members to lay claim to "large sums of money which they knew Mr. Kemp regarded as his."

Considering the contributions made by the plaintiffs to the music and their claim that they were entitled to joint copyright as collaborators, the judge said of Hadley that he sang the songs "in his own memorable style", but if he did introduce changes they were too small to make him a joint author. Keeble's contribution, "excellent though it was", was to the performance rather than to the creation of the composition, while Norman's "impressive contribution" included "elements of a performer's creativity" but "it did not significantly change the songs".

Summing up the situation regarding the group, the judge declared, "Sadly they have comprehensively fallen out now, but to me a heartening feature of the evidence was how they remained committed admirers and defenders of each other's artistic qualities." He added that the three plaintiffs were "honest, able and engaging witnesses" who had given an accurate account of events but they were "mistaken".

After the judgement, Hadley told waiting reporters that he was disappointed but added, "I think we had every right to bring this case and we live to fight another day. Let this be a lesson to any upcoming bands. No matter if you are school friends or have spent years touring together, make sure you get something down on contract."

Norman said the decision came as a "bombshell" and he was "baffled and confused" by the ruling. Keeble added, "The three things bands usually get into trouble over are women, drugs or financial matters."

The victorious Gary Kemp declared that he saw the decision "as a victory on behalf of all songwriters", while the British record industry heaved a mighty sigh of relief that the judge's verdict would block a possible flood of copycat claims.

At the end of the case, the three defeated former members, who were each left facing a legal bill of around £200,000, were thrown a potential financial lifeline when a promoter floated the idea of a Spandau Ballet tour – with all five original members. This would involve just two weeks of shows but, despite Hadley, Norman and Keeble being understandably keen, it all fell through when Martin Kemp refused to disrupt his important *EastEnders* schedule, and that was before his brother had even been approached.

All the three musicians could do was to consider dropping their appeal against the April 1999 court case in an effort to persuade the Kemps to allow them to tour as Spandau Ballet. When that failed, Hadley, Norman and Keeble came up with another plan. Under the name HNK, with the extra tag "ex-Spandau Ballet", they attempted to go back on the road to play their old hits, until a writ arrived from the Kemps, plus Dagger, withdrawing permission for the trio to refer to themselves as "ex-Spandau Ballet", even though they had spent nine years in the band.

A clause in the original contract the band members had signed with Marbelow related to use of the band name, forcing HNK to split before a settlement could be reached. Hadley then embarked on a TV talent series called *Reborn In The USA*, which he eventually won, while Norman and Keeble pursued separate musical ventures.

While Martin Kemp continued with his acting career, surviving two brain tumours along the way, Gary recorded an unsuccessful solo album, appeared alongside Whitney Houston and Kevin Costner in the film *The Bodyguard*, and continued to write and broadcast.

In his 2001 autobiography, *Martin Kemp True*, the younger Kemp sibling reflected on the court case. "For me the whole thing was extremely sad. Not only were my closest friends in court with my brother, but it was also closing the Spandau book. Would there be a Spandau reunion at some point? Would we ever get back together in the years to come and play a couple of shows or even to make the odd record? After this, the answer is definitely no."

Bizarrely, in the aftermath of the bitter 1999 court battle, Hadley had brought up the subject of the band's reunion. "The Eagles once said they would reform when hell freezes over but they ended up touring together again, and we have been talking about a Spandau Ballet reunion tour and album."

Some eight years later, in 2007, it seemed that the major players in one of Britain's most successful bands were in conversation again, but this time Hadley was being a bit more cautious. "The next window of opportunity that I see would be our 30th anniversary in about four years' time."

Chapter 18

THE SPICE GIRLS

The sponsorship deal that became a legal battle

Five years after they were created through a "wanted" advert in an entertainment newspaper, The Spice Girls embarked on their ambitious, money-spinning Spice World Tour. In addition to the obvious increase in sales of records and concert tickets, this was also an opportunity to tie up major sponsorship deals along the way.

Victoria Adams, Melanie Brown, Emma Bunton, Melanie Chisholm and Geri Halliwell found each other in 1993 via the theatre journal *The Stage*, where an ad asking "R.U. 18-23 with the ability to sing/dance? R.U. streetwise, outgoing, ambitious and dedicated?" appeared.

From there, Ginger (Halliwell), Sporty (Chisholm), Scary (Brown), Posh (Adams) and Baby (Bunton) went on to become the fastest-selling act since The Beatles. By the time their global domination with "girl power" was in full swing in 1998, the five girls had become Britain's most successful female group. Their first six singles all made it to number one in the UK, they had two chart-topping albums, plus enormous success in America. As the femme five continued to rule the world's teenage and pre-teen female market, they embarked on plans for the European leg of their world tour with high hopes of signing a significant sponsorship deal.

The company they eventually linked up with was Aprilia World Service (AWS), a member of the Italian Aprilia Spa organisation and the producer of a range of motorbikes, scooters and mopeds. The deal, signed in March 1998 and announced two months later, involved Aprilia paying The Spice Girls a sponsorship fee of £400,000, in return for the company being able to use their name and image to promote the company's latest range of Sonic scooters, aimed directly at the teenage market.

The "Spice Sonic" scooter range would carry images of all five girls plus Spice Girls logos. In return the group members would also receive a royalty of £15 for every sale of the first 10,000 Spice Sonic scooters, and a further £10 for each sale after that. The Italian company also agreed to hand over £112,500 as a "guaranteed payment" of royalties, and to personally deliver a number of Moto bikes and Sonic scooters to the five Spice Girls.

However, between the European and US tours, Halliwell had decided to leave The Spice Girls, throwing the Spice World Tour and the sponsorship deal into confusion. The Italian company had planned a multimillion-pound campaign for their scooters based on the five members and now, out of the blue, came the news that there were only four of them. More bad news soon followed for Aprilia, which had handed over £300,000 as the first two instalments of the agreed £400,000 sponsorship fee. Suddenly, the company was accused of not paying the final £100,000 or the "guaranteed" royalty of £122,500, and of not delivering the full quota of scooters and Moto bikes (valued at over £6,000) to the five Spice Girls.

In October 1998, through their company Spice Girls Limited (SGL), the remaining members of the group announced that they were intending to sue Aprilia over the alleged unpaid amount and issued a writ against the long-established Italian motorcycle company. The company's response was to counter-sue for damages of either £434,564 or £1,016,541 – depending on whether they established either misrepresentation or breach of contract over the fact that Halliwell had left during the world tour and the company's campaign.

By the time the action came to the Chancery Division of London's High Court in February 2000, the case had become a complex two-way hearing before Mrs. Justice Mary Arden, with Ian Mill QC appearing for the claimants Spice Girls Limited, and Andrew Sutcliffe representing defendants Aprilia World Service.

Among the first witnesses to give evidence on February 9, Rosanna Fuzzi, advertising manager for Aprilia, outlined the campaign for the company's Spice Sonic scooter, which was aimed at a young market. Explaining that in many European countries 14-year-olds can legally ride 50cc machines, she stated that Aprilia had signed a £500,000 contract with The Spice Girls. She said the logo on the new model would feature a design incorporating a silhouette of all five. "When Geri left, all our brochures, advertising material and the logo became obsolete," Fuzzi said. "Young people would not want to be seen riding a product carrying a logo which was considered out of date. This is what I would call a marketing flop."

Fuzzi added that it would have made no sense in marketing terms for Aprilia to enter into the agreement knowing that there would be a change in the line-up, particularly taking into account the amount of time involved in redesigning the graphics.

The head of marketing for the Italian business, Roberto Brovazzo, confirmed to the court that had the company known "from the outset" that Halliwell was going to leave during the campaign, they would not have signed the deal and not invested several hundred thousand pounds in the project. The Spice Girls were the creators of a new "girl power" concept and were "symbolic for the fashionable, fresh and a bit cheeky image that Aprilia wanted to convey for their Sonic scooter".

Brovazzo added that Halliwell was "a core member of The Spice Girls and the embodiment of the girl power concept in the public eye". Aprilia had wanted to use the images of The Spice Girls to promote its product worldwide. It had expected to sell 10,000 scooters but only 200 were produced and sales, according to Brovazzo, were "disappointing".

The first of The Spice Girls to enter the packed Court 19 on February 9 was Emma Bunton, who began her evidence by confessing that she had "a terrible memory" and had initially "not remembered" the two occasions when Halliwell told the other girls of her intention to leave – firstly on a coach in Germany, and then in a dressing room in Italy.

"I just know that when I looked at Geri's statement, then I did remember the conversations," she told the court. Asked by Sutcliffe if this was not "a major piece of news" for the all-girl group, Bunton replied, "I never took it that seriously because things were said quite frequently."

However, she did admit that when Halliwell told her bandmates on a coach from Frankfurt airport to a hotel, there was an element of shock. "But it was something that we just took in because we had arranged to do this tour until September. We never believed she would go."

A few days later, in Milan on March 8, 1998, Halliwell spoke again about leaving and Bunton told the court, "I don't remember her saying it was definite. I just remember her mentioning it again."

Sutcliffe than asked the youngest Spice Girl a series of questions about Halliwell's proposed departure. "Do you remember Victoria asking Geri why and Geri saying, 'I've had enough and just want to finish with a big finale at Wembley'?

"Do you remember Mel C saying, 'This feels like a Take That moment' [when Robbie Williams left the boy band] and asking Geri, 'Are you doing a Robbie on us?' and Geri saying, 'No I am not. I'm going to stick it out until September. I am committed to the band'?"

In reply Bunton declared, "It was just jokingly said. And we were just about to go on stage. I think we were laughing. Again, we didn't seem to take it seriously." She then added that Halliwell had not outlined any plans for her future away from The Spice Girls.

"She never said she wanted to do something else. I think one of us asked her why and she said … Oh, I can't remember what she said, but I never remembered her having other plans."

The Spice Girls' former lawyer, Andrew Thompson, told the court that Halliwell had told him and Nancy Phillips, a director of Spice Girls Limited, of her intention to leave the group at an informal meeting on April 25, just before the group went on stage at Wembley.

Thompson said that he agreed that his initial idea to put out a press release was "ludicrous", and that the news should be kept confidential "as [Geri] may well have changed her mind". He claimed that the contracts with Aprilia were written in such a way that there would be "no breach of contract" should the group's line-up change in any way.

On behalf of the group, Mill argued that Halliwell had simply said that she might leave the group and the other four members hoped that she might change her mind. The news of her departure was reported in the media on May 31, and the next day Aprilia was assured that it could continue to use Halliwell's image in the campaign after her departure.

In addition to claiming that its range of Spice Sonic scooters became obsolete "overnight" when Halliwell left, Aprilia also claimed that a £150,000 television shoot for a commercial was delayed for several days at some cost because Victoria Adams had a private engagement she did not want to cancel. It also claimed that when the commercial was finally shot, the group members left early, causing body doubles to be used to complete the shoot.

The company also alleged to the court that full-page advertisements it had hoped would be included in the official tour programme did not appear, and that the band did the minimum in promotional photo opportunities and "meet and greet" events. In response to this, Bunton said, "We were always professional. We gave 100 per cent."

At the completion of her day in court, Bunton told waiting reporters, "I'd rather do a show. I was nervous. Going on stage is much easier."

Halliwell was called to give evidence on February 10. She told the court that her memory of the Aprilia dealings was "hazy".

Questioned by Sutcliffe, she agreed that following the departure of manager Simon Fuller, she was put in charge of organising sponsorship deals while Bunton was put in charge of charities and personnel. She also told counsel for Aprilia that the idea that she became "unofficial leader" of the group and was "perhaps more business-minded than the others" was "a media perception. I am a very directional [sic] person. But there wasn't one more prominent than the others. It was a joint collective".

Halliwell told Judge Arden that she had doubts about leaving The Spice Girls. "I knew at the back of my mind, instinctively, I wanted to leave, but I didn't know whether I was brave enough to do that – leave the security of such a big band." She added that there was not one occasion when she could say she had definitely decided to leave.

"I was drip, drip, drip-feeding the idea to the others as well as myself. That's why there wasn't one defining moment when I can say I consciously made that decision. It was like leaving a marriage. You get such mixed feelings. One part of me wanted to stay but the other half said it was time to go."

After confirming that she had told the other members of the group in Frankfurt of her plans to leave, Halliwell added that she didn't think they took her seriously. Aprilia's counsel suggested that by the time of the television commercial shoot in May 1998, she must have known that the scooter company was investing a great deal of money in the sponsorship deal.

"I'm sure I would be aware," said the singer, "but it was not the most prominent thing. When you're an artist, you're an artist."

Asked whether it concerned her that Aprilia might be producing scooters with an official Spice Girls logo on them and trying to sell the scooters when there were no longer five girls in the group, Halliwell replied, "I felt that The Spice Girls were strong enough and had momentum to go on as a four-piece."

Halliwell also recalled the meeting on April 25 at Wembley, where she told the tour manager that she was intending to leave the group and it was agreed to keep the news a secret.

After five days of evidence, the hearing came to an end on February 14. Mrs. Justice Arden adjourned the two-way lawsuit in order to consider her judgement, which she returned to give 10 days later. Her decision was that The Spice Girls had unintentionally but unlawfully misrepresented themselves as a five-girl group when they signed the sponsorship deal with Aprilia World Service, knowing that Halliwell was about to leave.

Explaining that she accepted the evidence of Halliwell and Bunton that references Halliwell had made to the other group members about leaving had not been taken seriously, the judge said, "I do not consider that The Spice Girls or, through them, Spice Girls Limited, appreciated that Miss Halliwell was going to leave the group as a result of those brief conversations. All that they knew was that she was thinking about it and there was a risk that she would leave."

The main issue for the judge was the Wembley meeting, when Halliwell's intentions were made clear to the other members as well as their solicitor. This was a month before the contract with Aprilia was signed and, had the Italian scooter company known she was leaving, they would have had the chance to renegotiate.

By entering into the agreement with Aprilia knowing that one of their members was planning to leave, The Spice Girls were guilty of misrepresentation, ruled Judge Arden. "There is no suggestion whatever that the misrepresentation was intentional," she added, and concluded that Aprilia was entitled to recover the £300,000 sponsorship money it had already paid and also damages for expenses and lost profits on the scooters.

The judge dismissed Aprilia's claim for breach of contract and £1 million damages, and announced that the exact amount of damages and costs would be settled at a later hearing in 2000.

After the case, Susan Barty from Aprilia's London solicitors, CMS Cameron McKenna, confirmed that the Italian company would not have taken action against The Spice Girls if the band had not sued for unpaid sponsorship fees and royalties.

"Aprilia would just have put it down to something that had gone wrong, written it off. But they were forced to counterclaim when The Spice Girls sued them," she confirmed.

For their part, The Spice Girls issued a statement saying they would decide whether to appeal against the judgement after a final decision had been made as to the extent of their liability. They also emphasised that the judge had only upheld one of the allegations made against the group, of unintentional misrepresentation, and had dismissed the £1 million breach of contract claim. "It is, as yet, unclear whether Aprilia will, in fact, be awarded any part of the £430,000. Indeed, Spice Girls Limited may yet end up with a judgement in its favour. However, if the claim is dismissed an appeal is highly likely."

During the summer of 2000, Judge Arden decided to refuse damages to Aprilia for the group's misrepresentation, but awarded the company £45,550 in damages for scooters delivered to The Spice Girls. She also ruled that Aprilia should pay 10% of both its own costs and The Spice Girls' costs of the action.

The group's threatened appeal became reality in November 2001, when once again both The Spice Girls and Aprilia launched claims against the judge's rulings, including her decision not to award the company damages for the unintentional misrepresentation.

The members of the group argued in the Court of Appeal that they were "innocent" of misrepresentation, and maintained that they should have won their original claim for £218,000 from the Italian business. They also wanted the Appeal Court to quash the order for them to pay the damages for scooters supplied by Aprilia and the legal costs of the original hearing.

While the women did not appear at the appeal hearing, their counsel, Ian Mill, told the Appeal Court judges, Vice-Chancellor Sir Andrew Morritt, Lord Justice Chadwick and Lord Justice Rix, that there had been no discussion about Halliwell's departure before the agreement with Aprilia came into force.

He added that Halliwell had then said that she would not be leaving until the end of the US tour in September 1998, but changed her mind and quit without warning in May. However, the Appeal Court judges declared that the fact that The Spice Girls, mistakenly as it turned out, did not take Halliwell seriously in March 1998 when she said she was leaving was immaterial.

The judges also viewed that Judge Arden, in connecting the sponsorship contract and access to promotional material only to the New York shoot in May, had seriously understated the significance of a Heads of Agreement document signed on March 4, 1998. They also considered the sales figures for original Sonic scooters and Sonic Spice scooters, both in Europe and in America, and accepted that there was some dispute over the exact numbers sold and the profits earned, which contributed to Judge Arden's ruling over damages.

The judges dismissed the appeal, finding The Spice Girls liable to Aprilia for misrepresentation, and dismissed their claim for £218,000, allowing the scooter company the £45,550 damages. They also ordered The Spice Girls to pay all the legal costs of the hearings, which lawyers for the Italian company estimated could run close to £1 million, while the girls' solicitors suggested that it would be no more than £500,000.

Either way it was an expensive and disappointing result for The Spice Girls, who had set out to sue their sponsors for non-payment of just over £200,000 and ended up losing their claim, having to fork out hundreds of thousands of pounds in costs and damages.

In March 2000, just one week after the original hearing ended, both The Spice Girls and Geri Halliwell were on the same bill for the first time since their well-publicised split two years earlier. At the BRIT

Awards, Sporty, Scary, Posh and Baby closed the show and took home the award for Outstanding Contribution (managing a "big thank you to Geri" along the way). However, the former Ginger Spice-turned-solo singer stole the show, stunning the live audience and TV viewers by emerging from between a giant pair of inflatable legs that were encased in Union Jack knickers. The show's producers described it as "a risqué performance that was a throwback to the days of Hollywood".

The Spice Girls signed off in 2000 with a final ninth UK number one single and a top two album, which brought their worldwide record sales to more than 55 million. Solo careers beckoned and, while Emma Bunton, Mel B and Mel C all notched up number one singles, the now Victoria Beckham's best effort peaked at number two.

But the lure of The Spice Girls proved too much for the five and, in December 2007, Ginger, Sporty, Scary, Posh and Baby set off on a massively successful, sold-out world reunion tour. Halliwell, avoiding the issue of lucre, claimed it was about "celebrating the past, enjoying each other".

There was not a Sonic Spice scooter in sight – it was replaced by a 757 jet dubbed Spice Force One.

Chapter 19

NAPSTER

When a college dropout upset the US record business

A lot of years span the histories of the Recording Industry Association of America (RIAA), the legendary rock band Metallica and the California-based online music service Napster, but over two short years they were linked in a blaze of publicity and a huge amount of acrimony.

The RIAA was set up in 1952 to represent the biggest music companies in the world's largest market for recorded music. Today, it focuses on the interests of the four majors – EMI, Sony/BMG, Warner and Universal, which between them account for over 90% of the US music business. The RIAA also lobbies Congress over copyright issues, protecting free speech and handing out certified sales awards on behalf of what is called "the most vibrant national music industry in the world".

The thrash metal band Metallica owe their existence to the efforts of Danish-born drummer Lars Ulrich, who formed the band in Los Angeles in 1981. Since then he has steered them through line-up changes, relocation to San Francisco and a host of award-winning, number one albums. Classed as an "unstoppable metal monster", Metallica's inventive thrash metal brought about worldwide album sales in excess of 70 million.

The third cast member – whose activities so upset the other two – is Napster, which was founded in 1991 by 19-year-old Shawn Fanning. A dropout from Northeastern University in Massachusetts, Fanning was introduced to computers at an early age thanks to his uncle John, and it didn't take him long to understand the merits of the new MP3 development and its compressed digital music files. Perfectly legal in its own right, MP3 technology creates reduced files that can reside on a hard drive and require less time to transfer, making them perfectly suited to sharing over the Internet.

However, the company that took its title from Fanning's school nickname – it was to do with having thick, curly hair – was soon to find itself in deep water as music fans swarmed to the Napster site to share and swap thousands of songs stored as MP3 files. By providing an index allowing users to access hard drives and copy files, Napster never actually copied any music itself but simply allowed access for file sharers. It was this facility – coupled with claims posted on its website that it was the "world's largest MP3 music library" and "ensures the availability of every song online" – that incensed the RIAA.

The Napster service became available on June 1, 1999. It quickly became a hub for hundreds of thousands of songs made available by music fans that could be downloaded by other fans ... the business of peer-to-peer file sharing had begun. Within months of its launch, Napster collected literally millions of users, with students from some of America's leading universities and colleges at the heart of the revolution. Within four months of its start-up, Napster was reported to occupy 10% of Oregon State University's Internet bandwidth, while at Florida State the figure was approaching 30% and at the University of Illinois it reached a mighty 75%.

In the early part of 2000, regardless of its legal status, the sheer popularity of Napster forced universities to start banning the service. New York University took action followed by Hofstra, Indiana and Oregon, along with nearly 200 other places of learning. Elsewhere, the likes of MIT, Stanford, Harvard and Washington State refused to ban it, citing as reasons academic freedom, the exploration of ideas and the modern learning environment. While many of these academic centres allowed Internet access – including the use of Napster – they covered their backs by condemning copyright infringement at the same time as confirming that they were not about to monitor students' use of the college Internet service.

Not surprisingly, the students did not run scared. They launched protests and help set up systems that got around the bans urged by some colleges and universities. The long arm of the law was getting ever closer, however, as both the record industry and the artists who made the music took action.

At the outset, the major music companies had begun negotiations with Fanning in an effort to put the new service on a legal footing but, by October 1999, the record business had ended the discussions. The RIAA filed suit against Napster in December, accusing the company of encouraging and facilitating the widespread practice of illegal copying and distribution of copyrighted music on a massive scale. The recording organisation also asked for damages of $100,000 per recording copied, and accused Napster of "creating and operating a haven of music piracy on an unprecedented scale".

The first hearing took place in the US District Court for the Northern District of California on March 27, 2000 before Judge Marilyn Patel, who listened but gave no decision. Also listening were some of popular music's leading players, who decided the time had come for action. A statement was issued on April 11 in which artists such as Elton John, Lou Reed and The The spoke out against Napster.

Two days later, thrash giants Metallica took things one stage further and filed a $10 million copyright infringement and racketeering lawsuit against Napster and the universities of Southern California, Indiana and Yale. The band were moved to act by the fact that they found 100 Metallica tracks on the site, including five versions of a previously unavailable track destined for the *Mission: Impossible 2* soundtrack.

Filed in the Central District of California, the suit alleged that Napster had distributed numerous Metallica tracks without compensating the band, while the colleges "have knowingly sanctioned and encouraged students to pirate" the tracks by allowing them to access Napster through university computers. The ominous-sounding reference to racketeering in the lawsuit was based on the band's belief that Napster was an "enterprise" that had allegedly participated in the interstate transportation of stolen property.

"Metallica has sued on copyright infringement and other things before," manager Cliff Burnstein was quoted in US music magazine *Billboard*, "but this is a whole different deal because the Internet is infinite, and it gets worse every day because Napster's user base is growing."

On the other hand, Napster's counsel, Laurence Pulgram, made the company's position clear. "We regret that the band's management saw fit to issue a press release and to file a lawsuit without even attempting to contact Napster. Many bands who have approached us, and learned about Napster and how to leverage what we offer, understand the value of what we do."

The final word in the opening round of the legal battle went to Metallica founder Ulrich, who stated, "From a business standpoint this is about piracy – a.k.a. taking something that doesn't belong to you – and that is morally and legally wrong."

Before the month was out Dr Dre, whose lawyer, Howard King, filed the original suit against Napster on behalf of his clients Metallica, also filed his own $10 million action against the music service. One of the biggest artists to add his name and voice to the anti-Napster movement was leading rapper Eminem, who argued that he was due a reward for his work and that students and young people with computers could be expected to pay for music. "If you can afford a computer, you can afford to pay $16 for my CD," was one of the comments attributed to the Detroit-born rapper.

The row with Napster ultimately and unsurprisingly led to a split in the artists' camp, with the likes of Chuck D and Limp Bizkit among those arguing in favour of the web service. In fact, the nu metal/rap outfit from Florida went one stage further and signed Napster as the $2 million sponsor of their next tour.

During the first week of May, Ulrich and Metallica took drastic measures and, with the help of an Internet private detective service, tracked down over 300,000 fans of the band who, they alleged, had used the Napster service to illegally download their music. The drummer and his lawyer delivered a 60,000 page document, including the internet addresses of 317,000 fans, to Napster's headquarters in San Mateo, California, and demanded that the company ban them from their service.

While Napster argued that it was merely an Internet service provider, or conduit, and not liable for piracy by its users, it was required by law to bar users who were proved to be infringing copyright via its service. Napster's response to Metallica's direct action was for Pulgram to announce that the company would review the list of fans' names as soon as possible and, "if the claims are submitted properly, the company will take the appropriate action to disable the users Metallica has identified".

Whether they anticipated a backlash against their actions or not, that was exactly what Metallica got, as former fans ironically used the Internet to post their attacks and grievances against the band. They urged a boycott of concerts and the burning of CDs in a concerted anti-Metallica movement.

Resuming the earlier hearing in May 2000, Judge Patel rejected Napster's claim that it was a "mere conduit", and ruled that the suit brought by the RIAA should proceed to the next stage. At the same time, Ulrich continued Metallica's Napster onslaught by testifying before a Senate Judiciary Committee discussing intellectual property rights on the Internet. The drummer travelled to Washington and told the political high-flyers, "If you're not fortunate enough to own a computer, there's only one way to assemble a music collection the equivalent of a Napster user's: theft. Walk into a record store, grab what you want and walk out."

By the time the RIAA and Napster returned to court in July 2000, it was estimated that there were over eight million Napster users in the US, exchanging on average around 20 songs per month, while in the UK, Napster had attracted close to 500,000 users.

On July 26, Judge Patel reached a landmark decision regarding the future of Napster. The company's attorney, David Boies, argued that while sharing music was legal for consumers not engaged in profit-making, there were plenty of significant legitimate uses for Napster. Furthermore, as an ISP (Internet Service Provider), it couldn't be held responsible for the listings that appeared in its directory.

However, the judge was clearly unimpressed by these arguments and posed the question: if Napster offered so many significant uses other than trading copyrighted songs, why would an order suspending trading of songs force the company out of business? "The evidence establishes that a majority of Napster users use the service to download and upload copyrighted music. This, in fact, should come as no surprise to Napster since that really was the purpose of it.

"And by doing that, it constitutes – the uses constitute – direct infringement of plaintiffs' musical compositions – recordings that are copyrighted. And it is pretty much acknowledged also by Napster that this is infringement unless they can fall back on the affirmative defence because of the warnings that were given to the users of the system that they may be infringing."

While suggesting that as much as 87% of the music available on Napster was probably copyrighted material, the judge confirmed that the defendants had put forward a defence of fair use and substantial non-infringing before declaring her ruling.

"The court finds that ... the potential non-infringing uses of the Napster service are minimal, the substantial or commercially significant use of the service was and continues to be copying popular music, most of which is copyrighted and for which no authorisation has been obtained."

Having concluded that Napster users were engaged in "wholesale infringing", Judge Patel issued a preliminary injunction that ordered Napster to stop allowing its users to exchange copyrighted music owned by the major record companies represented by the RIAA. She gave a deadline of midnight two days later, pending a full trial hearing.

However, within the two days set by Judge Patel, the United States Court of Appeals for the Ninth Circuit gave Napster an unexpected reprieve, when the three judges agreed to grant the company's request to overrule the judge's injunction.

The Appeals Court accepted that Napster had raised substantial questions about "both the merits and the form of the injunction", and allowed the company to continue in business until at least October 2000, when a hearing to reinstate the injunction would be held.

Before the appeal was granted, Hilary Rosen, president of the RIAA, told reporters, "They're throwing the same reasoning at the court of appeals they tried at the judge. The judge's reasoning was solid and this won't be successful."

There were those who believed that simply closing down Napster was not the main issue facing the record industry. It had to find a way of meeting the now obvious demand for music to be supplied online to the millions of customers who had been attracted to the company.

Record industry analyst Michael Nathanson chose the eve of the Appeals Court hearing to warn the music business. "They have got to fill the vacuum. They can't just keep stopping these things."

Finally, on October 2, 2000, the Ninth Circuit Appeals Court convened in San Francisco to hear the appeal.

Chief Judge Mary Schroeder sat with Circuit Judges Richard Paez and Robert Beezer. They heard Boies state that the plaintiffs (the RIAA's member companies were collectively gathered under the name A&M Records) were asking the court "to do several things that no appellate court has done in the history of copyright". He outlined that they wanted the court to hold a company liable for infringement when the direct infringer was not engaged in any commercial activity, and added that Napster also supplied a technology capable of commercially significant non-infringing use.

Boies also argued that there would be no case to answer unless the court found that consumers sharing music was illegal. He concluded that, as an ISP, Napster would have to be found liable for the infringing activity of its users when it could not know what they were doing, even after it had suspended service and when infringement was brought to its attention, as in the case of Metallica.

"The plaintiff asks this court to reach each one of those four unprecedented holdings, and this court must reach each of those to find liability," Boies said in conclusion.

Judge Schroeder took the opportunity to suggest that Judge Patel's reasoning in the earlier hearing seemed sound when she said it wasn't fair use when someone made music anonymously available to anyone in the world. In the final part of Boies' 20 minute submission, a lengthy discussion occurred as to whether Napster was a service or a technology. For the RIAA, Russell Frackman seized on the service or technology debate and claimed that only Napster's servers could be reasonably compared with the mechanical videotape recorder. The rest, he said, was a service, programmed to infringe. "We're not talking about technology, we're talking about a business plan."

Frackman added that it was Napster's own fault if its technology had to be shut down. "No one can get that material without Napster using its server for this service," he pointed out. "Whether or not Napster chooses to suspend what they're doing is not relevant. If they have created a situation where they either choose not to, or cannot continue operation because of the massive infringement involved, then we as the copyright owners are entitled to injunctive relief expressly permitted in the copyright act."

When Judge Beezer offered the suggestion that Napster had been designed for "fair use", Frackman explained that was not Napster's original intention, although "that may be what they tell you now". He added that the company was "integrally involved in the distribution to millions of people of millions of recordings, the overwhelming number of which are copyrighted recordings owned by our clients."

Within days of the hearing ending and the judges adjourning to consider their verdict, Shawn Fanning elected to speak at a congressional hearing held at Brigham Young University. After running through the history of Napster, he made an indirect reference to the legal arguments that had been running almost from the day he started his business. "Once there is collaboration and not litigation, we can come to a peaceful conclusion and everything will work out."

By the end of October, Fanning received some good news when the German media and music giant Bertelsmann announced an alliance with Napster that would result in a legal, subscription-based music service allowing users to swap songs copyrighted by the company's BMG record division. Reports suggested that Bertelsmann, which, at the same time dropped its lawsuit against Napster, had loaned the company an estimated $50 million to develop the legal file-sharing system. Bertelsmann, which described the controversial deal as "a milestone in the history of the music industry", also negotiated an option to buy a stake in Napster, and urged its rival record companies to drop their lawsuits and work with Napster to establish a legal paid-for service.

The downside of the deal was the resignation of BMG founder Michael Dornemann and president Strauss Zelnick, who had been kept out of the Napster loop by Bertlesmann CEO, Thomas Middelhoff, as he secretly negotiated with Fanning and Napster CEO, Hank Barry. Middelhoff was convinced where the future of the music industry lay.

"The great message of today is that we found a great way that content, that intellectual doing, even with file sharing, will be an important part of the media entertainment industry."

But even with Bertelsmann on its side, Napster still faced the wrath of the remaining music companies and the RIAA organisation, all of whom were anxiously awaiting the next legal move. It finally came after a further three months, when the three judges from the Ninth Circuit Appeals Court finally released their findings on February 12, 2001. Basically, they agreed with Judge Patel's original ruling and reinstated the injunction, but allowed Napster to continue to operate while the law ran its course.

The judges agreed that Napster should be held liable for copyright infringement, but sent the case back to the lower court in order that the injunction could be refined. In the judgement, Judge Beezer wrote, "The district court correctly recognised that a preliminary injunction against Napster's participation in copyright infringement is not only warranted but required."

All three judges held that using Napster to "get something for free they would ordinarily have to buy" was a commercial use and an infringement of copyright, and concluded that Napster "bears the burden of policing the system within the limits of the system."

The panel acknowledged that Judge Patel's preliminary injunction was "overbroad because it places on Napster the entire burden of ensuring that 'no copying, downloading, uploading, transmitting or distributing' of plaintiffs' works occur on the system." They also rejected Napster's claim for a court-ordered royalty payment instead of the injunction it faced, saying that there were no special circumstances and describing it as the "easy out" for the defendants, who could either choose to continue in business and pay royalties or simply shut down.

"We are disappointed in today's ruling," said Hank Barry. "Under this decision Napster could be shut down before a trial on the merits." He vowed to pursue "every legal avenue to keep Napster operating".

Fanning, too, joined in the media frenzy, stating, "Napster works because people who love music share and participate. Along the way, many people said it would never work. Today we have more than 50 million members and we'll find a way to keep this community growing."

The outcome brought a degree of rejoicing from Napster's arch enemies, Metallica, who said, "We are delighted that the court has upheld the rights of all artists to protect and control their creative efforts," adding, "We have never objected to the technology, the Internet or the digital distribution of music."

From the Artists Against Piracy movement, which boasted support from acts such as Garth Brooks, Christina Aguilera and Bon Jovi, came the opinion that, "We hope the message is clear: artists' rights must be respected online."

The RIAA was also satisfied with the outcome, and Hilary Rosen commented, "This is a clear victory. The court of appeals found that the injunction is not only warranted but required. And it ruled in our favour on every legal issue presented."

A week later, the RIAA issued a plea for Napster to accept the ruling and get on with setting up a legal business. "Stop the infringements, stop the delay tactics in court and redouble your efforts to build a legitimate system," was the message from Rosen. "Our member-company plaintiffs have always said that they stand ready and willing to meet individually with you to discuss future licences. This path would be more productive than trying to engage in business negotiations through the media."

On March 2, the modified injunction ordered by the Appeals Court was considered by the US District Court. Within a few days, Judge Patel ordered that Napster remove all copyrighted material from its service within 72 hours.

For their part, the record companies were required to provide Napster with lists of the songs they wanted removed from the system. Napster confirmed that it would "take every step within the limits of our system to exclude their copyrighted material from being shared".

The online company still harbored hopes of a settlement with the major music companies, but while Judge Patel acknowledged that tracking all the copyrighted material might be difficult, she added, "This difficulty does not relieve Napster of its duty."

But even with the judge's decision fresh in their minds, coupled with their own efforts to comply with the court order, Napster's executives still found themselves on the wrong side of Metallica and the RIAA.

Both the band and the industry organisation alleged they had found no evidence of compliance, and that Napster had failed to block access to music as ordered. The charge was that Napster users were circumventing the newly installed screening process by changing the spelling of a song title or artist.

This issue brought Napster back into court in front of Judge Patel on April 11. Confronted with evidence that thousands of copyrighted songs were still available via MP3, she declared the company's efforts to filter music as "a disgrace". The judge warned that if Napster failed to comply with the injunction she had handed down a month earlier, then it "may be the system needs to be closed down". She agreed to talk with technical experts about music filtering, while Napster also welcomed the outside adviser, who, it claimed would validate that the company was removing songs as quickly as possible.

Lawyers for the record companies that had sued Napster presented to the judge lists of copyrighted songs that remained on the defendant's system, specifically, 6,000 that Napster had been asked to remove by March 24, of which 84% were still available.

With an end almost in sight, in June 2001, the Ninth US Circuit Court of Appeals confirmed that Napster could no longer knowingly trade in copyrighted material, and that it could be held liable for users of the service who swapped copyrighted songs. This decision confirmed the courts' support for an amended injunction and rejected Napster's request that the case be reheard. In its 58-page ruling, the court made it clear that Napster knew its users were swapping copyrighted songs. "Napster has knowledge, both actual and constructive, of direct infringement of copyright law. Having digital downloads available free on the Napster system necessarily harms the copyright holders' attempts to charge for the same downloads."

Judge Patel was back on the case in July 2001. Once again, she considered that Napster's efforts to block users sharing unauthorised files had been unsatisfactory. As the company failed to show that it was unable to completely block copyrighted material from its system, the Federal Court judge ruled that the Napster service should be suspended.

The RIAA saw this as yet another nail in the coffin of the song-sharing operation. Rosen was quick to point out that, "while we appreciate that Napster is attempting to migrate to a legitimate business model, its failure to prevent copyright infringement from occurring on its system has only hampered the development of the marketplace in which it now hopes to compete".

She added a warning: "Today's ruling sends a clear signal to all infringers: any attempt to hide illegal activity behind the shield of technological innovation will not be tolerated."

While Napster immediately announced its intention to appeal, industry speculation was that the end was nigh for the world's most famous and notorious file-sharing system. It was thought it could only return when it was a fully legitimate and legalised service with authorised deals in place with the industry's major music companies.

On July 13, 2001, the day after the court's ruling, both Metallica and Dr Dre announced that they had settled their outstanding lawsuits against Napster for copyright infringement. "Our beef hasn't been with the concept with file sharing," said Ulrich. "The problem we had with Napster was that they never asked us or other artists if we wanted to participate in their business."

Dr Dre concurred. "I work hard making music, that's how I earn a living. Now that Napster agreed to respect that, I don't have any beef with them."

While both acts agreed to make "certain material available from time to time" on Napster once an acceptable system to ensure payments was in place, details of the financial settlement remained undisclosed.

Napster agreed to identify and block access to any music files the two acts did not want shared. "We respect what they've done," Barry said in his statement of apology, "and we regret any harm which this dispute may have caused them."

On the other hand, speaking on behalf of both his clients, King made it clear that the settlement had come about because the two artists had accomplished everything they set out to do, which seemingly included drawing attention to artists' control and compensation concerns, spurring action from the RIAA and receiving an apology from Napster. He also confirmed that the financial settlement would "more than cover" the cost of the lawsuit.

Quite how much the two artists suffered will always be in question. Certainly there was a backlash against Metallica, with cartoons posted on websites portraying them as selfish rock stars, while US magazine *Blender* listed them at number 17 on its list of the "biggest wusses in rock". Others referred to Ulrich as "Lar$".

Despite the protests, Metallica's success continued to increase. Their 2003 album, *St. Anger*, topped the charts in 13 countries, while 2004 saw them embark on a world tour on the back of a Grammy win for Best Metal Album.

For Dr Dre (born Andre Young) things slowed up on the recording front after his hit 1999 album *2001*, but his business acumen brought him new success as he concentrated on launching his Aftermath Entertainment operation, including best-selling rap artists such as Eminem, Busta Rhymes and 50 Cent.

For Napster, the ultimate and most damaging aspect of its failed lawsuit was the settlement, agreed in September 2001, of reportedly $26 million to be paid to the music creators and owners for the company's past unauthorised use of copyrighted tracks, plus a further $10 million advance against future royalties.

In January 2002, Judge Patel agreed to suspend the three year-old lawsuit brought against Napster by four of the major record companies (AOL Time Warner, BMG, Vivendi Universal and Sony) in the hope that all issues could be resolved and that Napster would be reactivated as a legal site. The fifth major, EMI, declined to go along with the request and announced that it was pursuing settlement talks with Napster.

By May things had gone from bad to worse for Napster, when a proposed sale of its assets to Bertelsmann was blocked by a US bankruptcy judge. Instead, Napster was forced to liquidate its assets under Chapter 7 of the US bankruptcy laws. As a result, most of the company's staff members were released, while a notice posted on the website declared: "Napster was here".

The Napster brand and logo ended up on sale at a bankruptcy auction where they were bought by American software company Roxio Inc., which used them to launch the legitimate music service Napster 2.0.

So, nearly 10 years after launching the illegal, albeit immensely popular, peer-to-peer music file-sharing service, the new Napster found itself trailing in the emerging digital music business. According to figures issued by the IFPI (International Federation of Phonographic Industries), this business was busy making inroads into the traditional multi-billion dollar record industry.

In 2006, sales of music online or through mobile phones reached an estimated $2 billion, which accounted for 10% of the global music market. While the industry estimated there were about 795 million single track downloads, the number of tracks available topped four million, via 500 online services in 40 countries worldwide.

Arguably, all this was the result of an upstart American teenager's dream to simply make music available to music fans, but he overlooked one crucial thing – paying the pipers who owned the tunes.

Chapter 20

THE BLUEBELLS

A falling-out over the fiddle intro to a two-time hit

Such are the vagaries of pop music that the biggest chart success in the career of Scottish band The Bluebells came close to a decade after the five members of the group had parted company. It was the second round of success for their song 'Young At Heart' and was thanks to a major television advertisement for a brand of German car, which prompted the record company to reissue the previously deleted single.

However, while the band were not moved to reform in the light of their new-found fame and fortune, a major dispute developed over the record's renewed success. It took a further decade before it was sorted out in an English court of law.

At the heart of the Glasgow-based Bluebells was singer and guitarist Robert Hodgens, who seemingly went by the name Bobby Bluebell, and brothers Ken and David McCluskey on vocals/harmonica and drums respectively. They were joined in 1982 by bassist Lawrence Donegan and guitarist Russell Irvine, who were subsequently replaced within a few months by Neal Baldwin and Craig Gannon.

Even in their earliest days together the band managed to attract the wrong kind of attention. There were reports that the world-famous

French dance troupe of the same name had sued the band over use of the name Bluebells. It seems that the leggy Parisian hoofers felt that the somewhat scruffy image of the Scottish pop band was less than appropriate, and perhaps even damaging, but their 1982 legal action failed.

Undaunted by the attention of the dancing girls, a year later the five-piece band won a recording contract with London Records as a result of a successful demo session overseen by Elvis Costello.

In the same year, The Bluebells reached the lower reaches of the UK pop chart with the singles 'Cath' and 'I'm Falling'. At around the same time, Hodgens started a relationship with singer Siobhan Fahey, from the successful all-girl group Bananarama, which also involved them writing songs together. One of their joint compositions, 'Cheers Then', was the fourth hit single for the trio of girls, who went on to become Britain's most charted female group; the song also featured on their Top 10 album *Deep Sea Diving*. The album also included the first version of another song Hodgens and Fahey co-wrote, entitled 'Young At Heart'.

Following the modest success of 'I'm Falling', which made the Top 20, The Bluebells selected 'Young At Heart' as a song with hit potential, but it needed something extra. A session musician was recruited to add a distinctive violin introduction. The fiddle player was Robert Beckingham, known professionally as Bobby Valentino, who was booked for a recording session at Red Bus studios in London in February 1984. He was paid £75 for his performance on 'Young At Heart' and received no royalties from the song, although he did sign a consent form covering the use of his performance on the record.

Within a few weeks of being recorded, 'Young At Heart' entered the UK chart on June 23, 1984. However, when the record was listed in music industry magazine *Music Week* – just two weeks after being released – only Hodgens was named as composer. The listing credited Clive Banks/ATV as publisher. Things stayed that way until July 14, when the record reached 14 in the chart. Now the *Music Week* composers listing carried the names Hodgens/Fahey, and the listed publishers were Clive Banks/ATV and In A Bunch – the latter presumably representing Fahey's newly acknowledged interest in the song.

The single, which remained in the chart for a total of 12 weeks and peaked at number eight, was the band's only Top 10 hit. Within a year The Bluebells had split, with the McCluskeys becoming a folk duo, Hodgens starting Up and Gannon became temporary guitarist with The Smiths. However, the McCluskey brothers were quickly reminded that they were in fact still under contract to London Records. This meant that their 1987 debut album had to be deleted just two weeks after release, and it wasn't until 1990 that they were released from the existing deal.

Fast forward to 1993, when the German car company Volkswagen chose 'Young At Heart' as the theme tune for a major television advert. This in turn prompted London Records to reissue the original single, resulting in a number one hit that April. But even as The Bluebells enjoyed their moment of recognition, they steadfastly refused to reform, although they did get together for a *Top Of The Pops* appearance to promote the record before returning to their new careers, which included life as a folk singer, a club owner and a chef.

During the record's 12-week stay in the charts from March 27, 1993 – when sales topped 400,000 and earned a gold disc – the song was again listed in *Music Week* as being written by Hodgens/Fahey, with the publishers now credited as CBanks/ATV/In A Bunch/Warner Chappell. The *NME*, meanwhile, speculated in its Public column (dated April 17) on who wrote what with regard to 'Young At Heart'.

The report read: "Forget sex let's talk about luurve which, as the saying goes, can make one do very strange, and in the Bluebells' case, occasionally very dumb things. Everybody has been impressed with the band's recent number one but think twice before you try to touch songwriter and frontman Bobby for a tenner in the pub.

"It seems that when Bobby wrote it many, many moons ago he was courting one Siobhan Fahey and in a lovestruck moment signed over the publishing rights to her despite her allegedly minimal input. So when you hear reports of Shuv being delighted for her old beau's success take it with an EEC mountain's worth of salt."

On the back of the song's renewed success, London Records also quickly compiled a Bluebells *Singles Collection* album, which entered the chart on April 17 and climbed to number 27 during a five-week stay.

More than 15 years since playing on the original Bluebells session, Bobby Valentino launched an action against Hodgens in 1999, claiming infringement of copyright over the violin part, which Valentino (listed as claimant under the name Robert Beckingham), was now claiming he also wrote. In the time between recording his contribution, Valentino had continued his career as a session musician, playing for artists such as Haysi Fantayzee, The Christians and The Style Council, in addition to touring with the likes of Bob Dylan and Tom Petty.

There were five other defendants, in addition to Hodgens, facing Valentino's action – Siobhan Maire Stewart (Siobhan Fahey, who had subsequently married Eurythmic Dave Stewart), Universal/Anxious Music, Clive Banks Music, Universal Music Publishing, and London Records 90. Under a legal order issued in January 2000, however, the action against them was stayed pending the outcome of Beckingham v Hodgens.

Hodgens denied Valentino's claims of copyright infringement and, once again, professional musicians were all set to go to court to sort out who had contributed what to a song and which parts of a song justified a composing credit and a share of any subsequent royalties.

The action began in June 2002 before Christopher Floyd QC, sitting as a Deputy High Court Judge. Hodgens maintained that Valentino had merely followed instructions in the studio to play the violin part Hodgens had written with Fahey in a London flat in 1982. In his evidence, Valentino stated that he in fact wrote the violin part during his time as a session musician with The Bluebells. He said he took his instructions from the producer, Colin Fairley, who asked him to perform something "jiggy" to fill the gaps in the song, in addition to providing background violin and a solo.

To emphasise his claim, Valentino gave a live performance in the Chancery Division of the High Court – using violin and acoustic guitar – of the four-bar section in 'Young At Heart' that was repeated three times during the song. In his evidence, Hodgens claimed that when he composed the song, "I wrote it on the guitar and there was a motif on the introduction, which is being called the 'violin part' in these proceedings, which I wrote at the time I wrote the song."

The judge, however, pointed out that when Hodgens first performed the song with The Bluebells in 1983, they played it in a Northern Soul style without Hodgens' introduction, which also did not appear on a taped demo played to Bananarama. Hodgens told the court that he had made a video of himself performing the original introduction and it was his gut feeling that it would always be played by a fiddle.

Kenneth McCluskey told the court that the first time he heard the riff was a couple of days before the recording session, while his brother, David, said he didn't think he had heard it until the day of the recording.

Evidence was also given of an earlier recording session at the Highland Studios, Inverness, in November 1983. Hodgens claimed that at those sessions he "wanted the introduction line to be on a fiddle and to play a very simple part which reflected what I had come up with when I wrote the song originally". He added that he consciously decided not to play the fiddle part on the guitar at that time.

Also given in evidence was a witness statement from Roger Ames, who was head of London Records at the time the song was recorded and had been present at the sessions in Scotland. When counsel for Valentino applied for an order calling Ames to court in order to be cross-examined, it was agreed that he would appear by video link from America, where he was employed at the time as Chief Executive Officer of Warner Music. This plan was further compromised when the court heard that Ames was too busy to even give evidence by video, but an earlier statement he had given to a solicitor was allowed.

In this statement, Ames – who is today a senior executive at EMI Music – was asked whether he recalled hearing the violin riff at the sessions in Scotland. He said, "When the song was played back to me in the studio no violin part was incorporated on to the track. Instead, the version I recall being played back to me constituted only vocal, guitar, drum and bass parts. No violin part formed part of the track. Moreover, I distinctly recall that the melody, the part which was subsequently played on the violin in the final version of the song, was played on the guitar."

This evidence failed to impress Judge Floyd, who told the court that he had no hesitation in rejecting Ames' account as being inconsistent with other oral evidence given about the backing tracks laid down in

Scotland. "Whether Mr. Ames was simply mistaken or deliberately setting out to mislead the court is something that I cannot decide in his
absence. What is clear is that it would be entirely unfair to the claimant
to place any weight whatsoever on Mr. Ames' account of events."

The judge was also unconvinced about the evidence given by the
McCluskey brothers as to events at Red Bus studios. "Whilst I do not for
one moment think that they were setting out to mislead the court, I cannot place much weight on their belief, 18 years later, that it was Mr.
Hodgens who came up with the violin part on the day. It would have
been hard to distinguish between Mr. Hodgens indicating the sort of
thing he wanted and Mr. Valentino coming up with the riff, and the
more explicit instructions which are the subject of Mr. Hodgens'
account."

In court, Valentino accepted that he had, from 1984 onwards,
allowed The Bluebells to assume that he was not intending to make any
claim for a share of royalties in the song, nor did he suggest that he was
"a joint author". However, counsel for the session player stressed that
from that time, by virtue of Valentino signing a consent form, an
"implied gratuitous" licence existed allowing Hodgens to exploit the
copyright of the song.

However, it was claimed that in March 1993, at the time of the reissued single's success, Valentino gave Hodgens notice of his intention to
revoke the licence and make a claim as co-composer of the song.
Hodgens denied this suggestion, claiming that it was not until
November 1997 that Valentino first indicated he was intending to make
a claim as co-author and for royalties. There was a further suggestion
that the two musicians had met at the *Top Of The Pops* studio in 1993,
where the song was discussed, and Hodgens had told Valentino that he
would "see him all right".

The court then heard evidence that Hodgens repeated this assurance
to Valentino's then girlfriend at dinner after a *Top Of The Pops* appearance. When asked later about the assurance he had given, Hodgens had
replied that he had not yet received any royalties.

Valentino's response to this offer was to say to Hodgens that if nothing was forthcoming, he would turn to the law for satisfaction.
"Although I had not taken any action before, I would 'go to law' this

time," the violinist told the court. "I was not prepared to let him continue to make money for a second time out of something that I had written."

After this exchange, there was virtually no contact between the claimant and the defendant other than a number of telephone calls from Valentino to Hodgens, which apparently went unanswered. However, in November 1997, the two musicians did speak on the phone, and Valentino made clear his intention to claim a credit and royalties on the basis of the contribution he had made to the song. Formal documents were then issued by the violinist in February 1999.

Counsel for Hodgens said that Valentino's claim should not be recognised, pointing out that it was made after a delay of at least nine years (March 1993) or at worst almost 14 years (November 1997) depending on whose account one believed, and because Valentino had indicated that he would not make a claim in 1984.

There was a further challenge as to exactly what was said between the pair in both 1993 and 1997, with Hodgens' counsel claiming that it was never sufficient to amount to a revoking of the "implied" licence. There was also a suggestion that Valentino's 1993 claim was a case of him "jumping on the bandwagon", and that it would affect Hodgens' professional reputation. There was a further assertion that had Valentino made clear his claim to joint authorship in 1984, it would have allowed his violin part to have been removed from the recording of 'Young At Heart' in order to head off any potential dispute.

Again, Judge Floyd was unconvinced with the defendant's argument, and pointed out that there would have been little time between the recording and the release of the record to make the change. "I doubt whether, in fact, had Mr. Valentino asserted his rights at the time, the group would have changed the violin part on the recording," he said.

At the end of the hearing, the judge was left to decide whether Valentino had in fact composed the violin part and, if he had, whether he should be considered a joint composer of the song and therefore entitled to a joint credit and a share of the royalties.

Giving his judgement on July 2, 2002, the judge announced, "I have not found the process of resolving this conflict easy. I believe it is made difficult because both the principal participants have to some extent exaggerated their evidence, making it more difficult to decide between them. I have explained that I reject some of Mr. Hodgens' evidence about how he composed the riff in 1982. I also feel compelled to reject Mr. Valentino's evidence that somebody other than Colin Fairley had any real discussion with him at the recording session. The critical question is this: where did the violin part come from?"

Announcing that he was finding in favour of Valentino, the judge said, "In the end I have come to the conclusion that Mr. Valentino's is the more probable account. I am satisfied that Mr. Hodgens gave Mr. Valentino an idea of the sort of thing he wanted, by indicating the country style, the underlying chords and the rhythm. That, however, does not mean that Mr. Hodgens was the author of the violin part...

"Having heard the piece played and reflected on the evidence given, I conclude that the violin part does make a significant and original contribution of the right kind of skill and labour to The Bluebells' version of the song. Thus Mr. Valentino is a joint author of the copyright in that work."

"I'm absolutely delighted with the outcome," Valentino gushed to the waiting media. "It is probably fair to say this is my biggest ever payday."

Valentino's lawyers announced, "This case highlighted the plight of session musicians, whose creative contribution to the songs they perform is rarely recognised."

The musician and professional Clark Gable look-alike also mentioned the courtroom performance of his violin solo. "The court was the oddest venue I've played in but I thoroughly enjoyed it – the acoustics weren't bad."

With the media putting estimates of his potential earnings in the region of £100,000, Valentino's legal team readied themselves to search through record company sales figures in order to draw up a claim for royalties.

A week after the hearing, the defence lawyers announced their intention to appeal. The appeal was launched in February, 2003, but Hodgens was left with limited options. With the original judge finding that the three requirements for joint authorship had been satisfied – there was collaboration in the creation of a new musical work, a "significant and original" contribution from each author, and each author's

211

contribution must not be separate – Hodgens had only two main grounds for his appeal.

Firstly, he prepared an argument that a fourth requirement for joint authorship should be introduced, saying that there had to be a joint intention to create a joint work. Secondly, he said the judge was wrong to have allowed Valentino to lay claim after such a long delay.

The hearing came before Lord Justices Ward, Laws and Parker in the Court of Appeal on February 19, 2003. Handing down the court's judgement, Lord Justice Jonathan Parker said there was no basis to challenge Judge Floyd's finding – that what Valentino said to Hodgens in March 1993 was sufficient to revoke the implied licence.

He added that the claim (no evidence was allowed in the original hearing to establish the point, as it was deemed too late) that Hodgens had spent the royalties he received pre-1993 had no bearing on the issue, as Valentino's claim was only concerned with future royalties post-1993.

Dealing with the question of the time-lapse between the original recording and the successful re-release in 1993, when Valentino first made clear his intention to revoke his licence, the appeal judges were again in agreement and again came down on the side of the violinist.

"I see no reason," said Lord Justice Parker, "why Mr. Valentino should not be entitled to say at that stage, 'I have let you have free use of my composition until now. But this new success is different and I claim my share of it'. I believe that Mr. Hodgens recognised this in 1993, and his statements to Mr. Valentino and his then girlfriend were a recognition by him of the fairness of such an approach."

The judges also dealt with the issue of Hodgens, during the time when Valentino made no claims as a joint composer, giving warranties to music publishers and other interested parties as to his ownership of 'Young At Heart', and giving them indemnity against any third-party claims.

"I remain wholly at a loss to understand in what respect it could be alleged that Mr. Hodgens has suffered detriment in this respect by reason of Mr. Valentino's claim to a share of future royalties," was Lord Justice Parker's summary.

Finally, the Appeal Court judges ruled that there was no need to add a fourth requirement to establish joint authorship. Lord Justice Parker confirmed that the existing wording required for a "work of joint authorship" was that the authors should have collaborated and their contributions should not be separate.

Not only did Hodgens' case end there but he was also refused a further application to appeal and ordered to pay costs, including an interim payment on account of £8,000. However, no reports have ever been published giving details of the final financial settlement in Valentino's favour regarding royalties earned since 1993.

In music industry legal circles, the outcome of the case caused some surprise. The reason for the concern was Mr. Justice Floyd's decision to overlook the time issues – the long delay from the original recording to the claim for royalties and a composer's credit – which, in normal circumstances, would have been a successful argument in Hodgens' favour.

Action against the five other defendants originally named in Valentino's lawsuit was further stayed by a second order in August 2001. It seems likely that the proposed claim against them was abandoned following the outcome of both the 2002 hearing and 2003 appeal.

Continuing life after The Bluebells, Hodgens, whose credits as a producer include Texas, Eurythmics and Sinead O'Connor, most recently formed The Poems in his native Glasgow. Their debut album, *Young Americans,* was issued in 2006.

Meanwhile, Valentino joined Los Pistoleros alongside pedal steel guitar legend B.J. Cole. He was featured violinist and vocalist on their two albums and regular live tours.

Ironically, the falling out between Valentino and Hodgens was in part reflected in the Volkswagon TV commercial: a smartly dressed young woman leaves a large official building, being congratulated by friends and family and showered with flower petals. She then gets behind the wheel of her new VW Golf, drops her wedding ring into the ashtray and drives off with a "Just Divorced" sign hanging from the back of the car.

Chapter 21

JIMI HENDRIX

His death started a long-running family feud

Between 1966 and 1970, Jimi Hendrix's legacy was a collection of groundbreaking and often breathtaking recordings and live performances, which have served to carry the American rock star's name forward for over three decades.

On the other hand, the gift the guitarist left to his surviving family members was an altogether more complicated affair. It was not helped by the fact that he died intestate, which resulted in nearly 15 years of legal battles involving Hendrix's father, his half-brother and his stepsister.

For a variety of reasons, Hendrix's estate was administered under New York State law of intestate succession. Jimi's father, Al Hendrix, who worked as a gardener and had no experience of dealing with serious amounts of money, inherited the entire estate – and all the squabbling and infighting that was to go with it.

Hendrix first rose to prominence when he was brought over to London from New York in September 1966 by Chas Chandler, bass player with the hit-making British group The Animals, who had just split up. Linking with bass player Noel Redding and drummer Mitch Mitchell, the guitar virtuoso created The Jimi Hendrix Experience.

In 1967, after three successful UK singles, the Experience signed a record-breaking $1 million, five-year deal for America with Warner Bros. Records, which included the highest advance – $50,000 – in the label's history. Hendrix's performances at the 1967 Monterey Pop Festival and at Woodstock and the Isle of Wight festivals in 1969 and '70 respectively, are now part of rock legend.

Burning guitars, allegations of drug use, stage walkouts and a final, desultory performance at a German festival invaded by feral bikers made Hendrix a controversial, occasionally unreliable, but always successful rock star. He took the highest fee – $125,000 – of all the acts at Woodstock.

But almost exactly four years after the Seattle-born musician arrived in Britain, Hendrix was declared dead on September 18, 1970, just hours after jamming on stage with former Animals singer Eric Burdon at Ronnie Scott's Jazz Club in London's Soho. An open verdict was recorded after it was decided that Hendrix had died as a result of inhalation of vomit due to barbiturate intoxication. The star's body was flown home and his burial took place in Renton, Washington in October, a month before 'Voodoo Chile' became Hendrix's only British chart-topping single.

A posthumous collection of recordings, *The Cry Of Love*, reached the top three on both sides of the Atlantic in early 1971, when Hendrix was also voted the second greatest guitarist ever (behind Eric Clapton) in a *New Musical Express* poll. And the classic 1968 Jimi Hendrix Experience double album, *Electric Ladyland*, finished sixth in a 1974 *NME* writers' poll of the 99 best-ever rock albums.

Over 20 Jimi Hendrix compilations and collections of unreleased material entered the UK album chart between late 1971 and 2006. Indeed, two decades after his death, the man who made just three studio albums during his lifetime was credited with a further 300 different titles.

Things became complicated for Hendrix senior in 1973 when Mike Jeffrey, who had initially co-managed Hendrix with Chandler but became his sole manager by the time of his death, died in a plane crash after a two-year dispute with Al Hendrix over his son's assets. The keys to the secrets of Hendrix's somewhat Byzantine business empire were lost with him.

Although there was a so-called "final settlement", Jeffrey's death confused the issue, and Al Hendrix appointed a lawyer named Leo Branton to take control of his son's legacy. In partnership with producer Alan Douglas, Branton effectively controlled the Hendrix estate, paying Hendrix Snr. an annual stipend of $50,000, plus occasional lump sums, for the next 20 years.

However, in 1993, Al Hendrix began to reconsider the long-standing arrangement. He became aware of Douglas' negotiations to sell the US rights to his son's catalogue to a major record company. While Al claimed he had never agreed to sell ownership of the rights, and had only signed licensing deals, the catalogue was eventually sold to MCA.

On April 16, Al Hendrix finally filed a lawsuit against Branton, Douglas and what were termed as various US and overseas corporations that had profited from sales of Hendrix-related material. The suit alleged fraud and malpractice and covered what was described as more than 20 years of "abuse of trust, misrepresentation, mismanagement, unjust enrichment and self-dealing".

This action came two weeks after Branton had filed a suit alleging that statements made by Al Hendrix were libelous and slanderous.

At that time, as well as Hendrix's released masters, the estate included recordings of concerts, studio and live improvisations, shares in Bella Godiva – the New York publishing company set up during the guitarist's lifetime to administer the rights to his compositions – copyrights, publicity rights, exploitation rights, photographs, films, writings and personal property.

Al's lawsuit was funded by a $1.6 million loan from Seattle billionaire businessman Paul Allen, a co-founder with Bill Gates of Microsoft and a huge Jimi Hendrix fan. The legal battle ran for over two years but, two months before an official trial date in August 1995, a settlement was reached.

Under the terms of the deal, Branton and Douglas gave up any future rights to the estate and transferred ownership of all Hendrix material to his father and other family members. While no details of the arrangements were disclosed by the court, there were reports that Al Hendrix paid the two defendants close to $9 million to get back what he had originally inherited when his son died in 1970.

216

Earlier, in May 1995, Al Hendrix had regained ownership and control of his son's musical copyrights and legacy as a result of an agreement with MCA. Two months later – with debts of around $25 million from the settlements with Branton, Douglas and MCA – Al set up Experience Hendrix LLC as the new family business. Al took the title of chief executive officer and named his adopted stepdaughter, Janie Hendrix, together with his nephew Bob Hendrix, to run the company, which was to look after the business generated by his son's estate.

The Hendrix family tree was quite convoluted. Al Hendrix married Lucille Jeter in March 1942. She gave birth to Jimi in November the same year, the couple christening him Johnny Allen Hendrix. Another son, Leon, was born in 1948, although Al Hendrix disputed that he was the father. After divorcing Lucille in 1951 and being granted custody of Jimi and Leon, Al married Ayako Fujita (known as June) in 1966 and legally adopted Janie, one of her five children.

With Jimi's natural mother already dead, after his son's death, Al wrote and re-wrote a number of wills during the following three decades. In January 1993, he signed a will that named his wife June, son Leon and stepdaughter Janie, plus her children, as principal beneficiaries. A year later, in a second will, he agreed to leave 38% of his estate to June, the same amount to Janie and 24% to Leon. In November 1996, Al executed a third will, which this time recognised the formation of Experience Hendrix, plus its related companies, and the birth of his new daughter, Corvina Pritchett.

By February 1997, he was busy discussing an estate plan, which resulted in him transferring his 49.4% interest in Experience Hendrix and the associated Authentic Hendrix into a newly formed limited company called Bodacious Hendrix. This allowed Al to profit from his son's legacy during his own lifetime.

A month later, irrevocable trusts were established for Janie, her cousin Robert and other beneficiaries of an earlier marital trust, while Hendrix Snr moved his entire interest in Bodacious to these trusts, which held Janie and Robert as trustees and co-trustees.

By April, Al had instigated a further change to his will. He bequeathed all of his stock in his own wholly owned company, Axis, to Janie, increased Pritchett's share to 10%... and left Leon Hendrix with a single gold record. In the few weeks between March and April, Janie's share of the estate had increased to 47.2%, Robert's had gone up to 17.7%, while Leon's inheritance had dropped from 24% to nothing but a souvenir disc.

Al's concerns stemmed from the lifestyles, criminal records and drug history of Leon and members of his family. In early 1997, Leon had agreed to undergo an inpatient drug treatment programme, which he failed to complete.

In July 1998, Al transferred his remaining interests in Experience Hendrix and Authentic Hendrix to the living trust he had set up in 1997 and, in September 2001, during a continuing long illness, he executed durable power of attorney and named Janie as his attorney in fact. Just over six months later, in April 2002, Al Hendrix died at the age of 82. That same day, Leon's lawyers sent a letter to his late father's representatives threatening legal action relating to the estate and personal property of Hendrix Snr., which was now estimated to be worth around $80 million.

Letters turned to action four months later when Leon filed lawsuits against Janie and the estate, arguing that the will and the living trust were invalid because Al had signed them under undue influence from Janie, the adopted daughter.

In addition to challenging the will and the living trust – alleging fraud, lack of capacity, undue influence, mistake and misrepresentation – Leon also filed a tort suit (a breach of legal duty with a liability for damages) against Janie for alleged interference with an inheritance expectancy. Described in reports as a struggling artist and musician, Leon claimed, "It's my legacy and heritage," and described his meagre inheritance as "a single gold record of Janie's choosing, and one of the most meaningless ones".

Janie, who had adopted the name Hendrix after her mother married Al, only met her famous stepbrother on just a few occasions, and was just nine years old when he died. In a war of words before the hearing began, she suggested that Leon's "upsetting behaviour" caused the breakdown in his relationship with her adopted father.

"My dad and I had a wonderful relationship and as far as what he chose to do, give or not give to Leon, my dad had all his wits about him. He did what he wanted to do."

Calling himself "the keeper of the flame", Leon led the action against Janie on behalf of 13 other relatives, including his six children plus cousins and other family members, who alleged that Janie had mismanaged the business of the Jimi Hendrix estate. The lawsuit filed by Leon's children claimed that their grandfather intended to provide for them even if he meant to cut their father out of his will.

Before the court action even commenced, Leon's lawyer, Robert Curran, said the lawsuit aimed to prove that Janie had influenced the redrafting of her stepfather's will "in a way that disinherited Leon and his children and gave Janie total control of his legacy. This is a very, very valuable estate but nobody but she and a very few other family members have benefited. That's not what Leon believes his father wanted".

John Wilson, counsel for Janie, asserted that she had not been involved in the drafting of the final will and there was "overwhelming evidence that the estate plan was the result of Al Hendrix's considered and independent judgement". He added that Leon had been excluded because of "major events in the months before his [Al's] decision that upset him in some way", and concluded by saying, "Janie feels it is her responsibility to defend her father's final wishes."

By the time the trial was set to begin on June 28, 2004, Experience Hendrix LLC had proved to be a lucrative enterprise. According to *Forbes* magazine, the production and sale of Jimi Hendrix memorabilia and recordings in 2003 totalled an impressive £3.8 million.

The case was heard at King County Superior Court in Seattle, Jimi's home town, before Judge Jeffrey Ramsdell. His first task was to deal with a surprise appearance from Joe Hendrix, who claimed to have been sired by Al Hendrix but given up for adoption 50 years earlier. He demanded to be involved in the case and made his own claim to be included in his father's estate.

The judge sent Joe for DNA testing; when it came back negative, his claim was dismissed. He also ordered Leon to undergo DNA testing, but ruled that the result would have no bearing on the case as Leon was legally Al's son under Washington state law. He was also Jimi's brother, as Lucille Hendrix had given birth to both boys.

The opening statements in the hearing covered allegations by Leon's counsel, Robert Curran, that Janie was guilty of excessive spending.

"This is about greed. Janie has lived a very, very good life. She travels the world first class. Her family goes with her. They get picked up in limos. They stay in first-class hotels."

Curran suggested that Janie had plotted for many years to have Leon disinherited.

There were further accusations that Janie and Robert had refused pleas for financial help from other family members and run up monthly credit card debts of $40,000. "Janie has treated Experience Hendrix as an ATM," said David Osgood, attorney for seven of the claimants contesting Janie's position as head of the trusts. Osgood claimed that Janie had spent over $1 million on herself, including $60,000 from the company for home improvements, $40,000 on rental property and a further $400,000 in personal loans.

"Al Hendrix thought she would be the person who would be responsible for taking care of his family and she got the lion's share in exchange," Osgood added. "But she has shown extreme disregard for the welfare of the family. This is not what Al wanted. He intended for those trusts to benefit the people he had taken care of during his life.

Osgood asked the court, "I want Janie's credit card taken away. They will tell you that the income over the past five years earned them $47 million, but what they won't tell you is that they spent $48 million, which is a huge operating loss."

John Wilson explained that his client had repaid some of the expenses referred to, and that her father gave her the controlling interest in Jimi Hendrix's estate because of her commitment to the family legacy and because he trusted her after she helped him regain the rights. Referring to Leon and his fellow plaintiffs, Wilson stated, "Their complaints are with Al. They may think there were bad decisions but they were made by Al. The bottom line is that Al Hendrix made it very clear that he did not want Leon involved."

Arguing that Janie had been an excellent manager of the estate, Wilson said, "Al Hendrix wanted to give the legacy to Janie for one purpose – to keep the legacy alive. She started from scratch with $26 million in debt, while everyone was waiting on the sidelines for her and her husband to fail. But they have been extremely successful."

In early July, during the second week of the trial, Diane Hendrix-

Teitel, a first cousin of the deceased rock star and now a Seattle minister, confirmed that the rock star barely knew his stepsister. "Jimi didn't know Janie back then, she was just a little girl."

Osgood suggested that Janie only met Jimi three or four times. "The longest she ever spent with him was when she tagged along with Leon to a concert when she was nine years old."

Hendrix-Teitel said that Jimi would have wanted Leon to have part of the legacy. "He was a giver, never selfish. He loved us all and he certainly loved Leon. He would have wanted him to have so much."

She suggested that the trial might allow Janie to see the truth in her wrongdoing. "She was blessed that she was adopted into a family that some people long for in life. She has the chance to make things right. I don't think you really know a person until they are given something like this."

C. Barry Ward, the attorney who represented Lisa Marie Presley in a court case over her father's legacy, took the witness stand to suggest that estates brought out the worst in people. "Greed gets in the way of family settlements. If everyone comes to an agreement in this Hendrix case, provided the court will agree, everyone could be happy."

Ward's idealistic view was seized upon by Wilson, who suggested that the ongoing success of the late guitarist's legacy owed something to Janie. Explaining to the court that Jimi Hendrix's legacy was ranked at number five in the all-time highest-grossing revenues for recording artists, behind Elvis Presley, John Lennon, George Harrison and Bob Marley, Wilson claimed, "What they [Janie and her husband] did as far as attaining income from securing new tapes not only helped current revenues, but will show in future revenues as well."

This prompted Osgood to claim that Janie had nothing to do with artistic creativity. "Jimi's fan base is one thing – it's about his genius as guitarist, musician and performer. All the work needed to solidify the fan base was accomplished in 1970 when he was alive, creating and creative. Nothing magical about Janie Hendrix adds to that legacy."

Called as the last witness in the plaintiffs' case, Leon told the court of his gradual estrangement from the Hendrix family. "We started being invited less and less, and then we were invited only at Thanksgiving and [my father's] birthday. And then we were invited but separated from everyone, and then we were not invited."

Leon revealed that it was a disagreement over the family's restored rights to Jimi's music that precipitated the rift. He said he thought he was doing what his father wanted when he signed away his early rights to Jimi's music. The court heard that, in wills drawn up in 1973, 1979 and 1987, Al included a bequest to Leon and Janie of a significant portion of his residuary estate (the amount left after charges and debts), which included a share in Jimi's music. While Leon signed over his copyright interests to Al's lawyer, Branton, sometime in 1992 for $300,000 in cash and a further $700,000 in trust for his children, Janie refused the offer.

Even though it was alleged that his decision went against Al's wishes, Leon claimed that he and his father shared a warm relationship. "He didn't care about all that. We'd still get together and gamble, shoot pool, hustle pool and play golf together," said Leon, who admitted that cocaine and alcohol addictions were responsible for much of his irresponsible behaviour.

At this point, Osgood revealed that Al was also an alcoholic and had sympathised with his son's problems. "He's not the only one who had addictions and Al never held it against anyone," the lawyer claimed.

In presenting Janie's case, Wilson said it was Leon's "hapless irresponsibility" that led to his father cutting him out of the will. Asked if he used his own money, given to him as an allowance by his father, to pay overdue property taxes, Leon admitted, "Janie was supposed to pay the taxes."

The man who oversaw Al's final estate plan was lawyer George Steers from Stoel Rives, who was retained by Experience Hendrix, Al and Janie in 1996. Steers told the judge that he conversed at length with Al to determine his wishes for estate planning, and he observed nothing that indicated Al was being pressured by others. He also stated that Al was concerned about ensuring that the family – and not creditors, companies or the government – benefited, and the estate plan he drafted was consistent with that wish.

At the same time as Leon was contesting his father's will, he and other family members continued with their claim that Janie and Robert were guilty of mismanagement of the estate and the trust funds. In evidence, Robert said that he did not understand his obligations as a trustee. He said that he asked Stoel Rives for guidance and was given 20 to 30 pages of notes on responsibilities. He accepted that in order to be a trustee "you need to know what you are doing, and we didn't".

Near the end of the trial, in late August, Janie Hendrix took the stand to tell the court that her job in the family home was to clean windows, carpets, laundry and prep for dinner. "That was my job. I had to do everything for my parents," she said, before denying ever attempting to influence her father over his will or to have Leon disinherited.

Janie outlined the work she had done in getting back the legal rights to Jimi's music after they had been taken from Al by an attorney, saying she read legal documents for as long as 10 hours a day over a two-year period. Answering questions about Leon's paternity and the suggestion that Al was not his biological father, she said it did not matter to her father. "Just because you didn't have the same blood doesn't mean he loved you any less."

She also denied allegations that she had claimed to be Al's biological child, and had produced a birth certificate and suggested to a biographer that he ask Al about Leon's real father.

On the question of her role as a trustee, Janie told the judge that she relied on accountants to advise her about personal charges, and was only made aware of any impropriety when she received differing advice from the accountants hired in 2001 to act for Experience Hendrix. She claimed that the reason no money was disbursed to the beneficiaries of the trust funds was because they were acting on Al's will that no money should go out until the estate was debt-free.

On September 24, 2004, nearly a month after the trial ended, Judge Ramsdell gave his ruling in a 35-page document. He decided that Janie had not unlawfully coerced her father into denying Leon, his children and other family members a place in the estate. Upholding Al's final will, the judge said, "Janie was the family member Al trusted the most."

He concluded, "Janie Hendrix did not want Leon involved in the family business. She did not like Leon and she disapproved of his lifestyle. She warned Al that if Leon was involved in the family business, he would cause trouble. She also raised concerns that if Leon had an interest in the business, that interest could be lost to an outsider."

The judge also pointed out that Leon's effort to sell his share of the rights to Jimi Hendrix's music, his threats to extort money from his father and his failure to get drug and alcohol treatment were among the reasons why Al might have legitimately wanted to cut him out of the will.

"Unfortunately for Leon, during the time that Al was considering these concerns and arguments, Leon embarked on a self-destructive journey to prove Janie right." The judge concluded that, while not healthy, Al appeared to know exactly what he was doing when he signed the 1998 will and estate plan.

However, other members of the extended Hendrix family received some satisfaction when the judge ruled that Janie and Robert Hendrix should be removed as trustees of the Diane Hendrix-Teitel Trust, the Linda Jinka Trust (Linda was another of Ayako Fujita's daughters) and the Hatcher Family Trust.

While Janie and Robert were left in control of the Hendrix companies, including Experience Hendrix, Judge Ramsdell concluded, "They appear to have been relying on the mantra 'Experience Hendrix must be debt-free' to justify their failure to exercise any discretion over distributions to the funds. This abdication of their duty as trustees is not justified by any reference to any directive from Al Hendrix." Despite the "financial improprieties that had occurred over the years, Experience Hendrix is currently far more debt-free that it was in 1999, yet no distributions have been made or even considered".

Announcing that the court would decide how payments should be made to these family members, the judge ordered Janie and Robert to pay court costs of the beneficiaries named in the three trusts. While refusing the removal of Janie as the personal representative of Al Hendrix's will, Judge Ramsdell retained jurisdiction to revisit the issue "should future circumstances warrant reconsideration". He also ordered both Janie and Robert to continue to co-operate in identifying personal expenses and loans that should be repaid to Experience Hendrix.

At the end of the judgement, Janie told reporters, "The judge has upheld my dad's will and the way it was written. I had a great partnership with my dad and now it's time to heal."

While aware the judge "recognised that Janie and Robert breached their duties", Osgood still questioned their ability to run the Hendrix companies. "Are they fit to run this company? Our position still is no, they are not fit."

Fifty-six-year-old Leon, whose $3 million legal challenge was reportedly funded by wealthy developer Craig Dieffenbach, immediately announced his intention to proceed with a civil suit accusing Janie of coercing Al into disinheriting him.

A spectator for most of the trial, Hendrix biographer Charles R. Cross said afterwards, "The sad legacy of Jimi Hendrix is that ever since his first record came out, people have been fighting over the money."

Even in death, the musician was seemingly a pawn in a game between family members. To the horror of Hendrix fans worldwide, in 2002, Janie moved his casket to a new resting place next to his father and the stepmother he hardly knew. At the same time, his birth mother continues to lie in an unmarked welfare grave in the same cemetery; nobody has paid the £1,000 it would cost for a headstone.

In 2006, Leon's appeal was heard by Judges Joseph Coleman, Ann Schindler and Ronald Cox in the Court of Appeals of the State of Washington. They upheld the original ruling and again denied Jimi's brother a portion of the rock star's fortune. The only bit of good news for Leon was that three judges denied Janie's request for attorney fees, deciding to "decline to award fees here because although we did not find Leon's arguments persuasive, we do not find his appeal to be devoid of merit".

Undeterred, Leon continued in his fight for a share of his father's will and took the case to the Washington Supreme Court in June 2007, asking them to review the original Superior Court decision. However, for the third time in just under three years, Leon was unsuccessful. The Supreme Court refused his request, finally bringing the curtain down on a family tale of drugs, greed, adultery and illegitimacy.

While the long-winded dispute between Leon and Janie over their father's will and Hendrix's inheritance was finally over, there were still other issues to keep them occupied, including a speciality vodka called Hendrix Electric. The drink, sold in a purple bottle with an image of Jimi Hendrix on the label, was produced by the Electric Hendrix company, co-owned by Leon and his friend and financial benefactor Dieffenbach.

In March 2007, Experience Hendrix filed a lawsuit in the US District Court in Seattle, claiming that the company owned numerous trademark images of Jimi Hendrix. The suit alleged that Electric Hendrix had committed trademark infringement and false advertising, and also described the use of Hendrix's likeness to promote alcohol as "a sick joke".

Three years earlier, in a case that had centered on different US state laws, the US District Court judge had ruled that Janie and her companies did not own the rights to Jimi Hendrix's name and likeness. In New York, where Hendrix's estate was originally administered in the months after his death, publicity rights could not at that time be passed down, which denied Janie ownership of the rights. In the state of Washington, however, where Experience Hendrix was located, the law was different, and stood in her favour.

However, the judge followed the New York ruling and found that Experience Hendrix did not own publicity rights to Jimi's image. Janie appealed against this decision to the Ninth US Circuit Court of Appeals, while also filing a new action against Electric Hendrix. She had also gone to arbitration in 2000 and won an intellectual property hearing over ownership of the jimihendrix.com Internet address, which had been established by an unrelated holder.

Four decades after his death, Jimi Hendrix's flame burns brighter than ever. In 1991, he was honoured with a star on the Hollywood Walk of Fame while the following year, Neil Young inducted him into America's Rock 'n' Roll Hall of Fame. In 2003, he took pole position in *Rolling Stone* magazine's list of the 100 Greatest Guitarists Of All Time.

That same year, Experience Hendrix linked up with McFarlane Toys to grant the rights for a Hendrix "action figure" to go alongside its existing range of music icons including The Beatles, Ozzy Osbourne, Alice Cooper, Jim Morrison, Jerry Garcia and Janis Joplin. The Arizona-based toymaker created a six-inch replica of Hendrix from his fabled Woodstock appearance, including trademark white upside-down Stratocaster, red bandana, bell-bottom jeans and white shirt with fringes. This standard version retailed at between $12 and $15, while a second version, complete with a stage modelled on Hendrix's set-up at Woodstock, sold for $20.

However, and most importantly, it's Jimi Hendrix's music that has made the most lasting impact, and sales of albums are still reckoned to exceed three million around the world each year.

Chapter 22

U2

*Fighting over ownership of an "iconic" hat
and a pair of trousers*

In the 30 years since they first got together as school friends in Dublin, U2's success can be calculated from albums sales in excess of 120 million and global music awards by the hundreds and while their sell-out concerts are famous for reaching new levels of ambition and excess. From humble beginnings and church hall gigs Bono, the Edge, Larry Mullen and Adam Clayton have been the biggest rock 'n' roll stars on the planet for the past two decades, ever since their fifth album, *The Joshua Tree*, topped the charts in both the US and the UK. In 1987, it became the fastest-selling album in British pop history.

At the same time as they were just about getting their first taste of true global superstardom, a young lady named Lola Cashman joined the 150-strong U2 entourage in the months leading up to the release of *The Joshua Tree*. Originally employed to replace an employee on maternity leave, Cashman was hired through an agency to be the band's stylist, and stayed on through the Rattle And Hum tour and album until late 1988.

Soon after leaving U2, she joined George Michael as the stylist on his

1988 Faith tour where, she observed, she was working with a very different family – "one that was warm and intimate". She later travelled to Australia to spend some time on a cattle station before writing a controversial tour book, *Inside The Zoo With U2: My Life With The World's Biggest Rock Band*.

Some 16 years on, the band worth an estimated £400 million that Cashman helped glam-up and turn out on tour every night, began legal proceedings for the return of a sweatshirt, a hat, a pair of trousers, costume earrings and a couple of souvenir mugs – all worth an estimated £3,500.

In December 2004, as their album *How To Dismantle An Atomic Bomb* sat at the top of the charts in over 30 countries, U2 lodged a case in Dublin's Circuit Court seeking the return of the goods from their former stylist, who had offered them for sale through the London auctioneer Christie's.

Having probably not helped her cause by writing a less than flattering portrayal of U2, Cashman claimed all the items were given to her by the band, who had even signed some of the items for her. Upon hearing that the band were disputing ownership, and after being contacted by Christie's for authentication, Cashman said, "I worked with the boys for two years and was very close to them, particularly Bono. He helps all these charities and is seen as caring and generous, but then he is getting funny about me selling some old mugs, for goodness sake."

The band said nothing. Christie's also chose not to comment, but retained the items in dispute while the question of ownership was resolved in the courts. Six months later, fresh from performing in front of 250,000 people in Dublin's Croke Park on June 27, 2005, U2 appeared at the Four Courts, where the hearing was set to open the next day.

With all four members named as plaintiffs, the first day's events saw Circuit Court President Mr. Justice Matthew Deery appointed as judge, with Paul Sreenan representing U2 and Hugh Hartnett as counsel for Cashman, who had also begun her own libel proceedings against the band in London in 2002. In addition to the items offered to Christie's, the band were also looking to get back around 200 Polaroid photos taken during the group's tours, but dropped their claim for the return of a pair of autographed boots when drummer Mullen acknowledged he had probably given them to Cashman.

Bono (listed in court under his real name, Paul Hewson) explained U2's actions in turning to the law to recover the memorabilia. "You may have wealth and power but when someone is trying to push us around, blackmail us and threaten us with books, at a certain point you have to say, 'Stop right there'." The singer described Cashman's claim that the items were gifts from the band as ridiculous. "They sound like trivial items, they're not really. They are important items to the group and we take them seriously."

Accepting that U2 memorabilia was occasionally sold for charity, Bono said the rest of the band already felt he had put up for auction too many pairs of his trademark sunglasses. Describing the Stetson hat he wore on the *Rattle And Hum* album cover as iconic, Bono commented, "It would be like the Edge giving one of his guitars away. It is not something which will happen", adding that if he had given the hat to Cashman everyone in the wardrobe department would have known. "And then I would have been in trouble with the band as usual."

It also transpired that while other members of the U2 crew had had some personal difficulties with the defendant, Bono had supported her because she had a good eye as a stylist. When negotiations over a new contract dragged on, however, the band let her go because they considered her demands excessive.

On behalf of Cashman, Hartnett suggested to Bono that the whole affair was simply a legal stunt, and that the band had instigated proceedings in the Irish courts to obtain a stay against the defamation proceedings begun by Cashman in London's High Court.

"How on earth can it be a legal stunt to protect your reputation?" asked the band's singer, who conceded that he might have told Cashman that she could have the earrings and sweatshirt. He also accepted that the defendant had bought many wardrobe items for the band to use on tour, and that she had also designed trousers for him in a variety of different sizes because of his changing weight.

However, he denied the suggestion that he had gifted the items to Cashman in a moment of "exhilaration and giddiness" during a period of "great excitement and extraordinary happiness" on the last night of the hugely successful Joshua Tree tour. Asked what he meant when he described the Stetson hat as iconic, Bono explained that the band was aiming for a certain status. "You attempt as a songwriter to place your work, not just on the road, not just in people's cars and homes but into the popular consciousness. It's what songwriters do – we want our songs to be remembered as part of an era."

When Hartnett suggested that there was less awareness of the band's iconic status in 1987 than in the following 10 years, the group's vocalist admitted, "Oh no, we had delusions of grandeur from the very beginning."

In her opening day's evidence, Cashman told the court that she had been employed by the band and not by the group's management company, which she suggested had "created problems from day one" as they felt she had been getting "too big for her shoes". She also said that Bono had a growing awareness of the audio–visual nature of rock and was keen to change U2's image, which resulted in her being responsible for how the band looked and for purchasing everything relating to their wardrobe.

Explaining how she came to have the various items listed in the plaintiffs' claim, Cashman said that the trousers and sweatshirt were piled on the floor at the end of the Joshua Tree tour and were going to be binned when Bono gifted them to her. "The band came off stage and Bono was running around in his underpants with his hat on," she claimed, saying that she asked him for the Stetson and he gave it to her. "To me it symbolised all I had achieved in my work, working on this amazing tour."

At the end of the two-day trial, Judge Deery took a week to consider his verdict before finding in favour of the plaintiffs. He ordered Cashman to return the items within seven days, plus the 200 photographs that the plaintiffs had asked for outside the items listed in the court action. With neither U2, who were playing a concert in Poland, nor Cashman in court to hear his decision, the judge said that he preferred Bono's testimony. "It seems to me that Ms Cashman's version of events, the giving of the hat, is unlikely to have occurred... the weight of evidence is entirely against the defendant's version of events. Bearing in mind all the evidence, it is highly unlikely that the items were given in this way."

The judge was not convinced by Cashman's claim that the band had brought the case solely to stop the defamation proceedings, but did recognise that the outcome of the hearing would affect that case. "It would seem odd if the group were to make a provision to pursue a claim of this nature if the subject was not of importance to the band."

Ordering the return of the Polaroid photos, Judge Deery was satisfied that they had been taken by Cashman using film purchased by U2, and captured intimate scenes such as band members dressing and undressing. "There was an obligation on Ms Cashman to respect the confidentiality and to respect the dignity of the plaintiffs," he said, as he set July 12, 2005 as the date on which he would decide on the issue of costs.

In a statement after their victory, U2 said, "This case was brought very reluctantly, in the context of a larger dispute which we never invited. The point of principle involved was of much greater significance to us than any item of memorabilia."

While they added their best wishes for Cashman's future, the band claimed they would eventually be able to return the goods to their archives or consider donating them to museums such as America's Rock and Roll Hall of Fame in Cleveland. Over a month after the court's decision, by which time Cashman had won leave to appeal the judge's decision, the former U2 stylist made her first public comments about the case. "Money is not my master, it was never what this was about. I was fighting to protect my reputation, to fight off accusations that I was a thief and a liar."

Despite the court ruling that the trinkets and clothing items were not hers to sell, Cashman remained adamant. "I have always known and will always know in my heart that I was given those items. I have no idea why they are saying otherwise now."

She was not surprised by U2's determination to pursue what many considered to be a petty case. "I know what they are like," she told *The Independent*. "The only reason I decided to sell [the items] was because I was in serious financial difficulty and needed to realise some cash. They were not worth that much."

Admitting to a determined streak, which led her to fight on against one of the wealthiest organisations in rock music, Cashman observed, "Some believed that if Bono was willing to get up in court for this case, then he must have a good reason to do so. But if someone like me, a middle-aged nobody from London, was willing to fly over to Dublin to fight the case, then she has a good reason to do so too."

Cashman's appeal began in October 2006 before Mr. Justice Michael Peart in Dublin's High Court. Dressed in a brown suit with rose-tinted spectacles, Bono confirmed that Cashman's arrival came at an important time for U2, as the band were moving from arenas to playing major outdoor stadium venues.

"It was a very big moment in the band's career. Everything had come right for us. We had a lot of songs on the radio around the world and particularly in the US, where we had a couple of number one singles."

Bono again acknowledged that Cashman had a good eye for detail, as styling was not the band's greatest strength, but added, "It was very clear on almost immediate arrival she wasn't good in dealing with personal relationships, and initially put a lot of people's noses out of place."

The singer added that he had thought of the idea of the Stetson before Cashman arrived on the scene, and that the image was supposed to represent American iconography. "It was always part of my idea of how I wanted to present myself to the world in an iconic sense."

Confirming that part of Cashman's job was to transport the band's wardrobe items, Bono added that it was also important to the band that they kept a record of their memorabilia to either archive or donate. "We thought it would have some importance of the history of the band. We hoped we would be around long enough to be part of that."

It also came out in evidence that Cashman took to wearing the band's clothing during the Joshua Tree tour, which Bono viewed as "funny", "Many people did it. She wore mine and other band members' clothes. It was eccentric but I did not see any harm in it."

Although they did not appear in the original list of items, Bono said that the Polaroid photographs were of particular relevance. "I especially want the photos back. I did not know they were missing." In his view, Cashman's book *Inside The Zoo* was "reprehensible. She worked with us for nine months. Taking advantage of her intimacy with the band for remuneration. I am very annoyed about the book and these items. It is why I am here. The book is an abuse of trust. It is a betrayal of small intimacies".

Bono told the court that the band had bought Polaroid cameras and film for members of their touring party to use backstage during the tours and, in his view, any photos taken on the road were the band's property. In the book, which was published by John Blake in 2003, there were over a dozen photographs taken during U2 tours, many of which featured members of the band. There was no photographic credit anywhere in the book.

Cashman wrote of Bono "feeling uncomfortable about his weight gain", and trousers that "although a size larger than his usual jeans were also fitting rather too snugly". She also wrote of Bono's "vanity still getting the better of him", and a stage meeting with Bruce Springsteen in New Jersey when Bono aired concerns about his height. "Then he turned to me and said earnestly that he had to be taller than Bruce Springsteen," she wrote, adding that when her idea that the singer should wear a pair of her own high heels didn't work out, it was agreed that on meeting Springsteen, Bono would "remain seated, standing only to shake his hand".

In a final reference to working with U2, Cashman wrote that, to her surprise, at the end of the Rattle And Hum tour, the band's manager, Paul McGuiness, asked her to stay on permanently and work solely for Bono and U2. There were no references to the alleged protracted negotiations or the excessive financial demands that Bono had mentioned in the original court hearing.

Bono stated that when the items in question were put up for sale at Christie's by Cashman, the band wrote letters to the London auctioneer making it clear that the memorabilia was their property. He said the letters were sent in an attempt to avoid "a courtroom drama and trying not to go heavy on it", but, according to the singer, Cashman brought defamation proceedings in the UK. He further acknowledged that there was a costs order in the London High Court against Cashman for about £40,000, which she paid off at about £1,000 a month after unsuccessfully opposing an application by the band to have the London case deferred until the end of the proceedings in Ireland.

Reflecting on the seemingly absurd nature of arguing over the ownership of a collection of souvenirs, Bono said, "We have tried to avoid this bizarre situation for many years. She likes this. We don't. It's our stuff, she has it and a lot more besides. We want our stuff back. We want her to stop selling it."

He reiterated to the judge that he had not given Cashman the Stetson on the last night of the Joshua Tree tour. "I knew [because] I was filming. I would remember giving her a gift like this. It is a key piece of staging. I did not gift it to her".

For her part, Cashman told the court that during one concert she was duped into going onstage with a bottle of champagne to toast Bono. Explaining that she felt embarrassed in front of 80,000 fans, she said she "ran onstage and kicked him in his manhood" as the champagne cork popped out and hit him in the face. "The video footage shows Bono saying, 'Lola, I love you, come back'", she said. "I think it's a demonstration of the special relationship Bono and I had."

Questioned by U2's counsel, Sreenan, she admitted approaching notorious publicist Max Clifford. "That's the agency you would go to if you wanted to dish the dirt on somebody," Sreenan stated. Cashman insisted that she needed somebody who was used to dealing with famous personalities as powerful as Bono to defend her side of the story, while denying she was planning to release a new "warts and all" book or that she was working on a film script about the band.

After continuing with her claim that she had been given the items by the band and was therefore free to put them up for sale, the appeal hearing came to an end after three days on October 19, 2006, with a reserved judgement. Nearly a month later, on November 15, Mr. Justice Peart returned to give his decision on the case, which he said boiled down to the credibility of Bono and Cashman.

The judge said he could not be satisfied that, in light of all the evidence, it was more likely that the account given by Cashman was more correct than that given by the band. He added that her evidence lacked credibility and plausibility and that "on the balance of probability" the items of memorabilia were not given to Cashman. Therefore the judge ordered that the hat, earrings, clothing, souvenir mugs, a Christmas decoration, two Polaroid photographs and a photocopy of a handwritten list of U2 songs had to be returned to the band, but that the stylist could keep a pair of black Converse All Star boots that had been given to her by Larry Mullen. He also ordered that Cashman should pay U2 £700 a month to cover the costs of the court action.

While neither U2 nor Cashman were in court to hear the judge's decision, Sreenan confirmed that the band would not be pursuing costs for either the appeal hearing or the earlier circuit court action. From Australia, where they were touring, the band issued a statement saying they were "relieved that this matter has now been concluded and hope that today's outcome brings closure to all issues between the band and Ms Cashman". The proceedings were brought as a "last resort and with great reluctance." The statement finished with "U2 wishes Ms Cashman well in the future".

While the case brought U2 a legal victory, it also earned them a poor press, with accusations of pettiness levelled against Bono in particular. Reports compared his sterling work raising money and awareness for charities around the world with his fight for the return of a hat. Even as the band urged support for the Irish Government's Ireland Aid project in support of developing countries, local politicians were quick to criticise U2's transfer of some of its business empire from the band's corporate base in Dublin to the Netherlands. There they would benefit from better tax laws following the introduction of a £170,000 cap on tax-free incomes in the Irish budget.

One column sarcastically offered the view that: "There are certain things that particularly matter to Bono. Selling records, the plight of Africa and making hat thefts history."

Chapter 23

KIRI TE KANAWA

When the diva decided the show didn't have to go on

Australian rock star John Farnham has been making hits for over 40 years. During that time he has shared the stage with such pop stars as Olivia Newton-John, Tom Jones and Stevie Nicks, but plans for a tour with a classical Dame came unstuck over the issue of ladies' underwear.

A Dagenham-born plumber turned singer, Farnham is in many ways Australia's very own Cliff Richard, in that he is the only local artist to have number one hits in five consecutive decades. He also has a legion of enthusiastic female fans who, as with Tom Jones, have a penchant for throwing their knickers onto the stage during his concert appearances.

After over a decade as a singer, Farnham joined the successful Aussie group Little River Band in the early Eighties before returning to his career as a solo artist, this time under the name John Farnham. He reached a pinnacle in 1986 with the release of the album *Whispering Jack*, which sold over a million copies and was, for a while, the biggest-selling album in Australian pop history.

Farnham was set to play three major outdoor concerts in February 2005 with the great New Zealand Maori soprano Dame Kiri Te Kanawa in Sydney and Melbourne, under the banner "Two Great Voices."

Te Kanawa was already an established international operatic star when she performed at the wedding of the Prince of Wales and Lady Diana Spencer in London's St Paul's Cathedral in 1981, which was seen by an estimated 600 million people. She was created a Dame of the British Empire the following year and continued to perform on the world's leading stages before agreeing to join Farnham for the concerts, which would earn them each a reported A\$200,000 (£82,000) per show plus a share of the profits.

However, somewhere along the way – even as ticket sales for the shows were booming, with corporate tables going for A\$9,500 apiece – negotiations ground to an untimely halt, and ended up in court when Te Kanawa withdrew from the concerts and was sued by the promoters. Leading Edge Events brought suits against the singer, her manager, Nick Grace, and her company, Mittane Limited, (also known as Matani), alleging breach of contract after the singer's company told the promoters that it was "no longer holding the availability for Dame Kiri's services".

In a fax dated March 30, 2004, Mittane (Te Kanawa's service company, incorporated in the Channel Islands) made its reason very clear for effectively pulling out of the shows. "Mittane Limited and related advisors on behalf of our employee Dame Kiri Te Kanawa wish to retain full artistic control of the event – evidence of which has not been forthcoming."

The court case began in Sydney in January 2007, with Justice Patricia Bergin of the New South Wales Supreme Court on the bench. Leading Edge, which claimed that Mittane had agreed to provide Te Kanawa for the concerts, made an additional claim for expenditure incurred.

The judge heard evidence of numerous meetings, e-mails and telephone calls between June 2003 and March 2004, as the various parties had tried to reach a deal. At the same time, Te Kanawa's manager, Nick Grace, and Farnham's manager, Glenn Wheatley, had also been in contact over creative and artistic issues to do with the shows.

Confirming that she had sung with a "pop singer before", Te Kanawa told the court, "I have great respect for Mr Farnham's talent and for his celebrity. He is a very nice person." However, on November 24, 2003, the singer saw a DVD of one of Farnham's concerts that showed his relaxed style and women's underwear being thrown on the stage.

The soprano, who told the court that she preferred to be called Dame Kiri rather than Ms Te Kanawa, adding, "I think a first name would be inappropriate", told the judge, "I was concerned about the knickers or underwear apparel being thrown at him and him collecting it and obviously holding it in his hands as some sort of trophy." She then pondered, "How could I, in my classical form, perform in that way; how could it be controlled? It was something that was disrespectful to me in particular."

She raised these concerns with Leading Edge director Frank Williams late in 2003, and was "very disappointed" when a proposed meeting with Farnham and Wheatley in Auckland, New Zealand in February 2004 was cancelled due to bad weather, which had caused an airport closure in Australia. The court heard that this non-meeting upset the opera diva, who learnt that the airport was not closed and that other people had been able to fly out. She admitted to the court that she was disappointed but denied suggestions that she showed it through bad behaviour towards a waitress. "I am a nice person," she asserted.

Counsel for Leading Edge, Richard Evans, told the court that Grace knew his client had some concerns about performing with Farnham. "On many occasions Kiri told Mr. Grace that she was not committed and had some reservations about co-performing with John Farnham, but those feelings were never relayed to the promoter.

"So the plaintiff was led into error in thinking if someone's pants ended up on the stage, that was not enough to dissuade Dame Kiri from performing with John Farnham."

The court heard Evans claim that the parties had an agreement and that tickets for the concert were selling well. He described Dame Kiri's withdrawal as "capricious", her reasons for withdrawing "spurious", and that it was "unconscionable for Dame Kiri to withdraw her services without reimbursing the plaintiff".

Leading Edge, which was seeking A$600,000 (£240,000) for breach of contract, also claimed it lost £400,000 in profits and £160,000 in organising costs. This included security guards who, said Evans, would ensure "propriety and decorum" at the concerts. While it was not in doubt that Te Kanawa had reservations over sharing the stage with Farnham, the issue to be decided was whether a legally binding contract had been agreed and signed.

While the opera singer had major worries about artistic control, there were also concerns about the plaintiff's reluctance to provide an irrevocable letter of credit in Te Kanawa's favour to secure her performance fee, plus the use of her signature as part of the sponsorship launch. While claiming there was a legally binding contract between Te Kanawa, her company and itself, Leading Edge accepted that it was not possible to "actually identify offer, acceptance or the precise time of meeting of minds", but based its claim for breach of contract on telephone calls, e-mails and a draft written contract.

Counsel for the defendants suggested that a draft contract merely reflected the terms and conditions "that the parties had actually agreed on", but no agreement had been reached on a number of outstanding issues including the letter of credit. It also became clear during the court hearing that Te Kanawa had filed her own lawsuit against her manager over the Farnham concerts.

Finally, on March 21, 2007, two months after the conclusion of the six-day hearing, Justice Bergin returned to court to give her lengthy judgement. Her conclusion was that Te Kanawa was not guilty of breach of contract because no contract had been finalised. "It was a draft contract, subject to further negotiations," she announced. Accepting that the singer had genuine concerns about the shows, the judge ruled that "the real reason why Mittane ceased negotiations was that Dame Kiri did not want to perform at these concerts".

The judge added that while Te Kanawa's company was entitled to withdraw from negotiations, "its conduct suggests to me that it had some real doubts about the fairness of such a withdrawal. Mittane was not truthful as to the real reason for its withdrawal."

Justice Bergin also found that Te Kanawa was "very disappointed" and "extremely resentful" that Farnham and his manager missed a planned meeting in Auckland, and judged that it was a "major factor" in the defendant's decision not to perform. In her judgement, the judge acknowledged that the difference in style between the opera singer and the rock star was a relevant factor. "Dame Kiri was far from silent about her concerns with Mr. Farnham's style.

"It is obvious that two highly successful performing artists would need careful management so that their respective needs were met. Mr.

Williams [Leading Edge's co-proprietor] knew there was a possibility that Dame Kiri and Mr. Farnham may not have the necessary rapport to assuage Dame Kiri's concerns."

Despite finding in favour of the defendants over breach of contract, Justice Bergin did award Leading Edge Events A\$128,063 costs. She ruled that Te Kanawa knew the company was incurring costs in promoting the three shows before she decided not to take part and commented, "In those circumstances, I find Dame Kiri's evidence that if someone was going to spend her money then they should have a letter saying they were justified in doing so, rather unhelpful.

"This is particularly so when Dame Kiri obviously demanded to be flown to the Bay of Islands in a helicopter, and I have no doubt that she knew that the plaintiff was paying for that trip."

However, the plaintiffs failed in their claim for a management fee and for a share of net profits from the proposed shows.

In the aftermath of Te Kanawa's initial withdrawal from the shows, Farnham had told reporters that he appreciated that there was a gulf between them as performers. The 57-year-old singer said, "Kiri is obviously a Dame and I mean that with great respect. She is probably not used to an audience being so demonstrative and demands absolute silence when she works."

While proceedings against Te Kanawa and her representatives were getting under way, the "Two Great Voices" concerts went ahead, with Tom Jones standing in for the opera singer and undoubtedly doubling the number of knickers on stage.

Wheatley, who proudly confirmed to the court that in his 25 years as Farnham's manager he had never had a written contract, also made it clear during his evidence that the great Welsh singer turned up, performed and did not sign his contract "until after he left the country".

However, Wheatley found himself in court again just five months after the case of Dame Kiri and her highly publicised concerns about "middle-aged Antipodean women tossing undergarments" – but this time he was in the dock pleading guilty to tax evasion charges. With Farnham once again having no part in the action or court case, Wheatley was sentenced in July 2007 to serve at least 15 months in prison.

Chapter 24

PROCOL HARUM

Arguing over the intro to a 40-year-old number one

That showpiece of the Essex Riviera, Southend-on-Sea, was the birthplace of Procol Harum back in 1962, although the group's first – and unsuccessful – attempts to climb the charts were made under the name of The Paramounts. Four years on, The Paramounts were no more, despite supporting The Beatles on a tour and The Rolling Stones once dubbing them as their favourite UK R&B group. However, founder member Gary Brooker had discovered a new songwriting partner in Keith Reid.

An advert in *Melody Maker* brought forth not just a bunch of new musicians, but also a new identity. Procul Harum was born as a vehicle for the songs of Brooker and Reid. History suggests that this new name was derived from the Latin *procul* meaning "far from these things"; or perhaps from producer and mutual acquaintance Guy Stevens, whose best friend's pedigree cat was called Procol Harun (sic).

Either way, the new group started in the spring of 1967 with pianist and vocalist Brooker recruiting Matthew Fisher on organ, guitarist Ray Royer, bassist Dave Knights and drummer Bobby Harrison, while Reid was the non-performing, creative sixth member of the group. Together, Brooker and Reid came up with a treatment of a surreal poem written by Reid called 'A Whiter Shade Of Pale'. Under the direction of producer Denny Cordell, Brooker set the words to music adapted from Johann Sebastian Bach's 'Air On A G String' and 'Sleepers Awake'.

It also featured a haunting organ solo and melody, played and created by Fisher, which was also inspired by Bach. The recording featured session player Bill Eyden on drums rather than Harrison. In May 1967, as the band performed the song at London's trendy Speakeasy club, Cordell took a demo recording to the Deram division of Decca Records, while also sending one to influential pirate radio station Radio London.

Running just under four minutes, 'A Whiter Shade Of Pale' – the title came from Reid overhearing a man say to a girl, "You've gone a whiter shade of pale" – caught the attention of *New Musical Express* singles reviewer Derek Johnson that same month. "A gripping blues-tinged ballad, warbled in heartfelt style by the soloist. The outstanding backing highlights some delicious organ work. Hummable and thoroughly impressive."

Listener reaction persuaded Decca to rush-release the song and, before the end of the month, Deram DM 126 was in the shops. The published credit for both 'A Whiter Shade Of Pale' and the B-side, 'Lime Street Blues', went to Reid and Brooker, with Essex Music listed as the publisher, and Denny Cordell named as producer for his New Breed Productions company.

By early June, 'A Whiter Shade Of Pale' was at number one in the UK, staying at the top for six weeks and selling over 600,000 copies along the way. It was dethroned by The Beatles with 'All You Need Is Love'.

At the time, the band were only the sixth act to hit number one in Britain with their debut single, and the haunting melody, plus the bizarre and baffling lyrics, turned 'A Whiter Shade Of Pale' into one of pop music's true classics. A top-five spot in America took the record's sales over the one million mark, with a further nine million to come over the following decades. The record, voted Best Single of 1967 in the *New Musical Express* poll and named International Song Of The Year in March 1968 at the prestigious Ivor Novello Awards, became a Top 20 hit again in Britain when reissued in 1972.

Five years later it was announced as joint Best British Pop Single 1952-1977 (alongside Queen's 'Bohemian Rhapsody') at the British Record Industry Awards to celebrate the Queen's Silver Jubilee. There have also been over 700 cover versions of the song over the years, including Annie Lennox's 1995 version, which reached the UK Top 20. From the outset, Fisher's Hammond organ introduction and melody played an important part in the song's distinctiveness. Forty years later, it brought Procol Harum's original 1967 hit back to centre stage – in a court of law.

In November 2007, organist turned computer programmer Fisher began legal action to get his contribution to the hit song legally and formally recognised. He also sought a share of the song's copyright and royalties earned from sales stretching back over four decades. He made the claim against Brooker and Onwards Music Ltd., leaving Reid out of the action as his role as lyricist was not in dispute. Although the song had originally been published by Essex Music, it subsequently assigned the rights to Essex Music International, which was renamed Westminster Music. In turn, it later passed the song on to Onwards Music Ltd. from December 1991.

Pop music has, over the years, been littered with claims and counterclaims as to who wrote which part of a song. Cases involving groups such as Spandau Ballet and The Smiths ended up going to court, while musicians and composers such as The Shadows, Chuck Berry, George Martin and Otis Blackwell have all accepted situations where their creativity was either overlooked on the credits or shared with a non-contributing partner for "political" career-enhancing reasons.

For bands such as R.E.M., Pulp, and Coldplay – and in the notable case of Lennon and McCartney – sharing the credits irrespective of who wrote the song has been the easiest and fairest solution. However, Procol Harum's singer and band leader, Brooker, stood firm in his resolve as to who did what and who was entitled to share the credit on 'A Whiter Shade Of Pale'.

Before the trial began in London's Chancery Division, he made clear his thoughts on his former bandmate's action in a statement on the band's *Beyond The Pale* website. "I am shocked and dismayed that, after Matthew had worked with us quite happily over the course of nearly 40 years without him once alleging that his role on 'A Whiter Shade Of Pale' was anything other than as a musician, it is only now that he claims to recall 'composing' part of the song. I think people will draw their own conclusion from this."

In response, Fisher's solicitor, Mike Shepherd, said that the time between the song's release and the court proceedings was irrelevant. "My client has always maintained he wrote the parts, or composed the parts, he claims he composed." Shepherd said that Fisher could claim royalties on the song for the previous six years, but declined to put a figure on the amount he might receive if he won the case.

Opening before Mr Justice Blackburne, the case began in the High Court on November 13, 2007, with Ian Purvis QC representing Fisher and Andrew Sutcliffe QC for Brooker and Onwards. Purvis opened the proceedings by asking the judge – in order to avoid what he called "a Beatles moment" – if he was aware of the band Procol Harum and their lasting hit from the Swinging Sixties.

"I am of that age, yes," said the judge, who revealed that an organ had been installed in his private quarters before adding, "It may be that at some stage, after hours, I may want to work through the sheet music evidence. The natural thing to do is play it to myself."

In fact, Mr. Justice Blackburne was well qualified to hear evidence in a case involving a Sixties pop song. Aged 61, he had studied both music and law at Magdalen College, Cambridge, and had heard cases involving Spice Girls manager and *Pop Idol* creator Simon Fuller and *X-Factor* creator Simon Cowell.

With the media suggesting that Fisher's claim for back royalties could be worth over £1 million, those present in court were treated to an impromptu performance by the organist. The introduction to the record featured Fisher's organ solo, accompanied only by a drum beat. Fisher gave a 40-minute rendition and bar-by-bar analysis, which the judge followed from a transcribed music score. The song features an eight-bar introduction, a 16-bar verse, an eight-bar chorus, a repeat of the eight-bar intro, a 16-bar verse, a repeat of the eight-bar chorus and a variation on the eight-bar intro, followed by a final two-bar reprise of the chorus.

On the record, Fisher's playing was heard for just two minutes and 36 seconds, but he confirmed to the court how he had developed the solo and melodies that appeared on 'A Whiter Shade Of Pale', using his enthusiasm for the works of Bach. He said he made chord changes to Brooker's original sequence and developed a counterpoint to the melody.

"How did they get there if it wasn't for me? I finished that organ solo at home, partly from ideas floating around in my head and partly from rehearsals, whereas the original organ melody arose purely from rehearsals. This was a song not for people who are used to listening to Schubert or Benjamin Britten, but intended for the man in the street. We didn't want it too adventurous or avant-garde."

Admitting that his relationship with Brooker hadn't always been ideal, Fisher said, "There's always been a tension between me and Gary. The whole question of 'A Whiter Shade Of Pale' has always been there. It's like walking into the room and seeing a dead person. He knew it was there, I knew it was there, but nobody mentioned it. There was a lot of subconscious anger."

Purvis explained to the court that the 60-year-old musician, who first left Procol Harum in 1969 after producing the band's acclaimed album *A Salty Dog* but had returned on various occasions over the years, had delayed making a formal legal claim for 38 years because he had been unaware of his legal entitlement. Purvis added, "We are dealing with one of the most successful pop songs ever written by British artists."

On the second day of the hearing, Fisher said that he felt aggrieved not only because of the alleged unpaid royalties, but also because he had lost his place in British pop history. "It was not until the Eighties that the song began to acquire its cult classic status. Here we have a song which is going to go down in history which ought to have my name on it and it doesn't."

When it was put to him under cross-examination that he was making his claim after nearly four decades of reaping the benefits in Procol Harum, Fisher replied, "That's the funniest thing I've heard. If I could go back in time I would not have joined Procol Harum, I would have joined another band."

Brooker's counsel, Sutcliffe, also suggested to Fisher that when the song was first presented at rehearsal it was complete, and featured the distinctive, Bach-inspired introduction. "The writing Keith and Gary were doing needed fleshing up. I reject any suggestion that there was any memorable tune," was the organist's reply, although he accepted that it had been Brooker's idea to compose a song based on Bach.

"I thought that was brilliant," said Fisher, "but he didn't really have the background to carry it through to its conclusion. I came in to finish the job. If you take out my contribution, you would have had a song that would never have been released. We're getting into this fiction that he wrote this tune and I just adapted it. That is completely false."

Following Fisher into the witness box was Procol Harum's former drummer, Robert Harrison, who talked about the "before" and "after" versions of the song. Although not on the original recording and only with the group between March and July 1967, Harrison gave evidence about how different the material he had heard sounded after the addition of Fisher's Hammond organ. Harrison recalled visiting Brooker in 1967, when the vocalist played him some material recorded before Fisher's arrival. "There was bass, drums and piano, but I don't remember a Hammond," said Harrison. "I think it is significant because it did not have the organ on it."

Hearing the song later at his audition to join the group, he said it had been transformed. "That's when I heard the difference." The drummer, who sued Brooker over royalty rights and reached a confidential settlement in 1969, said that while he always viewed Brooker as the leader of Procol Harum, he was always under the impression that "Matthew was one of the main writers in the band".

Coincidentally, Harrison drummed on Fisher's 1973 solo album, *Journey's End*, which contained the track 'Going For A Song'. "Please don't make me sing that song again ... I've sung it so many times," appeared to refer to 'A Whiter Shade Of Pale', although Fisher never actually sang it!

During his evidence, Brooker, who continued to perform under the group name Procol Harum, acknowledged that, during early rehearsals of 'A Whiter Shade Of Pale', he and Fisher had improvised their respective instrumental sections over the original chord sequence composed by Brooker".

He accepted that each musician in the band had their own ideas when improvising, and that the band's philosophy allowed group members to make their own musical contributions. However, both Brooker and

Reid in their witness statements remained adamant about the structure of the song.

"In spite of differences between the piano and organ, what was played by Matthew in rehearsal and on the recording, both in harmonic and melodic terms, was essentially the same as what I had composed at the piano," claimed Brooker. Lyricist Reid added, "The difference between the song as it was when Gary and I wrote it and the version released on the record was that the song was much longer when we first wrote it. Otherwise it's the same."

The band's wordsmith continued, "It had the introduction and melodies that everyone recognises. Of course, in the recorded version they are adapted and played on Hammond organ. And obviously the record has a full instrumentation – drums, bass, lead guitar, Hammond organ, vocals and piano. Even with a different organist, the record would have sounded essentially the same."

Under further cross-examination from Purvis, Brooker accepted that he had given Fisher the job of effectively creating the best solo he could, but he took issue with the suggestion that the introduction was the result of a careful composition process.

"Might I just ask this," said the singer. "When somebody says composing, is there really a definition of what that means?" Purvis suggested, "Let's use a more neutral term. A careful creative process?" Brooker accepted that. "It was a careful creative process, yes." At this point Mr. Justice Blackburne interrupted to ask, "On whose part?" Brooker replied, "On Matthew's part."

Asked whether the melody in the song was Fisher's melody ("It's his tune, he came up with it", Purvis insisted), Brooker answered, "Again I would say that not all those notes were thought of by Matthew. They were based upon what he had heard me play or even the way I had improvised it at times. He ended up with these notes, which he repeated."

Brooker conceded that he hadn't played all the way through the melody of eight bars in the form that Fisher wrote them. When asked directly by counsel, "It's Matthew's composition?" Brooker answered, "In this form on these eight bars, it is."

Before the hearing ended, Brooker's wife, Francoise, was brought into the case to be a witness as to how the song sounded in rehearsal and on record. "The song, as Gary played it to me on the piano, was the same as the recorded version and included the now famous introduction," she confirmed.

While the hearing ended in November, it was not until December 20, 2006 that Mr. Justice Blackburne gave his judgement. He quickly concluded that "the organ solo is a distinctive and significant contribution to the overall composition and quite obviously the product of skill and labour on the part of the person who created it.

"I do not accept that the existence prior to March 7, 1967 of a demo recording by Mr. Brooker of the song provides any defence to Mr Fisher's claim.

"Mr. Fisher made his contribution as part of a collaborative effort with Mr. Brooker and the other band members without anyone at the time considering what, in copyright terms, the consequence was of his so doing. The consequence in law was that he qualified as a joint author of what resulted."

The judge also referred to an interview given in 1982 by Reid in which he said there were three things about the recorded version of 'A Whiter Shade Of Pale'. "There's the song, Gary's singing and the organ playing … the organ player plays whatever he thinks of playing so Matthew contributed his organ part, just the same as if there had been another organist, he would have played something else … that particular song gave him [Fisher] probably the scope to write a part."

Commenting on the remarks, the judge stated, "It is clear that, at that time at least and in marked contrast to his evidence before me, Mr. Reid considered that it was Mr Fisher who wrote the organ part."

The outcome was not looking good for Brooker, although the judge admitted that he found both Brooker and Fisher to be "honest witnesses". Admitting that he found the delay between's Fisher's first claim of authorship – supposedly made informally to Brooker on a train journey in 1967 – and lodging an official claim in 2005 "quite extraordinary", the judge declared that it was not a barrier to the action as the main parties were still alive.

"Relevant to this is that Mr. Fisher's interest in the musical copyright is a property right. It has many years to run. The fact that, for whatever reason, he has not sought to establish that interest before now does not mean that, by declining a declaration, the court should make it difficult for him to vindicate and enforce that interest so longs as it lasts, in the future."

Explaining that it would be a "wholly extravagant and unjust result to deprive Fisher for the remainder of his life and 70 years thereafter of his interest in 'A Whiter Shade Of Pale''s musical copyright", the judge said he could find no reason not to grant the declaration that Fisher was the co-author and joint owner of the musical copyright of the recorded and released hit version of the song.

Settling the financial side of the case, Fisher, who had asked for a 50% share of the royalties with Brooker, was awarded a 40% share of the total musical copyright backdated to May 2005, when he had first filed proceedings in the case.

While Fisher was also granted a co-authorship credit on the song, the judge took the view that even though the organist's contribution on the record was "substantial", it was not as great as Brooker's.

However, while the judge decided that Fisher was not entitled to any past royalties, he allowed that, as he "was successful in establishing a copyright interest", he was due a share of Brooker's half of the song's royalties. He was granted a 20% cut, with Brooker's share being reduced to 30%, while Reid, who was not part of the action, retained his full 50% share as the song's lyricist.

As Brooker was granted leave to appeal the decision, payment of back royalties to Fisher was withheld, but costs – expected to be over £500,000 – were awarded against Brooker, who did not appear in court to hear the judge's decision.

A victorious Fisher, who had returned to play with Procol Harum on various occasions after his 1969 departure, told reporters after the case that he was "dazed" before adding, "I think I can assume that from now on I'm not going to be on Gary's and Keith's Christmas card lists, but I think it's a small price to pay for finally securing my rightful place in rock 'n' roll history."

Understandably less pleased were Brooker and his original co-writing partner, Reid, who issued a statement that suggested the ruling "creates a ticking time bomb ready to explode when the musician chooses".

Expanding on this theme, Brooker explained, "No longer will songwriters, bands and musicians be able to go into a studio without the spectre of one of them, at any future point, claiming a share of the publishing copyright. It is effectively open season on the songwriter. Songwriters and publishers will now have to view all musicians with suspicion as potential claimants to a share in their copyright."

Describing the judgement as "a darker side of black" for the music industry, Brooker went on to attack Fisher. "It's hard to believe that I've worked with somebody on and off since 1967 whilst they hid such unspoken resentment.

"If Matthew Fisher's name ends up on my song, mine can come off! I have to respect and acknowledge the people I write songs with. After all this time the case should never have got to court," he said, before turning his attention to the German classical composer whose music was at the heart of the court case. "Johann Sebastian Bach deserves the credit for his inspiration to all musicians."

While Fisher – after life as a rock star – turned to work as a computer programmer, Brooker remained committed to life both as a musician and as keeper of the flame for Procol Harum. And despite what the court said, he was not prepared to share either his royalties or composer's credit with Fisher without a further fight.

In October 2007 he launched an appeal, the result of which was announced in the High Court in April 2008. His perseverance paid off as the Court of Appeal overturned the 2006 ruling and returned to him the right to the full royalty on 'A Whiter Shade Of Pale' on the basis that Fisher took too long to make his claim.

Lord Justice Mummery ruled that Fisher "silently stood by and acquiesced in the defendant's commercial exploitation of the work for 38 years". As a result he was "guilty of excessive and inexcusable delay in his claim to assert joint title to a joint interest in the work".

In the appeal hearing, Brooker's counsel, John Baldwin QC, explained that Fisher had failed to take the case to court earlier because he knew it would be the end of his career in the group. "He wanted to stay in the band and live the life of a pop star. Being a litigant was not something he could do alongside that and he realised what he would have to give up."

While the three Appeal Court judges agreed by a majority that Fisher had contributed to the song and was entitled to a co-authorship credit, they ruled that he was not entitled to any past or future royalties from sales of 'A Whiter Shade Of Pale'.

After the hearing, Fisher's solicitor suggested the legal battle was not over and that the former Procol Harum organist would apply for permission to appeal to the House of Lords.

"The court has accepted the decision that he co-wrote it, which was the primary issue for Matthew," said Mike Shepherd, "but he is disappointed about the future royalties. It seems to us that if someone contributed a significant part to a composition, why shouldn't they get the future income?"

Understandably, Brooker was happier with the outcome and, in a statement, he described the claim by Fisher as "something I would rather have dealt with 40 years ago". He added, "I believe the original trial was unfair and the result wrong. Today the decision of the Court of Appeal has gone some way to putting this right, and I would hope that now we all get on with our lives."

But despite his request for a return to normality and with victory under his belt, Brooker is continuing his fight with Fisher over who should pay the estimated £500,000 legal costs of the lengthy action.

After Procol Harum split in 1977, the pianist and singer recorded three solo albums, toured with Eric Clapton and wrote music for a number of ballets before, together with Reid, Fisher and original Paramounts' guitarist Robin Trower, he reformed Procol Harum in the early Nineties.

Since then the band – with a varied collection of musicians not including Fisher – has continued to tour, and no doubt Brooker will feel happier about featuring one particular song in their set, knowing that irrespective of the composer's credit, he won't be sharing his royalties.

ACKNOWLEDGEMENTS

My thanks go to Chris Charlesworth at Omnibus Press for his support and to my wife Pat for her painstaking "subbing" of my text. Also to The British Library, the British Newspaper Library, the British Phonographic Industry and *Billboard* magazine for access to their files and back issues. In researching this book I visited back issues of *Music Week*, *Melody Maker*, *New Musical Express* and also called upon a host of official court reports and judgements.

BIBLIOGRAPHY

Adediran, Peter: *A Practical Guide to Business, Law & The Internet* (Kogan Page 2002)

Beatles, The: *The Beatles Anthology* (Cassell & Co 2000)

Bret, David: *Morrissey Scandal & Passion* (Robson Books 2004)

Brown, Peter & Gaines, Steven: *The Love You Make: An Insider's Story Of The Beatles* (McGraw-Hill 1983)

Buckley, David: *Elton: The Biography* (Andre Deutsch 2006)

Cashman, Lola: *Inside The Zoo With U2: My Life With The World's Biggest Rock Band* (Blake Publishing 2003)

Cross, Charles R.: *Room Full Of Mirrors* (Sceptre 2005)

Donovan , Jason: *Between The Lines* (HarperCollins 2007)

Garfield, Simon: *Expensive Habits: Dark Side Of The Music Industry* (Faber & Faber 1986)

Hadley, Tony: *To Cut A Long Story Short* (Pan 2004)

Harrison, Ann: *Music: The Business* (Virgin Books 2005)

Harrison, George: *I, Me, Mine* (Phoenix 2004)

Johnson, Holly: *A Bone In My Flute* (Century 1994)

Liberace: *An Autobiography* (Putnam & Co 1973)

McIver, Joel: *Justice For All: The Truth About Metallica* (Omnibus 2004)

Merriden, Trevor: *Irresistible Forces: The Business Legacy Of Napster And The Growth Of The Underground Internet* (Capstone 2001)

Middles, Mick: *Breaking Into Heaven: The Rise And Fall Of The Stone Roses* (Omnibus 1999)

Miles, Barry: *Paul McCartney: Many Years From Now* (Secker & Warburg 1997)

Norman, Philip: *Sir Elton* (Sidgwick & Jackson 2000)

Parkinson, Judy: *Elton: Made In England* (Michael O'Mara 2003)

Rogan, Johnny: *Morrissey & Marr: The Severed Alliance* (Omnibus 1992)

Shapiro, Marc: *All Things Must Pass: The Life Of George Harrison*
  (Virgin Books 2002)

Simpson, Mark: *Saint Morrissey* (SAF 2004)

Soocher, Stan: *They Fought The Law: Rock Music Goes To Court*
  (Schirmer Books 1999)